BECOMING
A TEACHER
THROUGH
ACTION
RESEARCH

BECOMING A TEACHER THROUGH ACTION RESEARCH

Process, Context, and Self-Study
Third Edition

DONNA KALMBACH PHILLIPS AND KEVIN CARR

Routledge
Taylor & Francis Group

NEW YORK AND LONDON

Third edition published 2014
by Routledge
711 Third Avenue, New York, NY 10017

and by Routledge
2 Park Square, Milton Park, Abingdon, Oxon OX14 4RN

Routledge is an imprint of the Taylor & Francis Group, an informa business

First edition published 2006 by Routledge
Second edition published 2010 by Routledge

Library of Congress Control Number: 2013954529

ISBN: 978–0–415–66049–5 (pbk)
ISBN: 978–1–315–86749–6 (ebk)

Typeset in Utopia
by Swales & Willis Ltd, Exeter, Devon

Printed and bound in the United States of America by Sheridan Books, Inc. (a Sheridan Group Company).

TABLE OF CONTENTS

4 ACTION RESEARCH DESIGN

5 ONGOING DATA ANALYSIS

6 FINAL DATA INTERPRETATION

7 TELLING THE STORY OF YOUR ACTION RESEARCH

8 LIVING ACTION RESEARCH AS A PROFESSIONAL EDUCATOR

ACKNOWLEDGMENTS

A thing done or given in recognition of something received; a declaration or avowal of one's act of a fact to give it legal validity . . . an open declaration of something (as a fault or the commission of an offense) about oneself

. . . see CONFESSION.
(Merriam-Webster Online Dictionary, 2005)

And so we acknowledge . . . that we have been given much by many and are unable to make a complete account for this generosity; we cannot trace completely the wonder of rhizomic lines leading to people, places, and situations influencing the writing of this book, or of the many discourses playing, seducing, and commanding our written words. We confess to writing this textbook while living somewhere in a zone of contradiction (Whitehead, 1989), practicing inquiry not only as stance (Cochran-Smith & Lytle, 1999) but as a run, a ride, a trek, and as a resting place—as a *koan* whose answer we have not yet worked through.

We wrote the first edition of this book in the act of doing life; we wrote the second edition of this book during the act of doing a re-visioning of both the text of the book and the text of our lives. We come to the third edition of this book at a time of doing re-imaging of our lives and understanding that text/life has never been a binary. We come to the writing searching deeper, listening more carefully, questioning more directly, feeling the urgency of *becoming*: "A line of becoming is not defined by points it connects . . . on the contrary, it passes *between* points, it comes up through the middle" (Deleuze & Guattari, 1980/1987, p. 293). And we confess: The "points" of first, second, and third edition are illusionary and we do not know all of the where and what and who and how that have passed through in it/our *becoming*.

We write this third edition in the company of students, former, current, and those students still to come, who challenge our thinking, our way of being, our comfortable and habitual zones of teaching. We write this book in acknowledgment that the world of teaching and becoming teacher is in upheaval: national standards and testing, merit pay, "data-driven," violence shattering illusions of safety–all are altering landscapes, creating pressure points and fissures, and urgency for teachers who are critical and creative thinkers and leaders; questioners and visionaries; advocates of children and adolescents; dreamers and believers in what school might *become*. The words of Archbishop Oscar Romero, "We are prophets of a future not our own" still whisper from our walls and we find a new commitment to these words, to our students and we confess: we do not know where their words, concerns, and passions become our words, concerns and passions and therefore encompass the text of this book.

We write this third edition in the middle and beginning of introducing new programs, developing innovative curriculum for learning to teach differently, *with* community partners who require us to practice the words of this book, critical-self-reflexivity-in-action-research, even as we write. These new colleagues, these altered visions of what "teaching" and "researching" as *different possibilities*, work at *us* and we confess we are learning (and experiencing) what Colebrook describes: "Learning to swim is not replicating the movements of the swimming teacher; nor is it feeling the waves that the teacher herself is responding to; it is imaging the response to new and different waves" (2008, p. 41).

We write this third edition with reminders of how little we control outcomes, goals: *life*. We confess Ellsworth's (1997) words inspire this third edition and encompass our hope for it: "We pitch our teaching into an abyss between self and self, self and other. And yet something, and hopefully not a repetitive echo, but an inquisitive, ironic echo—a difference that makes a difference—returns" (p. 158).

And we (still) acknowledge our struggle with the wise words of Lao Tzu, "In pursuit of knowledge, everyday something is acquired; In pursuit of wisdom, everyday something is dropped." And we know we could not have completed this project were it not for the gracious gift of time from John and Lisa (our spouses) and friends, colleagues who talked, read, listened and nudged us toward change, and the editors at Routledge in saying "yes" to a third go-around.

Yes, we acknowledge that we wrote this book while re-*imaging* life, while *in* question, while teaching with conviction/doubt; passion/apathy; hope/despair, believing in our students even as they and others gave us the gift of believing in us. We acknowledge the words of Maxine Greene (2001) in our own practice for our "notions of teaching are much involved with notions of human relationship, intersubjectivity, the pursuit of various kinds of meaning, and *the sense of untapped possibility—of what might be, what ought to be, what is not yet*" (p. 82—our italics).

We write this acknowledgment in gratitude—for relationships, shifting subjectivity, the cacophony/harmony of life, for the named and unnamed influences here; for the irony/illusion of wholeness that is found in incompleteness, for time of re-visioning, and for *the sense of untapped possibility.*

INTRODUCTION: BECOMING A TEACHER THROUGH ACTION RESEARCH

An Introductory Guide and Invitation

If this book could be more than just a text—if this book could touch, smell, argue, exclaim, sigh, even dance—then it might better represent action research as we have come to know it.[1] However, it is *a book*, and as such it is bound by linear structures of thinking that do not always reflect the cyclical and even messy processes of doing action research. Just the same, we have attempted to create a book that allows space for you to interact and to talk back, recognizing that as a reader you are always engaged, whether you are deeply connecting with the text or finding yourself somewhat disengaged with its content. In order to mirror both the linearity and complexity of action research we have formatted this book in a unique way: a "main road" or the action research project road, and two "side roads," focusing on the important areas of cultural context and self study. You will find materials and activities for these side roads at the end of each chapter. What follows are some general guidelines and tips for understanding and organizing your action research journey as you navigate the content of *Becoming a Teacher Through Action Research*.

Who Is This Book Written For?

Are you *becoming a teacher*? The title, *Becoming a Teacher Through Action Research: Process, Context, and Self-Study*, encapsulates both the book's purpose and audience. While *Becoming a Teacher Through Action Research* (*BTAR*) is written especially for people who are formally becoming teachers for the first time, it may be useful in a wide variety of settings. After all, becoming a teacher is a life-long process.

Becoming a Teacher . . .

Many countries offer teacher education programs for students working toward their first teaching certification or license in preschool through secondary school teaching. We use the term *preservice teacher* for the student pursuing teacher licensure for the first time. Most preservice teacher education programs include a substantial field experience component (often called *student teaching* or *clinical teaching*). *BTAR* is specifically designed for preservice teachers who are or will be engaged in student teaching, in *becoming teachers*. That said, we believe that all teachers, even veterans with decades of experience, are continually *becoming*; we never arrive at a final destination of *teacher*. Therefore, we also invite to this text any teacher who wishes to *become* a better teacher by doing action research in their own teaching context.

We believe that preservice teacher education programs and other routes to becoming a teacher facilitate a critical phase in professional life, one that includes not only technical training in the skills of teaching but significant creation and transformation of teaching identity as well. *Becoming* is a place of transition. This book acknowledges, supports, and intertwines teaching's technical and transformational elements; ultimately, what you bring to the book and take away is part of the individual/collective journey you will travel.

. . . Through Action Research

Action research, part of the broad universe of research in the social sciences, takes many different forms, some unrelated to teaching or education. Experienced teachers often do action research as part of advanced degrees or professional development. Some colleagues in teacher education have questioned whether preservice teachers are even capable of doing valid or trustworthy action research, given their novice status within the teaching profession. You may even have already asked yourself, "How can I possibly do real research about teaching when I haven't even taught yet?" or "How will I have time to do research with all the other demands of becoming a teacher?" These are valid questions; action research is work too hard to be viewed as "just another requirement for licensure". We hope that by the time you complete your work you will value its contribution to your professional growth and development.

Many preservice teacher education programs include an inquiry project, capstone project, teaching improvement project, or some other experience that could be framed as *action research*; this is why you are reading this book! By doing your action research project, you will become a teacher more equipped to thrive in a professional environment where teachers are sometimes undervalued, underpowered, and at times even silenced by the culture of schooling. The process of learning about and doing action research enables preservice teachers to grow a strong and trustworthy professional voice to engage students, parents, and colleagues in critical conversation for change. We know this because we have journeyed alongside hundreds of preservice teacher action researchers, taking a small role in *their* stories of growth and change. We believe that preservice teacher action research represents a unique genre within the action research tradition, and has the potential to shape teacher identity in powerful ways (Phillips & Carr, 2009). The central purpose of this text is to scaffold your action research process, not only to make the journey successful, but also to make it transformative, energizing you as you enter a teaching profession as difficult as it is rewarding.

In this third edition of *BTAR*, we have made substantial changes that we hope will enhance your journey. These changes reflect our own ongoing growth and learning as we continue to travel this action research road with both preservice and licensed teachers. During this process of listening to and learning with teachers, we've become more convinced that the tools and way of thinking required by sustained inquiry are those that mark intelligent teachers of influence. These are the tools and ways of thinking that allow teachers to talk back and take back their practice when government mandates assail them. They are the same tools and ways of thinking that create spaces for teachers to problematize practice in powerful ways, resulting in a better, more just education for many students. And they are the same tools and ways of thinking that challenge teachers, creating uncomfortable spaces of being that move them away from assumptions and routine thought and into active, revitalized engagement in their educational communites.

To support the acquisition of these tools and ways of thinking, we've continued in this edition the focus on elements of *trustworthy* preservice teacher action research. These elements, described below, are woven throughout the book—keep these central to your journey. In addition, we have included two new chapters entitled *Action Research Design* and *Final Data Interpretation*, convering in depth areas that deserve more intense focus and clarity than we provided in previous editions. Each chapter is framed with a roadmap to better identify where you are in the journey and keep you focused on where you are going. We have also added more examples and charts to support critical pieces of writing a critical question, data collection, data analysis and the use of analytic memos. Content and process questions are included at the end of each chapter as a way to create a pause, a moment to think, in the midst of the intensity of learning to teach and research.

You may still be wondering how your project can be much more than just another of the many tasks you must complete as part of becoming a teacher. How can "good" action research be completed in just a few months? Or, in the language of action research, how can preservice teacher-action research be *trustworthy*? We realize that preservice teacher-action research is unlikely to be as lengthy, or academic, as a doctoral dissertation or master's thesis completed by a practicing teacher. Action research done by preservice teachers may not be ready for publication in the same journals that contain work done by professional researchers. So, what does "good " or trustworthy preservice action research look like? By analyzing the work of our students over the years, we have come to realize that trustworthy projects are strong in some of the following ways (Figure 0.1):

- Trustworthy preservice teacher action research makes evident a *strong sense of connection* between becoming a teacher, the context of the school and classroom in which the work is done, the design of the project, and the literature base. This textbook is designed to help you make these connections.

- Trustworthy preservice teacher action research involves substantial, "thick" data of multiple types representing *multiple perspectives*. After all, quality data is the basis of all good research. This textbook will teach you to design data collection processes that will grow your ability to more thoroughly evaluate your teaching and understand student learning.

- Trustworthy preservice teacher action research shows evidence of *self-reflexivity* that challenges the researcher's basic assumptions about teaching and learning. This textbook will help you examine your own assumptions and learn to deconstruct problematic areas in light of your action research work.

- Trustworthy preservice teacher action research produces *meaningful action* and results, improving teaching and learning for students. This textbook will above all teach you to become more student-focused in your thinking and planning for instruction.

→ FIGURE 0.1: Elements of Preservice Teacher Action Research

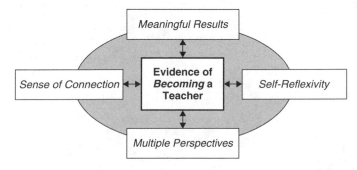

Taken together, trustworthy action research *shows evidence of becoming a teacher*. Our list isn't comprehensive. We have chosen to focus on this short list of possible outcomes not because they represent all that may be "good" about preservice teacher action research, but because we have found these to be central in our setting and context. We hope you find even more elements of "goodness" in your own work.

Process, Context, and Self-Study . . .

BTAR will support your preservice action research journey in three critical ways. First, and foremost, *BTAR* will guide you through the action research process in a linear fashion, from understanding teacher action research, discovering an area of focus, investigating data, designing a study and collecting data, analyzing and interpreting the data, and communicating your findings to others. To help you understand and trace your progress through this journey we include at the start of each chapter a flowchart marking the major phases and tasks of action research as they are laid out in the eight chapters of *BTAR*. A color version of the chart can be downloaded from the companion website, found at www.routledge.com/cw/phillips. The contents of each particular chapter are highlighted on the chart. In addition, *BTAR* includes critical "side roads" that you may follow to explore the larger context of action research, as well as the inner life of teacher action research. Each chapter includes a road map showing graphically the main route of action research as well as the side roads you may travel.

➔ FIGURE 0.2: Action Research Overview

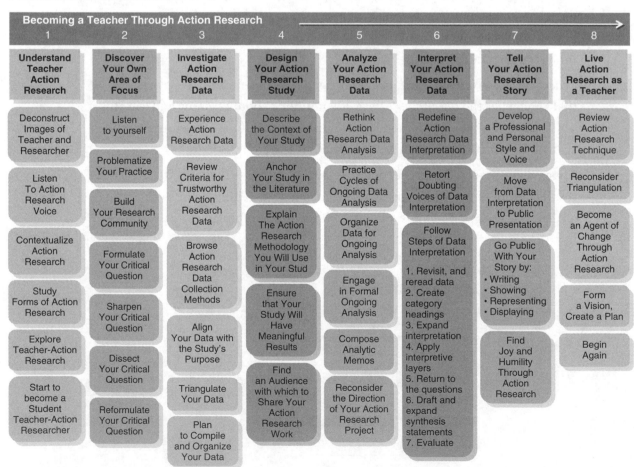

Organization and Navigation

This textbook contains a direct and concise description of the process of action research; you may work sequentially through these steps and arrive at the end with a completed action research project. We often travel with efficiency foremost in mind: we stay on the main road to get where we need to go. But we gain a more holistic view of the land if we take time to travel side roads. The two side roads designed to do this in *BTAR* are Cultural Context and Self-Study. On the Cultural Context side road you will consider carefully the cultural context of your action research project and how this influences everything from research design to data interpretation. On the Self-Study side road you will learn to practice self-reflexivity or probing how your values, beliefs and past experiences influence choices and interpretation made in action research. The side roads are marked with this icon:

> Travel the introductory cultural context side roads found at the end of this chapter on p. xvii.

> Travel the introductory self study side roads found at the end of this chapter on p. xviii.

This book is *not* written for the passive reader. We recognize that reading is a transacation between text and self; you bring your pardigms and experiences to the text and make meaning of it. Make this transaction as transparent as possible; interact with the text by taking opportunities presented to respond. These places are marked with this icon: 📓. Read with a dedicated spiral notebook, computer file, or journal close by. Taking time to respond will allow you to better construct your own meaning of action research.

In addition, *BTAR* provides opportunities for more practice in some areas, templates for particular activities, and examples of action research. These are housed at the *BTAR* companion website for this text. You can find this at www.routledge.com/cw/phillips. These opportunities are marked with this icon: 🖱 .

Published textbooks of knowledge are often outdated prior to publication. The postmodern information world we live in is an energizing place of change; knowledge is not static or a thing simply to memorize and store in a teacher toolbox. It is alive, organic, and evolving. This means learning to teach and becoming a teacher is more than accumulating knowledge and strategies. Becoming a teacher is the creation of new knowledges within the context of each teaching situation, it is learning to face the difficult, challenging and uncomfortable through critical thinking, examination, inquiry and questioning the taken-for-granted. It is honing skills of listening, observing, and deconstructing not only of our own work, but that of powerful structures of teaching and schooling that frame and influence our work as teachers. Action research is a process, then, not a set of knowledges. As a process, it is a way of thinking, a way of practicing teaching.

Taken as a whole, our intent is that this text serve as a flexible guide in your own journey of learning this practice, of becoming a teacher through action research. Read and interact with the text around, through, and in whatever way best suits you as a learner. Doodle, draw, argue, question. Risk, stumble, cheer your success. *Be* engaged. Live the process in becoming an empowered teacher who can learn the practice of action research as a way to teach *all* students in *all* contexts.

Welcome to the journey!

Note

1 We have borrowed the format and the sentiment of Gary Paulsen, young adolescent writer, in his description of the limitation of text as described in the preface to *The Winter Room* (1989).

Cultural Context: Introduction to the Cultural Context Activities

The schools and communities in which we work provide the living environment for our professional context (Gay, 2010). Traveling the Cultural Context side roads of *Becoming a Teacher Through Action Research: Context, Process, and Self-Analysis* will help you place teaching and action research within a greater cultural context. Even as you plan your lessons, design your research project, and daily attend a school site for a practicum experience, the larger cultural environments are present and powerful. Such influences are hard to define or categorize, but one can analyze, synthesize, deconstruct, and thus theorize about the influences around us. Taking a closer look at these forces allows us to re-create our own images, values, and beliefs about teaching and research.

We believe that this process of re-creation requires active, critical thinking and personal reflection. Therefore, the content of this strand comes largely in the form of questions rather than answers. You will be asked to observe, analyze, and interpret the cultural space around you to find clues about the nature of the context where you are journeying. These skills are, not accidentally, the same skills that teachers use in implementing action research.

The activities in this strand serve as a tangible reminder that we do not teach and do research in isolation. Our lives are connected through social histories, invisible genealogies that grow to tell the stories of teaching. These collective stories, be they interpreted as truth, myth, or merely fiction, swirl around conversations of education. This strand is a space in which to consider these stories more closely as part of your action research process.

Throughout the activities, deliberately resist the desire to say, "This is right," "This is wrong," or, "What's the problem with this?" The goal is *not* to determine "rightness," but to deeply consider public images, values, and beliefs about teaching and research. By identifying these themes among the discourse of dominant culture, we can better choose our own course of action: Why do we accept or reject these themes? What alternatives exist to define both ourselves, and our chosen profession? Do we wish to blend what we discover into some "new" construction for both ourselves, and our teaching identity? What will these new images, new stories be like?

Many of these activities will ask you to interpret data on some small scale. This is the same kind of interpretative work on you will be doing in your action research project. Don't be too concerned with being "objective" in these interpretations. Because of the way we are both consciously and subconsciously influenced by our culture, experiences, ethnicity, gender, and class, we cannot totally escape ourselves and claim to be "objective," at least not in in the usual sense of the word. As one of our colleagues often says, "It's hard to separate *you* from you." In order to develop trustworthiness in our judgments about the world around us, we must constantly and critically examine our own motives, biases, and desires.

Self-Study: Introduction to the Self-Study Activities

Self-study is a term used in educational research circles to describe teaching and researching practices in order to "better understand: oneself; teaching; learning, and the development of knowledge about these" (Loughran, 2004, p. 9). Self-study can take many forms, ranging from the simple keeping and study of a personal diary or journal to carrying out a more thorough examination of self and practice such as an "autoethnography" (Ellis & Bochner, 2003). What all self-study research has in common is its auto-biographical perspective—you the teacher-researcher becomes the subject of the study. Such study is embedded with deliberate acts of reflection that result in transformation of self, practices, and/or systems (Carr & Kemmis, 1986; LaBoskey, 2004; Schon, 1990; Zeichner & Liston, 1996). The self is not studied in isolation; rather, "understanding of teaching and learning derives from contextualized knowledge, by a particularly reflective knower in a particular teaching situation" (Bass, Anderson-Patton, & Allender, 2002, p. 56).

Self-study and action research share commonalities such as an emphasis on improving practice, interactive collaboration, and the primary use of qualitative methods (Feldman, Paugh, & Mills, 2004; LaBoskey, 2004). A certain amount of self-study is part of any action research project; after all, your own experiences, perceptions, and growth are all intimately entwined with your teaching practice. This is especially true as a preservice teacher—you will be *transformed* as a result of stepping into the classroom and working through the process of action research. Schulte (2002) defines the transformation process as the "continuous evolution of one's own understanding and perspectives in order to better meet the needs of all students. It is marked by a disruption of values or cultural beliefs through critical reflection with the goal of more socially just teaching" (p. 101).

Documenting and reflecting upon this transformation process is an important component of doing action research as a preservice teacher. It requires risk on your part, and finding some space and time to open yourself up to such interrogation; take a first step with the personal interview that comes later in the self-study activities in this book. O'Reilley (1998), writing about the power of quiet reflection on teaching, notes, "Sometimes I'm scared to do these quiet things because I might stumble on some data I didn't count on" (p. 15). Yet such data discoveries may be the beginning of a transformation.

CHAPTER 1
BECOMING A STUDENT TEACHER-ACTION RESEARCHER

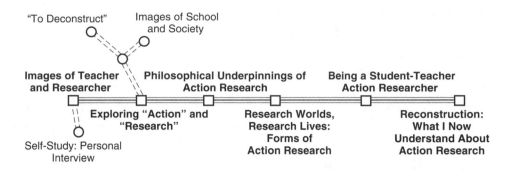

Chapter 1 is designed as a space for coming to terms with concepts and definitions of action research, as well as better defining your place as person/student teacher within the context of the greater society and your own personal universe in order to contemplate who you might be as a teacher-researcher. The main road and side roads bring together these ideas to mark a place of beginning. As you read, consider yourself (your context, values/beliefs, what you believe about teaching and researching) and your reaction to the text: How do your reactions speak of you? What do you immediately want to embrace, reject, learn more about?

You want to be a teacher. You come to this decision with your dreams and visions of what a "teacher" is. You aspire to certain standards, expectations, and desires. You know it will be hard work, but that's not a concern right now. You're focused on your dreams of what teaching will be like. Maybe you remember your favorite teacher: the third grade teacher who inspired you to become a mathematician, the middle school teacher who convinced you that you were an artist, or the high school teacher who took you trekking along fault lines and created a passion for geology. Or, perhaps what motivated you to become a teacher are your worst memories: you do *not* want to be like your boring ninth grade history teacher, the seventh grade teacher who used put-downs, or the first grade teacher who didn't believe you could read. You want to be different. You want to make a difference. We want you to make a difference as well, and we think the process of **action research** is one way of helping you achieve your dreams.

That's why we've written this book about teaching and research. It is not an "authoritative" account of either teaching or research, in which we as "experts" define teaching and research for you. Rather, it is designed to guide you through your individual process of *becoming* a teacher, a process that is different for everyone, and one in which we the authors are ourselves engaged. We've written in this way because we believe that action research is a powerful way of not only documenting your journey in becoming a teacher, but also a powerful way of *being* a teacher. The text is designed to be interactive, since this is how we view teaching, learning, and researching—as interactive process of discovery and inquiry. Becoming a teacher-researcher involves a thorough reexamination of taken-for-granted ideas, making possible new ways of thinking. This process involves risk, with the potential reward of both personal and collective transformation.

> We use the term *deconstruction* throughout this text. To learn more, travel the side road Cultural Context 1.1: *To Deconstruct*, found at the end of this chapter on p. 32.

Images of Teacher and Researcher

In this book, you will learn about *action research*, a category of research that can be defined and interpreted in many ways. We will be discussing the term *teacher-researcher* throughout this book. But these discussions often require a **paradigm** shift: "teacher as a researcher" is *not* an image our culture gives us. Rather, *teacher* and *researcher* are often constructed as figures in opposition, having very different traits, interests, and values.

It seems we all come to education with images and definitions of what "good teacher" and "good researcher" represent: how they act, look, and think. It is important to consider what our images are and how these images are shaped by our culture, gender, and ethnicity; our community and family values; and our experiences. Education courses and school experiences often change our ideas of both "good" teacher and researcher. Wherever you are in the journey of becoming a teacher, it is critical to consider your own ideas of what makes a "good teacher" and "good researcher."

What Is a Good Teacher?

Begin with your image of a "teacher." Start by defining a "good teacher" in your notebook or journal. Brainstorm as many different qualities, attributes, and skills you associate with someone who is a "good teacher." Then, compare and contrast your text definition to the drawings in Figures 1.1 to 1.5 completed by **preservice teachers** of a "good teacher." (If you have never drawn your own picture of a "good teacher," it may be an interesting activity for you to complete at this time.)

Drawings like these reflect the social values that surround us. In this case, the drawings of teacher mirror values portrayed in popular culture (Weber & Mitchell, 1995). Anthropologists have written extensively about how our perception of reality is shaped by media and literature. These sources teach us what is "normal" or "acceptable." In this way, such perceptions limit our boundaries of what is possible.

Many students notice that their drawings and definitions represent *the teacher they needed when they were in school.* Is this true of your drawing/definition? How does your own definition of a "good teacher" both limit and provide possibilities of who you might become as a teacher?

📖 Analyze further your definition and the drawings by preservice teachers by responding to the following questions:

- What themes appear among the drawings? What do the drawings have in common?

- What might be useful and dangerous about these themes?

- What is *not* included in these drawings?

- How do your own ideas about a "good teacher" compare with those shown?

→ FIGURES 1.1–1.5: Teacher Drawings

1.1

1.2

1.3

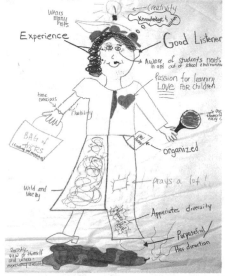

1.4

- How do own ideas represent the kind of teacher you needed when you were in school? What might be useful about becoming your own version of a "good" teacher? What might be dangerous?

- In your definition of a good teacher, did you include any attributes you might associate with *research*?

- Do any words represent **analysis**, decision making, or **synthesis** of information?

- Is the concept of "research" one you associate with the act of good teaching?

1.5

This is a good time to travel the side road Cultural Context 1.2: *Images of School and Society*, found at the end of this chapter on p. 34, and analyze how "school" and "teacher" are portrayed in popular culture.

What Is a Good Researcher?

Now consider your image of a "researcher." Start by defining "good researcher" in your notebook or journal. Brainstorm as many different qualities, attributes, and skills you associate with someone who is a "good researcher." Compare your definition to drawings of researchers we have collected from preservice teachers in our classes.

→ FIGURES 1.6–1.8: Researcher Drawings

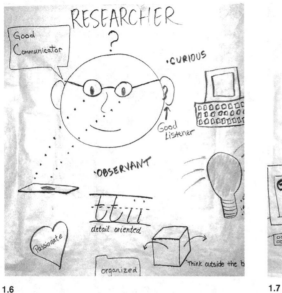

1.6

1.7

1.8

📘 In analyzing these drawings, you have engaged in *deconstruction*, a key element of doing action research that will appear as a theme throughout this book. Analyze both your definition and the drawings above by responding to the following questions:

- How does your definition of "researcher" compare or contrast with your idea of "teacher"? What themes seem to be present?

- What might be dangerous or useful about these themes?

- Why do you think these similarities or differences exist?

- What experiences have you had that define "teacher" and "research" for you?

Write a definition of teacher-researcher based on your work so far. You will return to this definition later.

Exploring "Action" and "Research"

Having considered the terms *teacher* and *researcher*, begin now to form a definition of *action research*, the genre of research this book explores.

Instructions

📘 In your notebook, create two "webs," one around the word *action* and the other around the word *research*. Try to connect the two webs showing the interrelationships between the two words as you conceive them.

Use the terms from your webs to create a Venn diagram of the concepts "action" and "research" (Figure 1.9), focusing on both their intersection (overlapping ideas) and complement (distinguishing ideas).

➔ FIGURE 1.9: Action Research Venn Diagram

📘 Based upon the webbing activity, write your initial definition of the term *action research*. Your definition will continue to emerge as you continue to work through this section. You will be asked to recall and revise your initial definition as you encounter new ideas. Allow your definition to evolve as you engage with the process of conducting your own action research project.

Voices of Action Research

Action research is most simply defined as a "practitioner-based" form of research. In other words, it is done by teachers in their own classrooms with the goal of improving pedagogy and student learning. We asked some of our former students to define action research while they were in their first year of teaching. This is what they said:

I believe that action research is the ability to daily recognize areas in your classroom that need improvement and then seeking to discover methods that will help make a needed change. I feel that it is a process that you are constantly going through by testing and trying out different methods and documenting what will help your students succeed. —Cole

Action research is everything a good teacher does . . . only documented! As a teacher, it is my job to identify a problem, make a plan of action, and watch carefully to see how my action influences the initial problem. If I never examine my work to see what worked and what didn't, both on a day-to-day basis, and in the larger spectrum of a year, then I am not teaching well. —Natasha

Right now I am researching how to survive my first year of teaching! Really, I am discovering when to rest, when to stay up past midnight to complete my work, how to learn from my fellow staff members, how to keep track of all the paperwork, and how to serve students from a background of neglect and abuse. Every day I am looking up ideas on the Internet, finding the right resources on my shelf of "teacher books," looking for student work or talking with my peers. I am always analyzing my practice. —Elena

How do these ideas prompt you to modify your initial definition of action research? Expand your definition of action research further by reading the following brief descriptions of projects our teacher education students have conducted.

Anna

Anna was a student teacher in a third grade classroom where most of the students were below grade level in writing, according to the state writing exam. Anna noticed that the students who had the most difficult time with writing were also those who had a difficult time just getting started. She wanted to explore how using prewriting exercises might assist these struggling writers. Anna began to implement several prewriting strategies. She collected three kinds of data: student compositions (each composition was scored using the state required scoring guide), student self-evaluations (inquiring about the writing process), and instructor **observations** with anecdotal notes.

At the conclusion of Anna's action research project, she wrote the following about what she had learned:

My research project was a journey that took me many places I had not previously envisioned. I not only learned more about how students write and how to assist them in becoming better writers, but also about my own teaching and learning practices. I am more confident in my abilities to assess the needs of a particular class and to adjust the lesson and assignment to meet those needs . . . I am confident my teaching career will follow a similar journey with new discoveries and unexpected side trips. The process of learning how to evaluate the progress of my class and my progress as a teacher has been invaluable.

Claire

Claire was a student teacher in a seventh grade social studies classroom with 22 students, representing a wide variety of learning styles, learning challenges, and reading levels. Claire wondered how using history/culture simulations in class might facilitate learning for *all* students.

She planned an action research project based upon six triangulated **data sets**; each data set included observations, student work, and student focus group **interviews**.

Claire discovered that history/culture simulations are beneficial for students in six specific ways. They provide focused learning; challenge students to take ownership of their learning; engage higher-level thinking; increase student engagement; trigger emotion, which in turn leads to increased learning; and encourage learning for diverse learning styles and intelligences. But she also learned things she did not expect. Here is an excerpt from her final reflection:

I discovered that action research is more about improving my abilities as a teacher and, in turn, improving the lives of my students than it is about becoming an expert in one specific area. Although I certainly learned much about the benefits and drawbacks of simulations as a teaching tool, the greatest lessons came in the areas of managing the classroom, being prepared for class, and redesigning lessons to meet individual needs. Not to mention the lessons I learned about Ryan's incredible acting abilities, Melissa's (who is at third grade reading level) capacity for reading difficult materials when she found purpose, and Sadie's sensitivity to being placed in a lower age-level class. Action research is not so much about the ultimate destination, but about the journey and the many companions, such as the three students just mentioned, who accompanied me on that journey.

Abby

Abby was a student teacher in English at a large suburban high school. She was interested in emphasizing critical thinking in her two American literature classes. She believed that Socratic questioning—one-on-one interrogative dialogue between student and teacher about literature—was the best way to facilitate critical thinking. Still, she wondered how could she hold one-on-one dialogue with 54 students within the confines of standard class time and space? She decided to implement online communication between herself and her students about class material, and study the interactions for clues about how critical thinking can be developed in such an environment.

Abby's results illustrated a three-stage critical thinking development process of "aesthetic response," "dialogical analysis," and "dialectical evaluation." Aesthetic response and dialogical analysis were successfully facilitated online—especially the latter. She discovered, through carefully studying and reflecting on the online dialogues she carried on with students, a depth of student experience and thinking that would not have taken place otherwise.

How do the definitions of former students and the examples of these action research projects inform your emerging definition of action research? How is action research similar or different to what you imagined? Add to these student voices definitions offered by published writers in the field of action research.

As you read these definitions, note words and phrases that either reinforce or challenge your concept of action research:

[Action research is a] form of teaching; a form of reflective practice and professional learning founded on an ethical commitment to improving practice and realizing educational values. AR involves individuals and groups identifying areas for improvement, generating ideas, and testing these ideas in practice. (Arhar, Holly, & Kasten, 2001, p. 285)

Action research is any systematic inquiry conducted by teacher-researchers, principals, school counselors, or other stakeholders in the teaching/learning environment, to gather information about the ways that their particular schools operate, how they teach, and how well their students learn. This information is gathered with the goals of gaining insight, developing reflective practice, effecting positive changes in the school environment (and on educational practices in general), and improving student outcomes and the lives of those involved (Mills, 2000, p. 6).

Action research . . . is about taking everyday things in the life of education and unpacking them for their historical and ideological baggage . . . . It highlights process with content, rather than content alone. It allows for a focus on teaching, in addition to student outcomes, and on the interplay between the two. (Noffke, 1995, p. 5)

Action research is a comparative research on the conditions and effects of various forms of social action, and research leading to social action. Research that produces nothing but books will not suffice. (Lewin, 1948, pp. 207–208)

Action research is systematic . . . It involves a self-reflective spiral of planning, acting, observing, reflecting and re-planning. It requires teachers to be acutely aware of a sense of process, and to refine their perceptions to account for that process . . . . action research raises to a conscious level much of what is already being done by good teachers on an intuitive level. It enables teachers to identify and come to grips with their practice in a human way which is at once supportive and critical. (McNiff, 1988, p. 7)

We see common themes in these definitions: Action research 1) involves a systematic or organized approach to problem solving, 2) requires active engagement and interaction between groups of people, 3) insists upon reflection, critical analysis, and revolving **assessment**, 4) analyzes systems of power, 5) deconstructs taken-for-granted assumptions, 6) results in *action* as a practical outcome, 7) results in transformation, in a rediscovered or new sense of self and other, in empowered teaching and learning, 8) relies upon democratic and ethical principles that value and respect all participants, and, finally, 9) focuses on a single place of inquiry.

Finally, our definition of action research merges with the thoughts of other writers, our own experiences as action researchers, and the experience of the preservice teachers with whom we work and learn. In alignment with the focus of becoming a teacher through action research, we've written our own definition of action research specifically for *preservice teacher action research*. The definition continues to evolve—we think this is indicative of the process of inquiry. At this time, our definition reads like this:

Action research for preservice teachers is a process of learning, in community with others, to think and act critically, to recognize and negotiate political systems, and to focus passion growing in one's identity as a teacher. This process evolves from a desire to become a caring, intelligent, transformative educator, and includes honing the art and science of planning, assessment, and a critical reflective practice. Action research includes the interrogation of one's own paradigm while in active exploration of ways of thinking and acting beyond one's own boundaries. The result of action research for preservice teachers is the beginning of a teaching-research journey, which simultaneously includes improving teaching practice, student outcomes, and systems of schooling to be more just and equitable for all children and adolescents.

The preservice teacher action-research process is like budget travel. We know the destination, at least conceptually, and we anticipate a successful arrival, but we realize we may need to be flexible in our journey. We lay out everything we would like to take with us, but then we leave much behind and take only the essentials. We include our camera and journal: photos will give **context**, and our written words will document the events, people, and places we visit and our reactions to them. Action research requires that we pack light, laying aside some of our assumptions and being willing to learn from those we meet along the way. We plan to pick up such souvenirs as language and experience along the way. We expect to come home changed because of our travels; in the end, we may find the destination is not what we thought and that arrival is an illusive concept.

Return now to your definition of action research. Add or delete text based upon the descriptions you have read. In the previous section, you defined the term *teacher-researcher*. As a closing activity for these first two sections, we suggest you revise your definition of a teacher-researcher based upon your new understanding of this term.

Philosophical Underpinnings of Action Research

Like our images of teacher and researcher, action research is the product of cultural history and takes its place among many other forms of research in the universe of possibilities. *Research*, in its broadest sense, could be used to name any systematic way of knowing. But not all research is the same. Each different genre of research was developed at its own point in history, incorporating its own set of philosophical assumptions and cultural norms. These assumptions and norms mediate to some degree how school has looked during different time periods. The work of philosophers, artists, scientists, and musicians provide us a window into cultural thought and paradigms. During times of transition, work in these fields often heralds changes that come much later in education. As teacher-researchers, we, too, reflect our collective and individual cultural time and place.

Figure 1.10 depicts three historical movements, or paradigms, of Western culture: the **Enlightenment**, **modernism**, and **postmodernism**. Each paradigm has defined and redefined a "good education" and has influenced the way educational research is conducted.

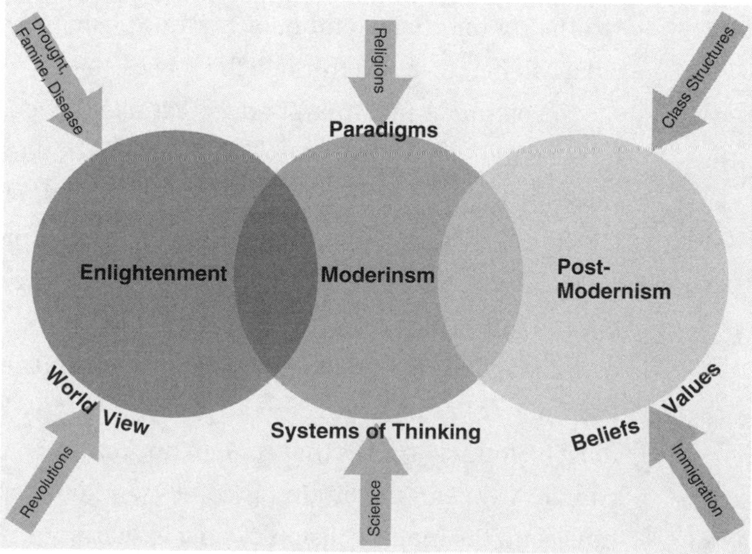

The Enlightenment was a time of intense knowledge production as Western civilization began to stress rational thought rather than religious belief as its cornerstone. The scientific method of deductive reasoning and logic still resonate in research today in

→ FIGURE 1.10: Paradigm Chart

its emphasis on objectivity. Classic art of this time reflects this kind of logic. Clean, orderly, and presenting a vision of clarity, it often reinforced the belief in rationality and the proper order of things. German Empiricist Johann F. Herbart (1776–1841) applied to education the early science of psychology. Science, in this way, was thought of as the means of developing students of good moral character.

The modernist period began with the intensification of Enlightenment principles of rational thought as a way to pursue and find truth. Building upon the deterministic foundation laid by Isaac Newton and others, science constructed a universal structure of **theory** that seemed unassailable in its ability to predict and control nature. Charles Darwin's *On the Origin of Species* (1859) provided the groundwork for the development of behavioral psychology, which in turn further reinforced the central role of objective observation in research, along with the rejection of non-empirical evidence. The subjectivity of personal experience was seen and explained through the objective and rational tools of science. Empirical educational research is still firmly rooted in beliefs from the modernist time period.

Horace Mann (1796–1859) proposed during this period the "common school," suggesting that public education serve as the "great equalizer." School could be the place where, through group education, all children could learn to be moral, thinking citizens. Art began to reflect some of the dilemmas of this thought. Édouard Manet's *Olympia* (1863), for example, depicts the human body no longer perfect or rationale but maintains the scientific tradition of "objectivity" by attempting to show truth through stripping the subject of emotion and moral judgment.

World Wars I and II devastated many of the hopes of the modernists. In the words of Kurt Vonnegut (1970), "Scientific truth was going to make us *so* happy and comfortable. What actually happened when I was twenty-one was that we dropped scientific truth on Hiroshima." Existentialists began to question the role of free will. Albert Einstein had reformulated Newton's laws into a new theory of gravity; his theories led to troubling problems in the field of physics, mapping a new view of the universe through quantum physics. The ideal of an "objective observer" was questioned, and the concept of the individual as a unified whole began to crumble. Art by Pablo Picasso, such as *Weeping Woman* (1937), questions the "truths" of rationality and objectivity, exposing the limitations of viewing the world through what can be perceived through the senses alone.

Postmodernist thought deconstructs the ideas of the Enlightenment and modernism by rejecting the concept of a unified self and exploring how historical and cultural voices and values work to socially construct the individual. Philosophers such as Ludwig Wittgenstein (1844–1900) described how language is not as a picture but a "box of tools" that forms our image of self. Michel Foucault (1926–1984) further explored how language frames our thinking and thus what and how we observe. The "objective observer" becomes a human-designed myth. Many of these changes in thought are spurred by the realization of physicists that the fixed narratives of "truth" are no longer reliable. "New" science recognizes that new stories must be found—stories that contain not contrite narrative with a fixed plot line, but tales that contain mystery, uncertain outcomes, and connections among characters and events that transcend the modern vision of what is "natural."

Such major shifts have influenced educational research in powerful ways. No longer are the only "experts" those from outside the classroom who observe "objectively" seeking empirical evidence. The narrative stories of teachers and students tell the story of the school in many different, diverse ways, each reflecting a unique and valuable perspective. The influences of class, ethnicity, gender, and learning styles and challenges are seen as windows into understanding school life. School as the "great equalizer" is challenged by such viewpoints; Jonathan Kozol's 30-year work with inner city schools (1985, 1992, 1995, 2001, 2005), for example, demonstrates just the opposite. The factory model of schools and the use of applied behavior sciences are questioned and deconstructed (Giroux, 2003; Goodlad, 2004; Kohn, 1999; Smith, 1998). Students are seen not as a blank slate but as humans constructing reality within a specific cultural and historical place; multiple viewpoints are encouraged in the pursuit of truth. **Qualitative research methodology**, including action research, and many other forms of "coming to know" reflect these changes in thought.

What we hope to deliberately communicate through this sketch of time and thought is this message: *We do not teach and research in a vacuum.* Our constructed lives, values, beliefs, pedagogies, and methodologies are influenced by a multitude of cultural and historical factors. When we discuss concepts like *paradigm* and *theory* in education, it is too easy to come to understand these ideas as isolated or separated from those found in art, music, philosophy, or science. When we discuss modernism or postmodernism it is too easy to think in categories, conveying a sense that we have moved from modernism to postmodernism and somehow left behind all the thoughts of a "previous" era. But as Wink (1997) writes, our histories "tend to turn into behaviors that run around behind us and tell stories for all the world to hear" (p. 132). Hargreaves (1994) describes this overlapping of the modern and postmodern era and schooling in this way:

Schools and teachers are being affected more and more by the demands and contingencies of an increasingly complex and fast paced, postmodern world. Yet their response is often inappropriate or ineffective—leaving intact the systems and structures of the present, or retreating to comforting myths of the past. Schools and teachers either cling to bureaucratic solutions of a modernistic kind: more systems, more hierarchies, more laid on change, more of the same . . . . As time goes by, this gap between the world of school and the world beyond it is becoming more and more obvious. The anachronistic nature of schooling is increasingly transparent . . . the major characteristics of the era of modernity, an era which is generally on the wane but one which has set remarkably resilient assumptions and conditions within which schools and teachers now operate, and to which they continue to cling as the vortex of change swirls all around them. (pp. 23–34)

Engaging in the process of action research is a tool one can use to bridge the gap between school and the world outside school. Most important is that educators be aware of these conflicting modes of knowing, of the way paradigms influence not only our own ways of thinking and perceiving but those of others.

Certainly, those of us in education, as in any field, represent collections of many systems of thought. The paradigm chart seeks to present not only the collection, but also the overlapping nature of multiple thought-fields. The Venn diagram fades across the Enlightenment, modernism, and postmodernism, but the diagram is all a shade of grey. This is to represent how the Enlightenment is still with us, still influencing who we become as teacher-researchers, just as modernist and postmodernist thought influence who we become as teacher-researchers. For example, in the United States, there is a resurgence of strong belief in scientific research as the only valid form of evidence in education, as perpetuated by the No Child Left Behind Act (U.S. Department of Education, 2004).

As you travel the distance of thought presented in this section, don't think of "leaving something behind"; instead, think of packing your bags and finding them more full as the journey progresses. Finally, this is *just* a very brief overview. Whole books have been written about any one of the subjects presented. (See Linn, 1996; Palmer, 2001; Sharpes, 2002, for further introduction and exploration.) The goal here is to give you a sense of the whole, a sense of the way we are shaped and influenced by our history and our interpretation of that history.

Always be mindful of your own reactions to ideas: with what do you find yourself agreeing, disagreeing, being amused, wanting to know more? Why do you have this reaction? What might your reaction mean in terms of who you are becoming as a teacher-researcher?

Your Personal Paradigm

Our teaching practice consists of the concrete techniques and tools we use in the classroom. Our practice does not live, however, in isolation from our ways of seeing the world. Our classroom practices are grounded in abstract views of knowledge and learning of which we are rarely conscious. We use the term *paradigm* to describe the set unconscious philosophical assumptions that form the foundation of any body of practice (Kuhn, 1970). We each have within in us

→ FIGURE 1.11: Paradigm Self-Test

Paradigm Self-Test

Consider your level of agreement with each of the statement below.
Only check if you strongly agree with the statement

____1. Truth is a relative concept.
____2. Truth is absolute either in terms of divine revelation or the accumulated wisdom of the centuries.
____3. The only social constant, or absolute, is change.
____4. The value of an idea can be measured only in terms of its immediate usefulness.
____5. The basic purpose of formal education is to transmit the cultural heritage.
____6. The basic purpose of formal education is to assist in the creation of new culture.
____7. Morality arises from the quality of mutually shared experiences.
____8. The whole is the sum of its parts.
____9. Science is the most powerful way of knowing.
____10. There may be different, but equally valid answers to many questions.
____11. I like art that depicts life realistically, as it actually is.
____12. I like abstract art that is very open to interpretation.
____13. There is much truth to be gained through non-scientific means.
____14. Most of life is a matter of cause and effect.
____15. Most of life cannot be explained by cause and effect.
____16. Proof consists of well-reasoned, logical arguments and evidence.
____17. Proof is a very tricky concept because there are many equally valid forms of evidence.
____18. Knowledge is mostly discovered in the world outside the mind.
____19. Knowledge is mostly found inside the mind.

See Appendix A to interpret your answers.

---

a personal paradigm that influences our view of the world, what we think about teaching and learning, and—ultimately—the role and purpose of action research as described in this book.

How does your personal paradigm fit into the larger picture? How does your view of teaching and learning reflect central paradigms seen in music, art, science, and philosophy? We invite you to respond to a short, simple survey that may help you think about where your views align with two major paradigm movements—modernism and postmodernism—that have had a powerful impact on education (Figure 1.11).

> Go a little deeper discovering your personal paradigm by traveling the side road Self-Study 1.1: *Personal Interview*, found at the end of this chapter on p. 31.

Research Worlds, Research Lives: Forms of Action Research

Our personal paradigms influence how we approach life's dilemmas; just as our personal paradigms influence the way we approach research. Our purpose, setting, and needs also influence such decisions. It is little wonder that there are, then, multiple ways to do educational research. Action research is just one way of exploring teaching, learning, and school context. Even within the category of action research there are many definitions and multiple approaches to school-based dilemmas or questions.

The way we teach depends upon our personal paradigms. The same is true of the way we approach research. Our personal paradigm may be found in the way we answer questions such as these:

- What do you believe about the nature of knowledge?

- What do you believe about the nature of "reality"?

- What beliefs and values do you hold about teaching, learning and schools?

- What is the purpose of the educational research? What is to be accomplished and for whom is the research being done?

Influenced by paradigm (or **epistemology**), a researcher chooses a *methodology*, an approach to conducting the research (this is the **research design**). Paradigm and methodology then drive the choice of **methods** or techniques used to gather data. Research is often classified as being either *quantitative* or *qualitative*. This somewhat simplistic typology disguises the complexity of choosing a research methodology and methods, but since they are widely used, we will begin this discussion with these two terms.

Quantitative Research

Quantitative research is research that relies on numerical measurement techniques and mathematical analysis. Such research often uses statistical computations to determine whether a given hypothesis is supported by the research data collected (Coladarci, Cobb, Minium, & Clarke, 2004; Gall, Borg, & Gall, 2003; Gorard, 2001). Quantitative research designs attempt to reduce the many complex variables involved in understanding teaching and learning to objective, numerical measurements. Common quantitative approaches include *correlational, casual-comparative*, and **experimental research** designs (see Tables 1.1, 1.2, and 1.3). The objective positioning of quantitative research enables the researcher to observe and collect data in an unbiased way so as to further the understanding of what is being studied.

➜ TABLE 1.1: Correlational Research

Purpose	Methodology	Validity and Reliability
To investigate the strength of possible relationships between two or more variables in a given population.	Sample population is measured with respect to two or more variables. Statistical analysis of data shows the degree to which variables are related to each other within the population.	Established by calculating correlation coefficient using inferential statistics.
Snapshot Example Researchers wish to investigate possible links between grade point average and a variety of behaviors in high school seniors. A large population of seniors fill out a questionnaire in which they are asked to self-report the frequency and duration of many behaviors, including watching television, playing video games, doing homework, talking with friends, surfing the Internet, text messaging, and involvement in extra-curricular activities. The survey data are analyzed, and it is reported that a moderately strong correlation was found between extra-curricular involvement and grade point average, while a slight negative correlation was found between playing video games and grade point average. No other significant correlations were found. The researchers are careful to point out that no cause-and-effect relationship has been established, and that an experimental research design would be needed to make further claims about grade point averages and behavior.		

➜ TABLE 1.2: Causal-Comparative Research

Purpose	Methodology	Validity and Reliability
To explore relationships between specific conditions and a desired outcome in a population.	Sample population is assigned to two or more groups based on one or more criteria of interest. Group members are then measured with respect to one or more variables, and data analyzed to show possible relationships.	Established by using means and standard deviations in the data to calculate the statistical probability that outcomes were different between the groups.
Snapshot Example Researchers wish to investigate how kindergarten attendance affects academic success in first grade. A large sample of first graders is identified and assigned to two groups for analysis. One group consists of children who attended kindergarten, and the other consists of children who did not attend kindergarten. The academic achievement of all of the children is measured during first grade. The data are statistically analyzed to determine if there are significant differences between the two groups. It is determined that achievement was in fact notably higher in the "attended kindergarten" group, and that the difference was statistically significant. It was reported that kindergarten attendance may be an important factor in first grade success, but is noted that many other variables may play a role as well.		

➔ TABLE 1.3: Experimental Research

Purpose	Methodology	Validity and Reliability
To determine cause-and-effect relationships between specific conditions and a desired outcome in a population.	Sample population is randomly assigned to treatment and control groups. Group members are then measured with respect to one or more variables, and data analyzed to show relationships.	Established by using means and standard deviations in the data to calculate the statistical probability that outcomes were different between the groups.

Snapshot Example

Researchers wished to determine the effect of a new reading program on the reading ability of third graders. A large sample population of third graders was identified, and each teacher agreed to randomly assign half of their class to the new reading program for two weeks, while half studied an alternative, traditional reading program. After the two weeks the groups switched treatments.

A reading assessment was constructed. All students were pre-assessed on reading level prior to receiving instruction, and were assessed again at the two-week mark, and again at the conclusion of the study. It was found that reading scores on the assessment increased more when students were instructed in the new reading program. It reported that the new reading program had been scientifically proven to be effective in reading instruction in third graders when compared with traditional instruction.

Researchers using quantitative methods in school settings often strive for *generalizability*; the knowledge gained should apply in other settings as well as the research setting. Therefore, quantitative methodologies include the use of reliable research tools and sample sizes aimed at providing statistically valid judgments. If a teaching approach is found in a well-designed study to produce statistically better outcomes in a sample population, then it can be generalized that the approach will likely be successful when teaching the general population of students. Validity and reliability in quantitative research are generally established by 1) the presence of a **statistically significant** sample population; 2) the appropriate application of statistical analysis; 3) the identification of all critical and influencing variables; and 4) the objectivity of the researcher.

While rarely carried out by classroom teachers due to the complexity of design and the need for a sample size larger than most classrooms, understanding how to read and critically interpret quantitative research is an important skill. (Cultural Context side roads in Chapter 6 provide a discussion about statistical analysis in educational research. These side roads will explain much more about quantitative methods and how to interpret quantitative studies.)

As you read the tables, how did you respond? Be mindful of your reactions. Did you find this information intriguing? From these brief descriptions of possible research designs, what aspects appear useful? What might be dangerous about such designs? How possible would it be to use these designs as a classroom teacher? Your reactions may be indications of how this type of research fits your personal paradigm concerning teaching, researching, and learning.

Qualitative Research

Qualitative research embodies multiple methodologies—narrative, participatory, historical, and feminist inquiries (to name a few)—and therefore defies easy definition (Whitt, 1991). Qualitative research methods generally assume the nature of knowledge as fluid and subjective (as opposed to fixed and objective.) Such knowledge is enriched by multiple viewpoints and changes as these viewpoints are used to further construct a knowledge base. Reality is not only known quantitatively, but also constructed by culture, history, and specific settings. While beliefs and values about teaching and learning vary widely among qualitative researchers, there is a sense of respect for the complex and diverse factors influencing schools. Terms like *validity* and *reliability*, which have specific definitions within quantitative research, are often replaced by the term **trustworthiness** (Lincoln & Guba, 1985), or other constructs such as *goodness* (Arminio & Hultgren, 2002). All speak to the act of seeking a variety of voices and perspectives.

Qualitative research is generally considered trustworthy if it features 1) multiple viewpoints as represented in data sets from multiple sources (referred to as **triangulation**), 2) "thick description," or research narrative rich with contextual and situational details based upon well-documented raw data, 3) deliberate and systematic data collection and interpretation, 4) clarification of researcher own biases or positions, and 5) critical reflection or **reflexivity** (see Arminio & Hultgren, 2002; Lather, 1991, 1993; Lincoln & Guba, 2003; Whitt, 1991). The term *crystalline* has been used to describe trustworthy qualitative research, bringing to mind the notion that a single crystal presents many facets and reflects light in many different ways depending on one's visual perspective and the light in which the crystal is viewed (Richardson, 2003).

Examine three different qualitative approaches common in action research as shown in Tables 1.4, 1.5 and 1.6.

→ TABLE 1.4: Narrative Inquiry

Purpose	Methodology	Trustworthiness
To explore the experience of schools and schooling as an observer-member of the setting and context.	The researcher's goal is to determine a narrative view of the experience that is truthful, informative, and grounded in theory. Data sources include observations, interviews, and artifacts from the field.	Established by triangulation of multiple data sources and inclusion of multiple voices in the resulting narrative.
Snapshot Example A teacher wishes to better understand the transition between middle school and high school as experienced by her students. She senses that this transition is sometimes traumatic, and desires to increase her understanding in order to better design her instruction, particularly at the beginning of the school year. She intentionally collects narratives not only of herself through observation and journaling, but from students, parents, and administrators through interviews. She reconstructs the stories, collectively re-telling the narrative of "coming to high school."		

→ TABLE 1.5: Participatory Inquiry

Purpose	Methodology	Trustworthiness
To collaboratively work to answer a question, solve a dilemma or improve a situation.	The group gathers data and reads outside to inform them. A course of action is then determined. The results are then evaluated using narrative techniques, quantitative analysis, or a combination of the two.	Established by triangulation of multiple data sources and inclusion of multiple voices in the resulting narrative.

Snapshot Example

A group of elementary school teachers has become over the last several years dissatisfied with the science curriculum. They have observed that the children become increasingly bored with the textbook curriculum as they progress from first through sixth grade. They decide that changes are needed, but what? Through outside reading, analysis of the current curriculum, and dialogue among the group it is decided that more inquiry methods should be implemented, and that a year-end science fair might heighten interest in science for the students and their families. As the changes are implemented the group continues to collect data and meet together. During the following summer, a report is compiled and presented to the school board detailing the results of their changes, suggesting that other district schools adopt similar adjustments to the standard curriculum.

→ TABLE 1.6: Critical Inquiry

Purpose	Methodology	Trustworthiness
To address a social, economic, and/or political concern rooted in a form of injustice.	The teacher/researcher focuses on implementing an educational practice that he/she believes will make schools more equitable and just. Results are documented using narrative and/or quantitative techniques.	Established by triangulation of multiple data sources and inclusion of multiple voices in the resulting narrative.

Snapshot Example

A teacher is in a school that has recently undergone realignment due to redistricting. The school has experienced an influx of new students, resulting in a much more ethnically diverse population. The teacher realizes that the established curriculum doesn't reflect multicultural values or voices. He sets about devising a plan to implement multicultural components in his reading program. He will plan, implement, and assess the results in terms of vision, politics, and ethical responsibility. He will share his results with colleagues and the broader population in an effort to bring change to others.

As you did after reading about quantitative research, consider these questions: As you read the charts in Tables 1.4–1.6, how did you respond? Again, be mindful of your responses. Did you find this information intriguing? From these brief descriptions of possible research designs, what aspects appear useful? What might be dangerous about such designs? How possible would it be to use these designs as a classroom teacher? Your reactions may be indications of how this type of research fits your personal paradigm concerning teaching, researching, and learning.

One term used in both quantitative and qualitative methods is *power*. In both forms of research, power is the measure of a design's ability to detect important patterns and differences that exist within the data. In other words, is the design powerful enough to get to the heart of the research question, suggesting not only possible answers, but new questions as well? The point of differentiating between qualitative and quantitative methods is not to make an either/or distinction. Instead, making this distinction encourages a both/and approach to making action research as powerful and trustworthy as possible by seeking multiple ways of viewing research questions.

Mixed-Methods Research

It may have already occurred to you that one way of using quantitative/qualitative research methods is to apply *both methods* to the same research question. If so, you are in good company, joining philosophers like William James and John Dewey, who, as pragmatists, often eschewed ideologically pure solutions to problems. Pragmatists often propose combining different or even opposite solutions in order to use the strengths of one approach to mitigate or lessen the weaknesses of another, and vice versa. Pragmatists often leave aside the question of "which single approach is best?" in favor of the question, "what works?" Barack Obama invoked **pragmatism** in his 2009 inaugural address when he said, "It's not about whether we should have big government or small government, it's about what works." Obama again invoked pragmatism in his 2013 inaugural address when he said, "We must act, knowing that our work will be imperfect."

Pragmatic educational researchers have suggested **mixed-methods research** as one way to relieve the tension between quantitative and qualitative approaches, combining both types of methods within the same study (Teddlie & Tashakkori, 2009). Mixed-methods research recognizes, in accordance with pragmatic principles, that both quantitative and qualitative methods have inherent strengths and weaknesses. Qualitative and quantitative methods are regarded as complementary in mixed methods research, each method bringing into sharp focus information and insight left fuzzy or invisible by the other.

Often, qualitative data and methods are used to help support and better understand results first brought to light through quantitative analyses. Consider the following summary of a mixed-methods study.

Martha, a school district math curriculum specialist, became concerned about the ways in which the over 250 individual elementary math teachers in her district were implementing the district math curriculum. She had heard rumors and reports that teachers varied greatly in their implementation of the curriculum, and wished to gather information in order to be equipped to make recommendations to the superintendent. She began by developing and administering a quantitative survey in which teachers were asked to self-report, anonymously, their opinions and usage of the district math curriculum.

Results from the survey were tabulated and statistics generated, showing means, trends, and correlations between the survey items. Then, focus groups were held and recorded in which teachers discussed the district math curriculum, including their opinions about what they would change, what they like and dislike, and what they would need in order to be better prepared to fully use the curriculum. These conversations were transcribed to help Martha better read and understand the content, and a software application was used to highlight words and phrases of interest. Finally, Martha used both the quantitative survey results and qualitative analysis of the discussion data to draw conclusions about the math curriculum and make her report.

Some questions to consider about Martha's work:

- What was useful about the survey Martha gave? What was dangerous?

- What was useful about the focus group sessions Martha used? What was dangerous?

- How was Martha's work enhanced by her mixed-methods approach?

- What information and data might Martha still be missing?

Where Does Action Research Fit?

Action research is often categorized as a qualitative methodology, even though quantitative data may be included. In this sense, action research often mixes methods. However, in another sense, action research is inclusive of data, methods of analysis, and purposes not commonly used in "mixed methods research." Reconsider Martha's story, keeping in mind these statements of the purpose and framework of action research:

- Action research improves one's own teaching practice, increases the quality of education for students, and, more holistically, makes life in schools better.

- Teacher-researchers view teaching and learning as a dynamic process that can be informed, modified, and altered through intentional planning, data collection, analysis, and self-reflection.

- Teacher-researchers recognize school communities as being complex, and realize that multiple ways of looking and analyzing issues, situations, and questions require more than simple analysis of either quantitative or qualitative data alone.

- The process of action research is the process of co-creating meaning with students and often other members of the school and community resulting in action.

Suppose Martha wished to adopt a research stance more aligned with action research as discussed above. How would you advise her? First, Martha may wish to consider collecting data on an ongoing basis from a wide variety of participants in her setting, including not only teachers, but students, parents, and other administrators.

Second, she would begin to use this data not only to answer her specific questions about the math curriculum, but to engage in deeper self-reflection about her own practices, challenging her own assumptions and knowledge about math teaching and learning and her role as an administrator. Finally, Martha may wish to consider more clearly how her research work to create meaningful action—the "action" in action research—about the math curriculum. By now you may be getting the sense that teacher action research is about more than finding specific answers to well-defined questions about teaching and learning. Action research draws us into the complexities of teaching and learning, and encourages us to reconsider not only our own practices, but our identities and roles as teachers.

Frameworks for Action Research Commonly Used by Preservice Teachers

While the term *action research* is closely associated with integrating practice and research, there are other forms of school-based methodologies that support the same goal of improving one's teaching practice. Bullough and Gitlin (2001) categorize these approaches as follows: (1) methods of exploring self, (2) methodologies for exploring school context, and (3) integrating methodologies. These action research methods include **self-study** (educational autobiography), **ethnography**, **curriculum analysis**, and **design research**. Browse Tables 1.7 to 1.10 for more details about these action research frameworks.

→ TABLE 1.7: Self-Study

Purpose	Methodology	Trustworthiness
To deliberately trace the process of becoming a teacher.	Analyze values, beliefs, and personal metaphors for teaching. Collect multiple perspectives on practice. Track progress in meeting goals, changing values, beliefs, and personal metaphors.	Established through "thick" reflection and description, multiple viewpoints, data sets that support goals, connection to the stories of others and to the literature.
Snapshot Example		
Loren grew up in rural America and understood personally words like "poverty" and "hunger." Her desire to become a teacher came from her own belief, based on experience, that education is "the ticket" necessary to leave cycles of poverty. Loren reflected on and wrote on her experiences, analyzing critical incidents that led her to teacher education. She devised a schedule and plan for becoming the interactive, project-based teacher she hoped to become. Her research not only tracked her progress in becoming this teacher, but also the changes she made in her conception of school, teacher, and students. Her story, when shared with others, lends a strand to the rich tapestry of felt experiences shared by those who have become teachers.		

→ TABLE 1.8: Ethnography

Purpose	Methodology	Trustworthiness
To better understand the issues of students and schooling.	Select representative students to "shadow" during their school day. Interview students and collect artifacts of their lives. Make recommendations for future teaching within the school/community context.	Established through "thick" reflection and description; triangulation in data sets, connection to contextually relevant literature.
Snapshot Example		
Aaron planned to teach middle school. His own middle school experience was positive, but he was well aware that this not the case for all students. He really wanted to get to know his students, especially since the school where he was going to student-teach represented diverse ethnic groups. He used an ethnographic study to develop his own personal list of "things to remember about middle school students when I am a licensed teacher." His work, when shared with others, serves to illustrate in a general way the task of becoming a good middle school teacher.		

➔ TABLE 1.9: Curriculum Analysis

Purpose	Methodology	Trustworthiness
To analyze curriculum based on the literature in the area, and to ascertain the curriculum's strengths and weaknesses.	A specific area of curriculum is identified, and an analysis rubric is developed and implemented based upon the literature from the area. Recommendations are made for teachers using the curriculum.	Established by triangulation of multiple data sources and inclusion of multiple voices in the resulting narrative.

Snapshot Example

The school where Courtney was student teaching had recently adopted a new reading series that claimed as one of its benefits an increase in elementary children's reading comprehension. Courtney developed a rubric based on what the literature reported were essential characteristics to be included in an elementary reading series. She analyzed the curriculum based on these criteria. She held focus group discussions with third grade teachers in her team and tracked selected student progress during the curriculum. She discovered specific weaknesses that needed to be mitigated by teacher augmentation of the curriculum, as well as strengths that needed to be emphasized. Courtney's work became a powerful aid when shared with others using the same or similar curriculum.

➔ TABLE 1.10: Design Research

Purpose	Methodology	Trustworthiness
To specifically "try out" and evaluate a teaching method, practice, or approach in order to improve student learning, attitude, or motivation.	Identify the dilemma or concern. Devise and implement a prototype plan or strategy to address the issue. Collect data to analyze the success of the prototype. Consider what has been learned about teaching and learning. Adapt and modify prototype based on results.	Established through "thick" description, triangulation of data sets, conclusions grounded in literature concerning the method implemented and theoretical framework used to evaluate the method's effectiveness.

Snapshot Example

The students in Andrea's ninth grade basic math class had been taught the same math facts over and over again. They simply did not understand the larger concepts behind mathematics. The students seemed to "shut down" whenever they were asked about the process behind getting the right answers to math problems. After doing some reading and discussion with her colleagues and others, Andrea decided to implement, as a prototype project, certain "visual math" strategies to teach not just the math facts, but the concepts and processes behind the facts. By implementing her prototype and collecting specific data, Andrea was able to understand where students were having difficulties in learning. This knowledge enabled her to develop her own teaching skills to better facilitate learning for her basic math students. She not only discovered "what works" in visual math, but also how her implementation would be different next time. As she shared her experiences with others, she was able to serve as leader in implementing the "visual math" strategy.

While self-study is presented here as a specific action research framework you may wish to consider, all of these methodologies contain elements of self-study. They all allow the student teacher to critically reflect on the process of becoming a teacher. All of them allow the student teacher to reinvent his or her image of the teacher, and to deeply consider issues of teaching and learning. All of them provide a framework the student teacher can return to as a practicing teacher and use to approach dilemmas, questions, and complexities in the classroom. Ultimately, this is why we are teacher-researchers: to continually engage and delight in the learning process with the goal of improving our own practice, the learning environment for our students, and the greater school community.

As you read the descriptions of different types of action research, what approach seems most interesting to you? Why do you think you are drawn to this approach? (How does it reflect your paradigm?) What would be useful about this approach in your process of becoming a teacher? What might be left out by this approach? What does your selection of this approach say about your own values and beliefs about teaching and the teacher you want to become? Which of these approaches do you think would best "fit" with your student teaching and/or practicum experience?

Being a Student Teacher-Action Researcher

You were asked earlier in this chapter to reflect upon your images of *teacher* and *researcher*, reconstructing a unified concept of the teacher-researcher. You then developed a definition of action research that integrates the combined role of teacher-researcher into the context of schools and classrooms. If you are using this book you are likely also involved in another role, that of student. Your beliefs about what it is to be a good student will complicate and potentially enrich your action research project. The goal of the next section is for you to expand your definition of action research to include your role as a student teacher, a guest in a school and classroom.

To continue to develop your definition and understanding of action research, consider separately your image of a student. In your notebook, write quickly some descriptive words or phrases you associate with the term *student*. Recall some critical moments of your experiences as a student. In your notebook, record one to three examples of *yourself* as a student. Include how these examples represent you as a learner, the process of your learning, and the conditions for your learning. Combine your personal experiences as a student with your earlier descriptive words and phrases defining the term *student*. Write one or two sentences defining the overall label *student*.

Review your earlier definitions of *teacher* and *researcher* along with your new definition of *student*. Using this information and your continued thoughts on these terms, complete the chart in Table 1.11.

→ TABLE 1.11: Student Teacher-Researcher

	Key Defining Words	Public Image/Perception	Personal Metaphor
Teacher			
Researcher			
Student			

Consider your chart and respond to the following questions:

- How are the expectations for each role (teacher, researcher, student) similar?

- If these titles are combined for one person, what are some spaces of possible conflict?

- If these titles are combined for one person, what are the possibilities?

Assuming simultaneously the roles of student, teacher, and researcher involves substantial negotiations of complex political systems, boundaries of thought and expectation, and perceived notions of "success." It is critical that you consider the tensions embedded in being a **student teacher-researcher**. From one perspective, you are a student, a learner, someone who is acquiring theory, pedagogy, and image. From another perspective you are a teacher, categorized as the "expert," who "knows the right answer."

As researcher, you are asked to be the one who questions, inquirers, reflects, and considers possible alternatives. Furthermore, you have your own goals, dreams, and aspirations you want to try on and try out as a teacher. And you are doing this all as a guest in someone else's classroom. You may be asked to "conform" or use teaching strategies or classroom management techniques you find do not "fit" your belief systems. As Britzman (2003) writes, "Marginally situated in two worlds, the student teacher as part student and part teacher has the dual struggle of educating others while being educated" (p. 36).

Integrating the Roles

There is a tacit, or taken-for-granted, assumption that experience in the classroom (as opposed to course work, reflection, and/or theory) teaches one to teach. Most teacher education departments consider the centerpiece of their program to be **field experiences**. But consider this: If experience is the best (and only) teacher, why do you most likely know someone who has been teaching for 30 years that you consider an ineffective teacher? What hasn't she learned from experience? "Experience" may act more to teach you to conform, fit in, or *be* the existing system; for "experience" depends on what is already known, and not necessarily what might be known or could be known if the taken-for-granted assumptions of schools and schooling were further explored. Ultimately, "Learning to teach—like teaching itself—is always the process of becoming: a time of formation and transformation, of scrutiny into what one is doing, and who one can become" (Britzman, 2003, p. 31).

Your teacher-education lived experience will be a time of transformation (Beijaard, Meijer, & Verloop, 2004; Britzman, 2003; Coldron & Smith; 1999; Gee, 2001; Marsh, 2002; Phillips, 2002; Zembylas, 2003). Your own assumptions, theories, and beliefs may be questioned; indeed, you may wonder at times if you should continue the process of becoming a teacher. For others, the teacher-education program is a time of affirmation and the transformation from student to teacher-researcher is perpetually balanced by rewards of fulfilling one's dream. For most student teacher-researchers, there are times when the context of school and being a student teacher demands that ideals and dreams are set aside. Lacey (1977) refers to this as "strategic compliance." We agree with Bullough and Gitlin (2001), who write:

Whatever approach is taken, you need to be acutely aware of the process of negotiation itself if you desire to direct it. Beginning teachers must be not only students of teaching but also students of their own development . . . to be such a student requires knowledge of self and of context and knowledge gathered in systematic and ongoing ways about the interaction of self and context. (p. 48)

The process of action research provides such a space in which you may consider deeply who you are becoming as a teacher and why you are becoming that teacher. The cultural context section in the next chapter will better equip you for negotiating the role of student teacher–researcher. It will acquaint you with the culture of the school where you will be teaching-researching.

Critical Considerations for Being a Student Teacher-Action Researcher

To explore the complexities of being student, teacher, and researcher, we next consider the guest status of "student teacher." We then apply the work of Clandinin and Connelly (1994, 1995, 1996, 2000) by considering the concepts of secret, cover, and sacred stories.

Guest Status

As a student teacher, you are a guest in someone else's classroom. As a guest, there are certain procedures, processes, and rules with which you will need to conform. As a guest, you need to be mindful of your **mentor-teacher**'s role as "host" even as you are trying on your own version of what it might mean to be a teacher yourself. As a guest, you are not a permanent member of the classroom. You will leave and the mentor-teacher will continue teaching in the school and district. Mentor-teachers all share space and power in different ways; all mentor-teachers communicate in different styles. Learn to "read" your mentor-teacher and his/her classroom well. This will be important as you conduct your action research project.

Time Constraints

Time constraints will be major influence on your action research project. Some student teachers are in the classroom for a full school year; others are in the classroom for a much shorter amount of time. In almost all cases, student teachers are involved not only in teaching, but in coursework and program projects. Design an action research approach that is appropriate to the amount of time you have in the classroom and is compatible with other obligations.

Context Constraints

Most action research projects are subject to various types of context constraints. These include the student teacher's limited experience as a teacher and a limited knowledge/understanding of the school, district, and/or community where he or she is placed. Part of the action research process includes acquiring knowledge/understanding in these areas and scrutinizing the influences of the later on the teaching/learning process. Even in instances where student teachers are familiar with the specific school, district, and/or community where they are student teaching we often find that the change in roles from parent, instructional aide, or student to teacher requires relearning and deepening assumptions about the context. Activities in this book will help you do this.

Multiple, Uncontrollable Factors

Schools are places of chaos in which continual novelty is generated. Schools and classrooms involve multiple, uncontrollable factors; we argue that this is one of the reasons why they are such intriguing places for learning! For the student teacher-researcher, however, this can be a source of frustration. Plans are disrupted and schedules are changed. As a student teacher-researcher, document these "disruptions" and embrace them as sources of data and grist for reflection and change. Often these seeming distractions are simply life trying to tell us something important. Write in your notebook or journal about how they influence your project. And, constantly be in dialogue with your mentor-teacher. Be honest about your needs. Discuss the process. Be deliberate in your action research plan, but be flexible when circumstances merit modifications.

Aha! The Transformation Factor

Becoming a teacher is a process we hope continues for the life of your career in education. Can one ever "arrive" and stop learning the intricacies of what it means to be a teacher? We don't think so. Conducting an action research project as a student teacher-researcher can initiate a continuous process of transformation. This may mean that your carefully planned action research project takes an unexpected change when you study the data and find that your original assumptions must be discarded. It may mean that instead of one answer to your question, you have five additional questions and no "real" answer. It may mean that the entire framework for your project is based upon assumptions that have no substantial merit in the context of your teaching. Remember, in action research, the goal is not to *prove* something "true" or "untrue." Rather, the goals cluster around discovering yourself as a teacher, improving your own emerging practice as a teacher, and facilitating learning for students. This is a messy process; leave yourself open to this kind of open-ended process of discovery.

Leave Yourself Open for Transformation

Simply learning to adopt the multiple roles required of professional educators can be a catalyst for growth. For our student teachers, transformation occurs while being simultaneously a student, teacher, and researcher and a guest in a student teaching setting. Consider the following stories of student teachers negotiating their new identities.

Inside Track: Secret, Cover, and Sacred Stories

In this section, we tell the story of two student teachers as they grapple with the role roles of student, teacher, and researcher. Clandinin and Connelly (1994, 1995, 1996, 2000) use a narrative structure to describe the lived experience of teachers. Specifically, they identify three kinds of "stories," or narratives teachers use: *secret, cover,* and *sacred.* Secret stories are those the teacher lives out within the safety of the classroom. Cover stories are those a teacher might tell to disguise the secret practices within the classroom. Sacred stories are those imposed upon teachers via the district office or state or federal governments. The use of this narrative structure to tell the stories of teachers is useful in highlighting the dilemmas, contradictions, and demands teachers live among and around. Such a structure can also be instructive to preservice teachers, who enter the classroom of a mentor-teacher as both a guest and a student.

Phillips (2001) considers the use of narratives in a case study of two preservice teachers who were teaching in two different school settings. Both student teachers were asked to demonstrate competence in teaching as told by the schools' sacred story, and both struggled with feeling that the approach to teaching they were asked to adopt did not "fit" their teaching style or their beliefs about learning.

Given that our beliefs about what a "good" teacher is are very personal, it isn't surprising that most new teachers feel that they don't exactly fit the expectations and standards of the school or classroom in which they find themselves. In the two case studies above, however, one student teacher was able to observe, listen, and ascertain not only the sacred, but also the cover and secret, stories of her school. In this case, mathematics instruction using manipulatives was not encouraged by the school (sacred story). However, she found a closet full of math manipulatives in the classroom (secret story). And although the school had adopted a scripted reading program, she discovered sets of novels in yet another "hidden" space. She began careful, measured conversations with her mentor-teacher concerning these "other" teaching strategies, and soon, by using the language of the sacred story (state standards and federal mandated testing), she was able to participate not only in her mentor-teacher's cover story, satisfying the demand of the sacred story, but also the teacher's secret stories by using such mathematic and reading strategies in her teaching. This student teacher learned to negotiate power systems at her school by using the sacred story to adopt desired teaching strategies.

The second student teacher did not learn these skills of negotiation. In this case, the student teacher was asked to teach science in a traditional manner, rather than the open inquiry-based approach she favored. She was more direct and adamant about her philosophies of teaching, and was more open in her disagreement with the host school's apparent approach to teaching science. She was offended at the expectation that she, as a student teacher, had to teach science in a traditional manner when research supported an inquiry approach. As a student teacher she maintained that she should be able to explore multiple points of pedagogy. However, her directness, in this instance, forced her mentor-teacher to speak more firmly the sacred story, perhaps in order to protect her own secret and cover stories. Ironically, she was never able to discover the way her mentor-teacher cleverly infused inquiry into a traditional-appearing curriculum, creating powerful secret and cover stories.

The experience of these two student teachers cannot be generalized for all student teaching experiences, nor are they told here to say there is a "right" or "wrong" way to enter the classroom as a student teacher. They are told to illustrate the kinds of political landscapes that student teachers may be asked to negotiate. Student teachers often have competing demands: teacher-education program competencies, state and/or federal competencies, district and school expectations, and the mentor-teacher's own expectations of what a "good teacher" might be. These are not always aligned, and often represent different kinds of secret, cover, and sacred stories. Furthermore, student teachers are often asked to demonstrate the more traditional version of the "good teacher" before being allowed to deviate from this image. In other words, they must demonstrate their ability to tell the sacred story.

While such demands can certainly complicate the process of learning to teach, they also represent the systems at play for many in-service teachers. In this way, learning to teach *is* learning to negotiate the political landscapes of schools.

Applying the Three Stories to Action Research

Being cognizant of sacred, secret, and cover stories when conducting research in another's classroom can be critical. The student teacher may, for example, be excited about a certain approach to teaching and may anticipate "trying this out" in the mentor-teacher's classroom. If the mentor-teacher is resistant to the idea, the student teacher may too quickly decide that the mentor-teacher is "traditional." But many other factors may be at play: the sacred story of the school or district may not support such teaching methods; the mentor-teacher may use such methods as a "secret story" but does not feel comfortable having such a story be made public. It could be that the mentor-teacher feels threatened by such methodology for a variety of reasons. What we are suggesting is that student teachers may need to become students of stories. They may need to listen hard to what is being said around them. What "code" language, if any, is used? How are teachers at the school site negotiating government demands? How are they aligning themselves or resisting such demands? What are the differences in what is said publicly and what is done privately?

There are times when student teachers must be compliant in order to gain admission into the "teaching club." This can be painful; sometimes, it results in a temporary loss of idealism and hope. However, as teacher educators, we have found that action research is a process that student teachers can use in powerful ways to not only support their idealism, but also to learn to teach in an influential manner. Action research, if carefully negotiated, can be an acceptable space in which to try alternative practices. In many instances, this process is shared with a mentor-teacher who equally delights in such learning and supports the student teacher during the difficult times of becoming a teacher.

In your role as student teacher-researchers, we encourage you to enter the classroom as *story collectors*. Perhaps this is the first critical trait of all excellent teacher-researchers: the ability to hear in multiple layers the stories administrators, teachers, and students tell of their lives. Expect such stories to be contradictory—even as your own stories may be replete with such contradictions. And know that in the retelling of such stories we bring new questions into our lives that keep us intrigued with the teaching/learning process, even as such retellings help us to make sense of our lived experiences.

Reconstruction: What I Understand Now About Action Research

Throughout this first chapter, you have engaged in multiple ways of considering who you are right now as a student entering professional education, and who you might be asked to be as a student teacher. You've also considered what action research is and how action research might for you to be part of this process.

Here we've asked you to integrate your concepts of *teacher*, *researcher*, and *student* to create a more unified concept of *student teacher-researcher*. This is a critical moment in your journey since we join a long succession of educators who believe that *to teach is to do research and to do research is to teach.* This concept of *teacher-researcher* owes a rich history to such professionals as social psychologist Kurt Lewin (1948). While Lewin did not intend for his work to be used necessarily in education, his series of four cycling steps (*planning, acting, reflecting,* and *observing*) became useful to teacher research. Stephen Corey (1953) introduced the term *action research* to education, believing if teachers conducted their own research it would be more meaningful to them. Scholars and teachers such as Lawrence Stenhouse (1975, 1980; see also Rudduck & Hopkins, 1985) continued to encouraged teachers to see themselves as researchers and thus evaluate their own practice. Carr and Kemmis's *Becoming Critical: Education, Knowledge, and Action Research* (1986), followed by Kemmis and McTaggart's *The Action Research Planner* (1988) contributed to the rising tide of teachers who assumed the identity of *researcher* in their classrooms. There are many recognizable names in the action research field, such as Cochran-Smith and Lytle (1993), Elliot (1991), McNiff, Lomax, and Whitehead (2003), Noffke and Stevenson (1995), Schon (1990), and Ziechner and Gore (1995). All have contributed in demonstrating the positive influence of action research as professional development for both in-service and preservice teachers and as a powerful vehicle for altering the status quo of schools. Many others have since added to this rich tradition, including theorists, philosophers, educational researchers, and a host of classroom teacher-researchers, making the community of action researchers lively, diverse, and international (Kemmis & McTaggart, 2003; Zeichner, 2001).

There are some general themes across the various kinds of action research (participatory research, critical action research, classroom action research, and action learning, among others). These themes include the belief that research should involve teachers *inside* the classroom rather than solely by specialists from *outside* the classroom; therefore, teacher research is focused on teacher empowerment, giving voice to the experiences of practitioners. Another theme that resonates is that critical reflection doesn't just happen. Critical reflection must be deliberate and result in transformed practice. Action research is often done in collaboration either informally or formally; such collaboration is often a way to make the research more credible. Finally, teaching and research are viewed as involving a continuous cycle or spiral of planning, implementing, and reflecting and/or evaluating (Figure 1.12).

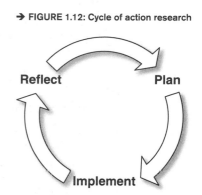

→ FIGURE 1.12: Cycle of action research

Reflect — Plan — Implement

Characteristics of "good teaching," then, involve the refined skills of observation and listening and the ability to place what we see and hear into the social, political, and economic context of both the local and broader school setting; hence the title of this book, *Becoming a Teacher Through Action Research: Context, Process, and Self-analysis.* For this volume, we have selected methodologies and methods from across the field of qualitative/action research (e.g. Clandinin & Connolly, 2000; Kemmis & McTaggart, 2003; Patton, 2002; Reinharz, 1992; Shank, 2002; St. Pierre & Pillow, 2000); we are not presenting here the "right" way or the "only" way to do such research. We have carefully limited and selected strategies we think will be most helpful to you as a student teacher-researcher. We invite you to continue to infuse the concepts of *teacher* and *researcher* as you progress through this text so that you might "own it" and, by taking it into the classroom, join a host of other teacher-researchers actively practicing research to make schools a better place for students. And in the future, we invite you to explore additional paradigms, methodologies, and methods for doing teaching-researching.

Based upon the introductory material in this section, here are additional questions for you to consider prior to continuing with the action research process. When you respond to these questions, include assumptions that you've had to think about as you've read this text, concepts with which you agree/disagree, new understandings you are now considering, and directions in action research you think you would like to travel. When considering the last item, include why these directions seem important and appropriate to your situation and in line with your personal paradigm. Save this response. It will provide a place you can return to in the future, to mark your own becoming a teacher.

- What do you expect to learn from your action research project?

- How do you think such learning should look?

- What complications and rewards do you anticipate during the action research process?

Before continuing through the action research process, you may want to read, meet, and be further introduced to the action research community. On the companion website you will find references and links to others in the action research community. Conduct your own web search, search your university's databases, and use library search engines to find additional resources to fit your interests and needs.

Chapter 1: Content Questions

1. Why is it important to consider our own views of "good" teaching and research in beginning action research?
2. Why does context matter to our work as teacher-action researchers?
3. What does it mean to "deconstruct"?
4. What is the difference between quantitative and qualitative research?
5. How does "mixed methods" research differ from action research?
6. Define: *Self-Study*, *Ethnography*, *Curriculum Analysis*, and *Integrated Action Research*.

Chapter 1: Process Questions

1. What contradictions are there between your images of "good" teacher and "good" researcher? What do the images have in common? How will you resolve these images as you continue your work?
2. Of the four types of teacher action research discussed—*Self-Study*, *Ethnography*, *Curriculum Analysis*, and *Design Research*—which make the most sense to you at this stage in your learning?

Self-Study 1.1: Personal Interview

To begin the self-study process, we suggest that you complete this self-interview. This interview probes the question of why you are becoming a teacher and who you are as you begin this process. Ask yourself the following questions, and save your responses for later use in other activities.

- Think back over your decision to become a teacher. List your top five reasons.
- Who and what kind of systems, situations, and experiences inform the above reasons?
- Consider your own career as a student. If you had to choose, what are five "critical moments" from your own schooling? How do these "critical moments" influence your image of "a teacher"?
- Describe your own cultural, ethnic, and socio-economic background. How does this background influence your decision to become a teacher?
- Describe in as little or as much detail how gender roles were determined in your family. How does this background influence your decision to become a teacher?
- Describe major factors in the development of your current belief/value system.
- How do these responses influence your view of what a teacher should be and the role of education in today's society?
- Do any of your responses indicate that part of the teaching process includes doing research? Why or why not?
- Why do you, or don't you, believe research should be/can be part of the teaching process?
- What, in your opinion, would make classroom research both beneficial and ethical?
- Do you want to become a teacher-researcher? Why or why not?

Read through the responses you have given in this self-interview. As you read, note and highlight any repetitive words, phrases or ideas in your responses. Summarize what the highlighted words, phrases, and ideas indicate about your image of a "good teacher."

Cultural Context 1.1: To Deconstruct

The term **deconstruction** is often associated with Jacques Derrida, the French philosopher, who used the term to refer to a "strategic device" used in reading, interpretation and writing (Derrida, 1983). This "strategic device" may be thought of as a "way of thinking"; as a *way of thinking,* deconstruction avoids asking what is "right" or "wrong," but rather instead asks "about the danger of what is *powerful* and *useful*" (Spivak, as cited in Lather, 1992, p. 120; italics added for emphasis). To deconstruct often means looking at oppositional or apparently contradictory ideas (sometimes called *"binaries"*) and resisting the tendency to think about them in either/or terms. For example, student teachers often find themselves facing these kinds of binary dilemmas:

- Teacher: friend/authority
- Learning: fun/boring
- Curriculum: textbook/no textbook
- Teaching method: inquiry/direct instruction
- Classroom environment: control/chaos

Many student teachers (and in-service teachers) feel the need to be on one side or the other of such binaries. For example, they must be *either* a friend or an authority; their lessons are *either* fun or boring; they must have control *or* risk chaos. With each of these, there is a sense that one of the sides is right and the other side is wrong. The side must then be defended; each side is isolated from the other. The result is a stagnant, single-view argument that is difficult to grow or expand.

To deconstruct these binaries, we might instead make a list of what is dangerous and useful about each perspective. We might consider the unthought-of assumptions we are making about each term. The goal of examining our assumptions in this way is to tease something out of the text (and our own thinking) that we may not have noticed before. Such deconstruction allows us to start all over again and to consider the dilemma from another viewpoint. In Lather's words (1991), this means to ". . . keep things in process, to disrupt, to keep the system in play" (p. 13). By doing this, we are continually revisiting dilemmas and continually discovering alternative ways to approach them. Rather than being "stuck" in one way of thinking, we open up alternative possibilities for approaching such issues. This is particularly important in the classroom.

For example, much has been written about the "reading wars." Such debates often play-out as "Reading: phonics/whole language." When this happens, teachers, academics, researchers, and politicians line up on one side or the other, each with their own stacks of "evidence." The result is a stagnant, entrenched and ongoing debate that doesn't move forward (or even backwards!). The war metaphor of "*entrenchment*" is used here intentionally. Oftentimes, this "debate" isn't even a dialogue or conversation: it is simply the two sides shouting at one another.

Yet, we know as teachers that each child approaches reading in unique ways, although patterns

continues →

of reading development do emerge. To be *solely* on one side or the other is to shut down possibilities of learning for some child. To deconstruct this debate, we begin asking: questions. What is useful and dangerous about phonics? What is useful and dangerous about whole language? In addition, we might look at the language being used on each side of the "war." How is each side describing "reading," and what do these descriptions assume? Again, the goal is not to arrive at one answer and stay there; the goal is to keep the dialogue moving, thus generating new understanding. Deconstruction, in this way, provides a "corrective moment" (Lather, 1991, p. 13). When we begin to see these assumptions, then we can begin to deconstruct and view classroom dilemmas from various viewpoints.

Here is a more personal account of deconstruction and how it might be used in the classroom. For example, Donna remembers the first time a student stood up in the back of her class and told her in no uncertain terms with an obscene gesture exactly what she could do with her life. At that point, there was a "show-down." Donna felt the need to assert her authority. The student had the same need. Although the student was sent from the classroom, no one "won." At first, Donna considered the student as "insolent" and "defying authority." By assuming and thus categorizing the student as "bad," and, therefore, other students as "good," the process of finding ways to work with the student was greatly diminished. Fortunately, Donna had a mentor who talked her through the incident, deconstructing the situation so that she could hear other points of view (like the student's) and begin to construct a learning environment where both the she and the student were affirmed and able to learn together.

As a way of thinking, deconstruction takes practice. Unfortunately, we are far more practiced in taking sides, "digging in," and "holding the line." However, through the action research process, learning to use deconstruction can be a powerful tool for thinking about teaching and learning.

A Way of Deconstructing

Deconstruction initially requires that we identify the opposites (or binaries) and consider this data from multiple viewpoints. For example, suppose you collect data about the on- or off-task behavior of students during teaching. You are surprised to find that many more students are off-task than you think is appropriate. Yet, this data is confusing because the students seem to be well engaged in successful learning. At first, you simply take the data at face value and conclude that something in your teaching practice needs to be changed in order to promote more on-task behavior. But later, you begin to ask yourself questions: What does on/off behavior actually *look* like? What assumptions about teaching and learning frames my view of on-/off-task behavior? What is dangerous and useful about my assumptions? What other story might be told about this data?

By considering such questions, you are able to view on- or off-task behavior from a different angle by deconstructing your own assumptions. There are numerous opportunities to practice the skill of deconstruction in the activities in this strand. As you practice, connect the stories and theories you create from the activities back to your own journey of becoming a teacher. How is the cultural context, the prominent power structures, shaping your experience of learning to teach, your image of *teacher*, *student*, and *school*?

Cultural Context 1.2: Images of School and Society

Have you ever said to someone, "I am going to be a teacher," and they replied, "You sure do look like a teacher"? Maybe this hasn't happened to you *yet*, but as authors of this text, we have heard this kind of a statement before. When we hear this, we ask, *"What does a teacher look like?"*

Perhaps you have found yourself making this kind of observation with your peers. For example, when meeting your fellow colleagues in the teacher-education program, did you find yourself more or less assuming someone "looked like" an English major, an art teacher, or a first grade teacher? What kinds of clues "told" you this? Where might you have learned such perceptions?

This activity looks at popular images of the "teacher." Again, you may agree or disagree with what you find, but we urge you to consider instead what might be dangerous or useful in the images you find and how these images influence the way you think about teaching.

Activity: Deconstructing the Public Image of the "Teacher"

In this activity you will search for, analyze, and interpret public images of the "teacher." The goal is to find as many images of teachers as possible and look for patterns and commonalities that provide clues into public perception of, and discourses surrounding, "teacher."

Instructions

Log on to Google (or another search engine of your choice). If using Google, choose the "images" button so you are only searching for Internet pictures. Search for images of "teacher"; or you can be more specific and search for "elementary teacher" or "high school teacher." (If you do not have Internet access, you may use the data we collected; see Appendix B, Table B.1. We have chosen Google for this activity because at the time of publication, it is a powerful and popular search engine, storing millions of images and other resources. As such, it represents a collective cultural museum of popular thought. It is one way we can find data to analyze about Western culture's perceptions of "teacher.")

As you peruse the images, look for the following:

- Is the teacher pictured male or female?
- What is the teacher's ethnicity?
- Is the teacher in the center of the picture, placed in a prominent position?
- Is the teacher in a non-traditional setting?
- Are there any pictures of students teaching students?

Considering the Results

What do you think the data you collected might say about the public image of "teacher"? How do these collections of images define a teacher? What are the teacher's attributes? What words would you

continues →

use to describe the collective, dominant image of a teacher from your Google search? Write down your responses and be prepared to share them with your colleagues.

Through Google we searched for "elementary teacher" and reviewed 38 images. Of these, 25 images were female and 7 were male. Of the teachers, 28 appeared to be white, while 4 appeared to be African American; there were no other visible ethnicities represented. All but one of the teachers was in the center of the picture, surround for the most part by children. At another time, we viewed 55 images from Google, but this time we searched for "teacher" alone. Of the teachers that we viewed, 21 were white; 25 were male. All of the male teachers were prominently featured in the middle of the picture or image. Nine of the pictures and/or images feature white, female teachers. One of the female teachers appeared to represent the Muslim faith, but her ethnic identification could not be determined. One female teacher was not centered in the pictures. Five teachers were in non-traditional settings (outside of a classroom or a lab). We found 6 pictures and/or images of students only, usually talking in a small group. Many of the male teachers featured were in very traditional settings—that is, in front of a chalkboard with chalk in hand, in a dress shirt and tie.

How do these results compare to your own results? Do you think the results would be different if we searched for "high school teacher"? Why?

Having considered both your own data and our collected data, write some **synthesis statements** about the image of "teacher" as represented in the Google search.

Our own synthesis statements and questions are as follows:

- The majority of teachers are white; we might theorize that when Western culture thinks of a teacher, it thinks of a white teacher.
- Female teachers are less likely to teach at the high school level. Male teachers, because of their dress, appear to be authoritative and more "content" or "business" orientated; female teachers, dressed in softer colors and styles and often placed in closer proximity to children, do not appear as authoritative. Perhaps they are perceived as being more concerned with the affective?
- Male teachers may be considered more prominently (even though they do not make up 50% of the teaching population) because men who teach are considered differently than women who teach. (Could it be that female teachers are considered to be more "normal" and male teachers more "noble"?)
- The public image of "teacher" may be "teacher-directed," "teacher-centered," or "teacher as expert." This is based upon the position of the teacher in the images.
- Teachers smile; most of the images included a happy, smiling teacher.

This brief sample of teacher images seems to define the teacher as one with authority based upon expertise. Thus, students might be defined as needing the teacher's expertise and knowledge. While the teacher is the authority, he is also expected to be cheerful and positive. Since the teacher is the center of the educational experience, success or failure appears to be located at the site of the teacher. Because the majority of teachers are white, it may be that the public image of authority and expertise is centered on dominant, white culture.

continues →

Activity: Teacher Gifts: How We View Teachers as People

We continue to explore images of teacher in Western society in this activity by again gathering images from the Internet. This time, use Google to search for "teacher gifts." Remember, this may or may not be your image of teacher, but you are exploring what society's image of "teacher" might be via public and popular sources.

Instructions

Go online to a search engine of your choice (we used Google), and search for "teacher gifts". (If you do not have Internet access, you may use the data we collected; see Appendix C, Table C.1.)

Select from the list of search results several different retail sites aimed at teachers. Observe the items offered for sale and categorize them using the following descriptors:

- the primary colors used;
- the approximate grade levels of any pictured students;
- symbols present;
- slogans present.

When you have completed collecting the data, consider these questions:

- To what kind of teachers do most of these items seem to be marketed (gender, grade level, and content area)?
- What are the recurring themes and symbols that appear to represent a teacher? What are your theories about why these themes and symbols are used?
- What might these images suggest about the public image of teachers and, perhaps, education? What is left out of these images (but in your opinion, should be included)?

Do you observe any incongruent themes or images in your search? What might these suggest?

Based upon your responses, write several synthesis statements regarding this data set. Return to the first activity in this section for examples of synthesis statements if you need them.

Activity: Teachers According to Hollywood

One more activity will allow us to triangulate our data, or collect data from three different sources, in our search for a public image of "teacher." Even with three different sources, we will not have a complete picture of dominant Western culture's perception of a teacher, but we will have enough data to raise questions and make tentative synthesis statements.

Movies tell us about our culture—especially movies that are box-office hits and remain popular long enough to be considered "classics." There are hundreds of movies about teachers; some of them are comical, some "made for children," and others marketed as drama. The ones that appear to most pull at our public imagination of what a teacher is are those based upon true-life stories. But with movies, fact and fiction become intertwined—we rarely know the "real" story a movie is based upon and those that are

continues →

fiction are so believable, they seem to become part of our "real" images. In this way, movies influence our way of thinking; they contribute to the images and expectations of education.

Instructions

Using your Internet browser, locate the following school-themed movies. We found all of the movies (and more) by searching amazon.com. Find a picture of the jacket artwork and the promotional description of each movie.

- *Dangerous Minds* (Simpson et al., 1995)
- *Dead Poets Society* (Haft, Wilt, Thorman, Schulman, & Weir, 1989)
- *The Emperor's Club* (Abraham, Karsh, Tolkin, & Hoffman, 2002)
- *Lean on Me* (Avildsen & Schiffer, 1989)
- *Mr. Holland's Opus* (Cort, Field, Nolan, Duncan, & Herek, 1995)

Study the artwork for each movie and read the promotional description carefully. Then, for each movie, answer the following questions:

- What key characteristics of successful teachers and/or principals are represented in the data?
- How do students appear to be positioned? What kind of students appears to be most "screenworthy"?
- What does the data suggest about schools in general?
- What in your opinion is left out of these representations?

When we brainstormed possible movies for this activity, we found we could not recall many, if any, movies featuring elementary teachers and children. The few we did remember took place in the early 1900s and featured single women teachers who ultimately found a husband and presumably left teaching. What other kinds of information about teaching and schools do you think is left out of the Hollywood depictions? Can you find additional data about elementary teachers and children to add to this data? You may also find it interesting to consider additional movies (including those from the comedy genre) to add to this data set.

Based upon the data collected, create synthesis statements summarizing the public image of the teacher as depicted in Hollywood.

Final Interpretation of Images of School and Society

Review the data collected throughout this section, read again responses to questions and synthesis statements. Using this information, conduct a final data interpretation by responding to these questions in your notebook or journal:

- What images of teacher are portrayed through the activities you have analyzed?
- What paradoxes and tensions appear to exist?
- What is a teacher supposed to do (and how should she look)?

continues →

- What attributes are most important to teachers?
- How does the public image distinguish between teachers of different grade levels?
- What additional "evidence" would you add to support or oppose the public images represented in the data?
- What are your theories regarding these images? Why have they become engrained in the public image of education?
- How might these images influence the lives of real teachers, students, and schools?
- How do you think these images might influence your own image of teachers, students, and schools?
- How do you think such images, representations, and symbols could influence your own process of becoming a teacher?

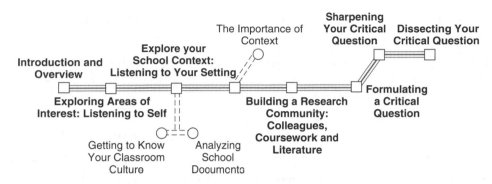

We do not plan our teaching and researching in a vacuum. The community and classroom context, and the children and adolescents in these classrooms, inform our research questions and teaching units. The combined main road and sides roads of chapter two support you in balancing your personal interest as it evolves into an area of focus and a critical question while considering the context of your teaching and researching. Read with both your personal and professional voices talking back and with the text. *Anticipate* the chapter: be willing to mine possibilities, take some risks, imagine what *might be* rather than focusing on what you think you already know or on what seems too hard or difficult.

———————————————

Introduction and Overview

What will your action research project be about? In action research, *we research our own issues, meaningful in our current life and practice. We pursue* critical questions *that resonate with our professional community and have the potential to improve teaching, learning, and life.*

You have begun the action research journey by surveying the landscape over which you will travel. You have also done some introspective self-study to become aware of where action research fits into your assumptions, beliefs, and values about teaching, learning, and the world in general. You have glimpsed the action research paradigm and read the "travel journals" of others who have completed the route now set before you.

You are ready to take the first step on your own action research road trip. This step involves determining the critical questions you seek to understand on your journey. We use the term *critical question* in place of the usual *research question* because, like the destination and goals for a road trip, we believe that the focus of your action research plays an essential, even critical role in your process of becoming a teacher. Your critical questions must be meaningful *now,* not in some distant, abstract, or imaginary future. Your critical questions must connect with the larger community of professionals to which you are becoming a member. Most important, your critical question must have the ability to make teaching, learning, and life in schools better.

This chapter lays out a process for helping you discover your critical questions and area of focus. You may not need to travel through this entire process. If at any time you experience an "Aha!" moment and the area of focus becomes very clear, feel free to skip ahead to the "Formulating a Question" section later in this chapter. If you do this, however, you will need to return to the section entitled "Building a Research Community: Colleagues, Coursework, and Literature."

Exploring Areas of Interest: Listening to Self

We research our our own issues . . .

The essence of teacher research is the pursuit of one's own issues and concerns. Throughout this and the next few sections, you will have the opportunity to brainstorm possible topics of interest for your action research project. We provide many different formats, prompts, and techniques for doing this. Not all of our ideas may resonate with you; you should feel free to pick and choose those which seem to be leading you in the right direction. Remember, there is no formula for finding your critical question. You must be willing to follow your intuition and hunches as well as listen to what your setting and practice are saying. We hope our activities help you do this.

Begin by returning to your notes and ideas from the previous chapter, particularly the "SS 1.1: Personal Interview" activity. Review some of your core values and beliefs about teaching and learning. As you review these ideas, do any stand out as possible areas of interest for your action research project?

Record these and any new ideas you have in your notebook or journal.

What are some political, social, and economic concerns you have that could be related to classroom teaching? What curiosities do you have about teaching and learning? Are there processes, issues, dilemmas you wish you understood better? Are there situations in the classroom with which you are dissatisfied? Do you wonder what happens when certain actions are put into play? What other concerns and/or challenges do you either personally face (or fear) in teaching? What do you want to achieve as a teacher? Who do you want to be as a teacher? What skills, content, and emotional fortitude do you need to become that teacher?

As you look over your responses, try to summarize your thoughts. What do the ideas share? What ideas strike you as worthy of pursuing and at the same time pursuable as you become a teacher? Write down notes about your initial thoughts.

In the next section you will continue to explore and brainstorm action research possibilities by problematizing your practice. You will return to these ideas later to further define your critical question.

Explore your School Context: Listening to Your Setting

. . . meaningful in our current life and practice.

For many of our students the most difficult phase in forming a critical question for action research is moving from broad concerns, curiosities, and wonderings to a focused question appropriate for the task at hand. To transform your personal concerns into a relevant question for study requires that you examine your current teaching practice and setting in light of your wonderings. We use the metaphor of *listening* to describe this process, sometimes referred to as *problematizing your practice* (Arhar, Holly, & Kasten, 2001). Learning to listen to your setting is the next step in giving your action research project a powerful life of its own.

Activity: Problematizing Practice Case Studies

Practice problematizing by reading through one of the student teacher case studies. We include early childhood, middle school, and high school teachers in this section; choose the one that best fits your interest.

More case studies may be explored at the *BTAR* companion website.

Case Study 1: Early Childhood Education

Today I tried to teach a lesson on sentence fluency. Not so good. I am not sure what happened. The material was prepared, the examples were given, maybe it was the assignment. I asked the students to create a four-sentence poem. I read them some examples; I modeled for them. I had a lot of questions, from all students. When I collected the papers, a lot had not followed a poem format, at least not one that I recognized. I am not sure if I thought the work was going to be extremely different from the five facts book (we did earlier this week), the two activities are very similar, in some way, identical.

Given the fact that it appeared to me as no one knew what they were doing, the classroom seemed to be on-task. Let me say that again: I think students thought they knew what to do; it was just different than I had perceived.

I am not sure if the objectives were met. After collecting the papers I just knew I had blown the entire lesson so I moved right into our reader's workshop. I was so frustrated with myself and the lesson that I just wanted it to be over. I figured that if I tried to have a closure with the students I would just be looking at blank faces. I thought that if I tried to have them answer questions about what good writers do they would mention all the previous points taught and they would miss today's objective. I didn't want to frustrate them or myself anymore.

The strength in today's lesson was the trust that I had from the kids. They so wanted to get it. While I thought it was confusing and the worst thing ever done, the students still stayed as busy as they could and only got out of their seats to ask me questions. I would send them back to their seats and ask for a quiet hand raised, they would comply, and I would work my way to them. They really wanted to do the assignment right.

Today I learned that no matter how good a unit is going, one piece of it will be your weakest link and hopefully you will have gained enough trust from your students so they will remain interested in the rest of the unit. I learned that each lesson requires a lot of thought and planning. I think this one may have been hastily thrown together in order to cover the writing strand. I think there was a better way to teach this point, maybe a different book and assignment. I think that if we had had an activity on the floor that was similar to the Delicious Words (the one we did last week) sentence fluency would be just as understood.

If I could redo this day I would not use *Animals Animals* as the read-aloud [text]. One thing that has been consistent in this unit is the tie from the book to the lesson. I think that this book was a bad choice. I am not sure what choice would have been better. I also would understand the importance of sentence fluency a lot more. I think that I went in today ready to teach sentence fluency and don't have a good grasp on what it is.

For the students I think today's lesson was a flop; for me it was a huge eye-opener. I was so happy with the way things were going that I let my guard down. I thought that every lesson was going to go as well as they had been—wrong. I think that because I thought that I came in less prepared today, not having given myself as much background on the subject as I had for others.

Case Study 2: Middle School

Today I was frustrated. For the first time I felt as if the kids had taken advantage of my "niceness." I gave them the whole class to work on their personal history projects as the presentations are due next week and Wednesday is grading day, with Thursday and Friday off for holiday. The students who were building their presentations on Apple Works or those who needed to scan in pictures went to the computer lab with my mentor-teacher. All others stayed in the classroom with me. This flexibility—because there were two of us—was wonderful, and breaking them into two smaller groups had its appeal by allowing more one-on-one time for students.

However, soon many started to socialize too much and some just put their work away and started goofing around. I asked them to get their work out and help each other if needed. They were allowed to talk quietly as long as they continued to work as several were making posters, etc. When this didn't happen I asked everyone to be quiet and gave them a quick talk about the time I was giving them to work and how we could be doing a lesson instead of talking. And then I gave them about three more minutes to get on-task.

When this didn't happen I told them all to be quiet and work. They were shocked that I was unhappy with them. However, two students continued to try to talk and so I gave a citation. It was the first citation I have given and I didn't want to give it. I have done citations before at previous schools, but these kids are good for the most part and I felt that I was being taken advantage of in my goal to give them the ultimate time to work on and finish their projects so they didn't have to do so over the holiday.

Another one almost got a citation for a chair incident but the other boy involved defended him, and though I wasn't sure he was totally innocent I let it go and discussed it with my mentor-teacher, who said I did the right thing. However, he (the student) hopefully now knows that I will not hesitate to use the citation option if I need to.

As tomorrow is grading day, I did grades for the assignments that I was responsible for, preparing them to give to my mentor-teacher. I carefully planned out everything in advance in our unit, assigning points for the work so that they would equal the total unit amount and be based on the project. But in reality, the family tree assignment seemed to be much harder for some of the students and should have been worth more points than I assigned. I adjusted the work by dropping one map assignment that somewhat duplicated what we did on another, which made something else that wasn't as difficult as the family tree worth almost as much. This seems to be a balancing act.

Case Study 3: High School

This lesson was designed to introduce students to the concepts around erosion, including types (wind, water, gravitational, etc.) and specific vocabulary related to the transportation of sediment related to river erosion (saltation, suspension, deposition, etc.). I presented a PowerPoint with picture examples of the terms and processes, and gave the lesson in discussion format, asking many questions and having students paraphrase definitions, versus allowing them to write a definition verbatim from one I could have provided. I also made sure to include examples of local erosion processes (Willamette River, Oregon Coast, sinking road ways, etc.) and emphasized ways such erosion can be prevented by minimizing clear-cut logging, replanting, respecting wildlife boundaries, etc.

Overall, this lesson was pretty effective, with a high ratio of student to teacher input. It was clear, by the discussion, that students were able to associate erosion processes by glaciation with river/water erosion, and began to understand how both processes can be con- and destructive forces at the same time.

It's clear some students are growing weary of studying land formation, but aside from the typical behavior management, I feel the class understands the concepts and are able to verbalize them, including using the vocabulary, when explaining their W. Valley models.

The biggest challenge today was getting the students to fill out their packets of their own volition. We reviewed their quiz results from two lessons ago, and told them that there was NO reason anyone should have had less than 100% on these quizzes because they are OPEN note, and if they fill out their packets in class like they are asked to, then the quizzes shouldn't be difficult at all. The results the second time around were still mixed, but overall had greater participation, mostly because we told the class they could not have a break until everyone at their table had completely filled in their tables and packets. It remains a mystery to me, how to get them self-motivated in this regard. They KNOW they'll do better on a test if they just fill out a few words on the packet, yet doing so still seems to be a challenge, and they don't seem to care about their scores. Frustrating.

[icon] Use the following questions to **problematize** the case study or studies of your choice:

- What are the student teacher's motives or goals for the lesson or teaching episode?

- What are the student teacher's biases revealed in her plans and approach?

- What problem(s) appears to have occured?

- What are some sources of the problem(s)?

- What biases and stereotypes are reflected in the sources you listed?

- How are the student teacher's actions or interpretations of the problem(s) useful and dangerous?

This is a good time to travel the side road Cultural Context 2.1: *Getting to Know Your Classroom Culture*, at the end of this chapter on p. 64. You 'll find specific strategies for gathering classroom data useful in forming a critical question.

Problematizing Your Own Practice

Of course, the real goal is to problematize *your own* practice. Think of instances from your own student teaching and/or observational experiences. Perhaps you have already begun writing formal observations of your classroom or have compiled a number of written reflections of your own teaching, your mentor-teacher's teaching, or about the classroom setting.

Using whatever data sources you have at your disposal, develop one or more incidents from your student teaching so far. Use formal observations, reflections, and memory to tell a story from your classroom experience. Return to the questions used above in "Problematizing Practice Case Studies." Personalize these questions and analyze your teaching incident.

Listening to Your Setting

In problematizing your own practice, you have spent some time engaged in what we call *listening to your setting*. As teacher/researchers it is critical that we learn to examine our settings—communities, schools, classrooms, and students—closely, with an ear to what direction our settings may be leading us.

What is your setting telling you? Have issues emerged that connect with your own personal concerns and issues in teaching, learning, classrooms, and schools? Take a moment to summarize your process to this point. What potential critical questions does your summary suggest?

> Listen to your school setting using the techniques in this side road, Cultural Context 2.2: *Analyzing School Documents* found at the end of this chapter on p. 67. Develop your understanding of the school context and possible critical questions.

Building a Research Community: Colleagues, Coursework, and Literature

We pursue critical questions that resonate with our professional community . . .

Teacher action research is most often focused on professional practice in classrooms. As such, it runs the risk of being isolated from the larger community of teachers, scholars, and other stakeholders in the process of teaching and learning. As teachers we must not allow ourselves to become isolated by our own theories, beliefs, and ways of teaching and learning. We believe that powerful action research is created at the intersection of the internal and external, the private and the public, and even the present and the past. In this section you will begin forming this intersection by building around the context of your action research journey a learning relationship with a trusted friend or colleague. You will also learn to find key **anchor texts** for your action research in the work of other, more "**distant colleagues**" found in the literature.

Establishing a Critical Colleague Relationship

Our action research doesn't take place isolated from those around us. Our friends, colleagues, students, administrators, and extended community all play a role in forming our questions, designing our studies, and interpreting our results. Many of those who influence us as we journey through action research do so in unintentional ways. However, we also meet fellow travelers who accompany us more intentionally as mentors, guides, muses, and—some-times—critics. These become our **critical colleagues**.

McNiff, Lomax, and Whitehead (2003) write the following about the role of critical colleagues in the action research process:

> Your critical friends should be willing to discuss your work sympathetically but critically. You and your critical friends choose each other, so you need to negotiate the ground rules of your relationship. They may turn out to be your closest allies, so never take them for granted. As well as expecting support from your friends, you must also be prepared to support them in return. This means being available, even in antisocial hours, offering as well as receiving advice, even if it is painful or unwelcome, and always aiming to praise and support. (pp. 38–39)

Identify a person who can be your critical colleague throughout the action research process. Find someone who you know will be honest and from whom you are willing to accept suggestions. Choose someone who is interested and knowledgeable about your potential focus areas. Begin your relationship by reviewing some of your notes in this section; discuss possible areas of interest and critical questions that you think may become your action research project. If your critical colleague isn't nearby, send an e-mail, set up a video chat, or use a social network– beginning this relationship deserves care and attention.

Applying Teacher-Education Course Knowledge

One of the most relevant places where the learning community is fostered is within your teacher-education courses. When considering a research topic, begin by thinking through courses you have taken (or are currently taking) and asking yourself, "How could the knowledge gained in these courses become an action research project?" For example, methods courses provide a plethora of specific teaching and learning strategies. Which of these strategies do you find yourself most curious? When you learn about some strategies, do you find yourself saying, "I wish I could have learned in this way!" or "I remember a learning experience using a strategy like this and it was so effective!" Other courses like those in human development, practicing diversity, or teaching in a inclusive classroom all provide not only strategies that are potential research topics but also frameworks for critiquing curriculum. Often teacher education programs include specialty courses in technology, multiple intelligences, or classroom management. If these topics interest you, consider exploring them further, first with your critical colleague, then through connections to distant colleagues.

Literature Review: Connecting to Distant Colleagues

Research projects require reading and review of published work related to the area of study. This review serves several purposes. In the beginning, the review of literature and theoretical perspectives assists the teacher-researcher in finding and refining the critical question for the study. Later, the review of literature becomes the framework for analyzing and interpreting data. This review is vital in grounding the assumptions, results, and conclusions of your research in the broader context of professional inquiry.

We conceive of the authors of published work to be our "distant colleagues" or "distant mentors." You don't have to "go it alone," you can rely on these distant colleagues, with their wealth of experience, to guide you in becoming a teacher. For this reason, developing a useful **literature review** is particularly important to your study as a preservice teacher.

What kind of literature will be most useful to you as a teacher-researcher? Avoid collecting literature just because it is about your topic and will fulfill a requirement for a literature review. Do collect literature that is meaningful and fills the criterion of "distant colleagues" providing guidance. A literature review for preservice teacher action research is somewhat unique, reflecting your position as "student" and "teacher." We suggest you gather guidance from the following sources:

- *Course textbooks.* If you find a topic you want to pursue in one of your courses, check out the reference list and see who else has written on the topic. Use your textbooks as a starting place.

- *Internet resources.* The Internet is a good place to begin to discover more about your topic of interest, find out more about distant colleagues, and even connect with other teachers doing research in your area of interest. How to do Internet searches is the topic of the next section.

- *Professional journals.* These are the journals published by professional content areas, such as National Council of Teachers of English, National Council of Teachers of Mathematics or National Science Teachers Association in the U.S. There are professional organizations for every content area and for various age levels (e.g. early childhood education and middle school education). Many of these are international organizations and all publish a variety of journals, newsletters, position statements, and other material. Check out these organizations; spend time with their publications. This is a good place to find a topic of interest and to refine a critical question.

- *Professional trade books.* These are books published specifically for teachers. They often are "how to" books, for example, how to organize cooperative learning science labs or strategies for organizing and evaluating literature circles. These books provide mentorship in trying out an innovative strategy.

- *Theoretical/research works.* While work in this category may not tell you how to implement a teaching strategy, it will give you a way of evaluating whether a strategy is successful and a way of thinking a teaching strategy. If you are doing a curriculum analysis or program evaluation, this is the work that will allow you to develop a framework for evaluating that particular curriculum or program. This is the larger work that surrounds much of the work in professional trade books. Having a few key pieces from this category will make your study more trustworthy since it will ground your assumptions and perspectives.

An Illustration

Megan knows she is interested in studying how to make the vocabulary of science more accessible to her eighth grade students, most of whom speak English as a second language. In her literacy methods course, Megan studies the Common Core State Standards (CCSS), Appendix A (http://www.corestandards.org/assets/Appendix_A.pdf) and is introduced to the concept of Tier 1, Tier 2, and Tier 3 vocabulary. She checks the bibliography of the CCSS Appendix A and finds multiple possible resources. She notices there are two references to the authors *Beck, McKeown, and Kucan* and decides to follow-up on these sources, as they seem most related to teaching. A quick search on the university's library search page reveals a second edition of one of these books, *Bringing Words to Life: Robust Vocabulary Instruction* (2013). The book is available as an eBook so Megan quickly downloads this and scans both the table of contents and the reference list.

In the same literacy methods course, Megan has access to two textbooks, *Academic Language for English Language Learners and Struggling Readers: How to Help Students Succeed Across Content Areas* (Freeman & Freeman, 2009) and *Word Wise and Content Rich: Five Essential Steps to Teaching Academic Vocabulary* (Fisher & Frey, 2008). As Megan reviews these books looking for sources, she notes any references mentioned in both books, for example, *The Vocabulary Book: Learning and Instruction* (Graves, 2006); she finds this book is available through her university library system and orders it as well.

Megan's primary dilemma is that between the above-identified sources, there are many more possible resources. To focus her search, she analyzes her current collection. She has sources that provide a broad understanding of vocabulary instruction, others that provide specific instructional strategies, and one with a specific focus on English Language Learning. While these are all based on research, she decides she might like to read some specific research studies related to English Language Learners. She returns to Freeman and Freeman (2009) and selects several sources that she finds through the database of her university. Megan also spends some time browsing the library's paper copies of *Voices from the Middle*, a journal publication of the National Council of Teachers of English, checking for articles or a special edition on academic vocabulary instruction and research.

For each article Megan reads, she completes an **annotated bibliography**. She keeps these in a dedicated file on her computer. Later, she will read across the articles, synthesize them, and group them according to common themes. (More about annotated bibliographies and synthesizing literature appears later in this chapter.) These common themes will focus her data collection and her data analysis and interpretation. In addition, as Megan reads, she will continue to focus on particular distant colleagues that will be most important to her action research project. The work of these authors will anchor her project.

Web Searching: Be a Critical Consumer of Internet Information

There are two challenges to finding information on the Internet using search engines: 1) knowing what key words or "search terms" to enter into the search form, and 2) knowing how to critically evaluate the information on the websites you find. The next section will help you evaluate the quality of the websites you find. To find search terms, review your notes both from this section and from Chapter 1 on becoming a student teacher/researcher. Generate a list of terms. Then, using the instructions below, proceed with your Internet search.

The Internet contains billions of webpages, and you need to find a small number that meet your needs. This is where search engines come to the rescue. From the nascence of the Internet, its engineers and users realized that searchability was the key to making it useful. There are many search engines; our favorite is Google (http://www.google.com).

Search engines work by automatically combing the entire Internet for content and indexing the results in a massive database. When you use a search engine, you enter "key words" or "search leads." The index is then searched, and you are returned a list of webpages that contain your search leads. If things go well, within the first few entries of the list you will find a webpage that contains the information for which you are looking and links to related material. Ineffective searches end with either 1) far too many websites to examine, or 2) no websites that have the right information. The search engine itself attempts to solve the first problem by ranking the search results in various ways in an attempt to send you the best pages for a given search. Of course, this doesn't always work, but it helps a great deal.

The second problem can be tricky to solve. You may need to modify your search terms(s) so you get the right webpages. For example, Kevin throws the discus, an Olympic track and field event. When he enters "discus" into the Google search engine, a list is generated of thousands of webpages about a tropical fish people like to raise, known as (you got it) "Discus." Now what? Kevin enters "discus throw" and gets better results (most people don't throw their fish).

The keys to effective web searching are patience, flexibility, and knowledge about the subject you are searching for. Notice that you need to *have* knowledge to *get* knowledge. The more you know about a given topic the more different search terms you will be able to generate, and the better your searches become. If you are searching in an area that is brand new to you, this process will take patience and flexibility.

Testing the Surf: Evaluating Internet Sources

Suppose you have a generated list of websites that seem to have the information you need. Now you need to evaluate the *quality* of the information you are getting. You already know that not everything on the Internet is trustworthy. It's time to become a critical consumer of all that information.

Most of the information regarding critical evaluation of Internet resources comes from libraries, which have an important stake in seeing that people become intelligent consumers of information. Libraries also (and rightly so) see the Internet as a tremendous resource, both for the good and for the erroneous. As Smith (1997) writes, you must learn to always be "Testing the Surf." Remember you are choosing to allow the authors of Internet information to influence your critical question, and therefore your process of becoming a teacher. Don't invite distant colleagues who don't prove themselves trustworthy and credible.

Consider the following criteria for judging Internet resources (Brandt, 2004):

- Who is the author?
  - Is she/he qualified to write this "article"?
  - What is her/his occupation, position, education, experience?
  - What are her/his credentials?
  - Are the facts accurate?
  - How does this information compare with that in other sources in the field?

- Perspective
  - Does the author have a bias?
  - Does she/he express a particular point of view?
  - Is the author affiliated with particular organizations, institutions, associations, etc.?
  - Does the forum in which the information appears have a bias?
  - Is it directed toward a specific audience (general public, scholars in a given field, etc.)?
  - Where is the information "published"?
  - When was it written?

- Purpose
  - To what audience is the author writing?
  - Is this reflected in the writing style, vocabulary, or tone?
  - Does the material inform? Explain? Persuade?
  - Is there sufficient evidence?
  - What conclusions are drawn?

Recording Information From Your Searches

As you begin to use your search terms on the Internet, be sure to 1) record information about useful websites you visit and 2) continually reexamine and modify your search terms. For recording your searches, create a table (see Table 2.1). Be sure to use the "favorite" or

→ TABLE 2.1: Recording Data From Web Searches

Title		URL	
Author		Perspective	Purpose
Summary			
Search Terms Used:			

"bookmark" functions on your Internet browser to store the links to useful websites. Above all, let what you find online speak to you with regard to your critical question. Let your distant colleagues further define your critical question and inspire you to know more. Note the searches and terms that seem the most fruitful as you begin to anticipate your action research project.

Re-Search: Digging Deeper to Find Distant Colleagues

In completing Internet searches, you have probably developed a good set of search terms. You can now apply these terms to searching databases that index the professional literature of education. Your college or university librarian is your best source of information about searching the many education databases (such as the Educational Resources Information Center), and acquiring materials from the vast universe of professional knowledge that exists. Depending on the resources of your institution, you may be able to complete much or all of the search and acquisition process online.

As with Internet searches, it is important and time-saving to record and organize the results of library searches. A common academic format for compiling research information is known as an *annotated bibliography*.

Activity: Annotated Bibliography

⌨ You may use the template found on the *BTAR* companion website to create an annotated bibliography, or make your own using the template in Table 2.2.

Annotated bibliographies done well save a researcher time later in the action research process when completing data anlaysis and interpretation and a final action research product. Here are some suggestions for writing useful annotated bibliographies:

- Make certain you have all citation information (see Table 2.2 for details).

- Use American Psychology Association (APA) formatting (or the citation format required by your instructor) from the beginning rather than waiting to format when completing your final action research product.

- Write a concise and complete summary. Include specific points or findings. You may want to reference these later in your final action research presentation. The trick is to write enough that you do not need to return to the original source.

- Include any significant quotations and the page numbers where these quotations can be found that you think you may want to use later. (It is not fun nor is it time efficient to scramble to find these later when completing a final action research project.)

- Double-check spelling and quotations: *are they accurate?*

→ TABLE 2.2: Annotated Bibliography Citation

Elements			
1. *APA Formatted Citation*			
2. **Describe type of article** (Academic research, practitioner, or trade)			
3. **Useful references included** (if applicable)			
4. ***Summarize the "story" of this article*** (*introduction/context/ background*)			
5. ***Research question(s), Problem(s), or Issue(s) Addressed***			
6. ***Who are the participants, audience, and/or subjects?***			
7. ***What forms of data (or information) help the author(s) answer the questions, problems, or issues?***			
8. ***What themes emerge about the original questions, problems, or issues?***			
9. ***What important and/or interesting in general about these results?***			
In what ways does this article connect to your personal understanding of being a student teacher/action researcher?			

The annotated bibliography will be used in Chapter 4 as you design your research project; in Chapter 5 as you conduct ongoing data analysis; and again in Chapter 6 during final data interpretation.

Building a Sense of Connection Through Synthesizing Literature and Finding Anchor Texts

Trustworthy preservice teacher action research shows a strong sense of connection between the teacher-researcher, the context of the project school and classroom, the project design, and the literature related the project. Each of these elements grounds or *anchors* your project, providing a solid base on which to build your interpretations and conclusions. Often, teacher-researchers find a single text or source in the literature that contains the major philosphi-cal foundations, theoretical framework, or core strategies that form the foundation of their research. We call these sources "anchor texts." Consider the following examples of teacher-researchers finding anchor texts:

Jeffery's Self-Study: A white upper-middle class male and self-described "high achiever," Jeffery student-taught in a community serving a significant minority/high poverty population. He was shocked that on his first math exam many students received "failing" grades, with an average of under 70%. Mentors and others assured him that this was normal for the students he was teaching, and that he needed to modify and reteach certain concepts. After a few weeks of disappointing (to Jeffery) results, Jeffery found himself awake at night, questioning his ability to teach; at times, he found it hard to get up in the morning and commute to the high school for his teaching day. He decided to make his action research project a self-study, starting with the critical question, "How do I maintain my motivation to teach when students don't seem to want to learn?" While doing background research about his student population, he re-read a chapter previously assigned in his education coursework entitled "Subtractive schooling, caring relations, and social capital in the schooling of U.S. Mexican youth" (Valenzuela, 2005). The chapter described, illustrated, and grounded philosophically the importance of developing caring relations in educating Latino youth, helping Jeffery shift from assuming that "good students care about school," to considering instead how to better care for students *so* that they will care about school. The chapter referred to the work of Nel Noddings and others on justice and caring (Katz, Noddings, & Strike, 1999). Noddings' work became for Jeffery an anchor text, providing Jeffery new language and theory in which to ground his journey.

Jeffery's experience is a reminder that "self" is a part of every action research project. Examine this in the side road Self-Study 2.1: *Images of Self as Student Teacher-Researcher*, found at the end of this chapter on p. 62.

Activity: Synthesizing Literature

In this activity you will syntheisze literature, looking across different articles, books (or chapters in books), and other sources to find common themes and make synthesis statements.

You may do this activity with as few as two or three sources, our students often do the activity using six sources.

1. Complete an annotated bibliography for each article, book chapter, or other source, using Table 2.2.

2. Review for each article the themes you found. Note any common themes shared by two or more of the articles.

3. Note common themes on a chart (see Table 2.3). Restrict yourself to the most relevant two or three themes. Consider whether these themes are or are not related to your image of "good teacher" and/or personal questions and concerns about teaching and learning.

4. Write each theme you are working with in the middle of its own large space on a large piece of butcher paper. We'll refer to this as your "theme map."

5. Using a highlighter or pencil, mark or underline quotes and ideas that specifically relate to each of your themes. Use a different color or some other marking for each theme.

6. Map the quotes onto the blank "theme maps" from Step 4, showing relationships and connections between ideas. Rather than rewriting the quotes onto the map, you might consider using scissors to cut out the quotes so that you can move them around before taping or gluing them to the paper.

7. Add information connecting to your theme images of "good teacher" and/or personal questions and concerns about teaching and learning. Use information from your prior pictures of teacher and researcher, self-study interviews, study of cultural context, work defining action research, and any new thoughts and insights you may be having.

8. View your map. Write a synthesis statement summarizing your learning and how this applies to becoming a teacher.

➜ TABLE 2.3: Synthesizing Articles

Theme	Connection to images of "good teacher" and/or personal "wonderings" or dilemmas about teaching and learning

Formulating a Critical Question

. . . and have the potential to improve teaching, learning, and life.

Bring together your thoughts from the beginning of this section, your initial conversations with your critical colleague, and the knowledge gained from your first Internet and library searches to begin drafting your critical question. Consider your general areas of interests and respond to the following prompts that most seem to relate to your emerging critical questions:

- What role does/should/might _____ play in the classroom?

- How can I _____ as a teacher?

- Will this teaching and learning strategy [name your strategy] . . . ?

- What happens when . . . ?

- How does this [name "this"] . . . ?

- I wonder . . .

- What are the consequences of . . . ?

- What is it like to . . . ?

- If this were changed . . . ?

- Why does this incongruence . . . ?

- Why is . . . ?

Spheres of Influence

As you responded to the above prompts, you may be worried that your questions seem "too big." Arhar, Holly, and Kasten (2001) suggest that teacher/researchers consider "areas of concern" as a way to conceptualize critical questions. Consider a layered depiction of areas of concern, sometimes called "spheres of influence" (see Figure 2.1). Note that we have placed *self* in the middle of the figure. We believe that change starts at the level of the teacher-self, informed by cultural context.

Now travel back through the prompts you completed at the beginning of this section. Label the sphere of influence for each of the prompts. In which spheres of influence does each lie? Do some cut across boundaries? In what way?

→ **FIGURE 2.1: Spheres of Influence**

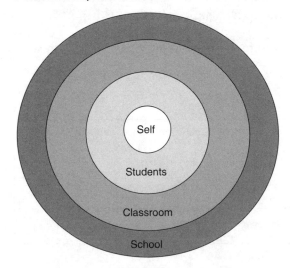

Self

Students

Classroom

School

Making Action Research Questions Workable

What makes a workable action research question? Your action research question has the power to energize and inspire. You may not have thought about research in these terms before (see Table 2.4). Begin to see your action research as a time of excitement, transformation, and even joy as you become a teacher.

→ TABLE 2.4: Qualities of a Workable Action Research Question

Important to you	Within your sphere of influence
Contains a good idea	Authentic
Focused	Compelling
Supports mission	Benefits students
Informs your work	Is your work—not more work. Has the potential to bring you joy and satisfaction

The Evolution of Your Critical Question

Most of our students don't feel like they know nearly enough about their placements, their settings, their classrooms, and—most important—themselves as teachers to create a critical question. What your action research is asking you to do is to risk a journey in which those questions (think of the meaning of the word *quest*) and many more may be answered or at least better understood. In teacher action research, the questions themselves are fluid. After you formulate your initial critical question, you will return to it for sharpening, modification, and, potentially, a complete rewrite as your project progresses. Consider the examples of critical question evolution represented in Tables 2.5 and 2.6.

Drafting Your Critical Question

In Chapter 1 we said that all action research studies completed by student teachers have elements of a self-study—all such projects will document your process of becoming a teacher. Therefore, use personal pronouns such as *I* or *my* in your question. Begin drafting your question with, "How can I, as a teacher, . . . ?"

→ TABLE 2.5: Evolution of a Critical Question: Elementary

What strategies do my first graders prefer in learning mathematics?	*First graders are not developmentally ready to articulate their preferences for learning mathematics. Even asking them what the like or dislike may not be particularly trustworthy data.* Question for the teacher-researcher: *If first graders could articulate a response to this question, what would you hope to discover?*
What strategies do my first graders prefer when learning mathematics and how are these strategies developmental appropriate?	*This question is getting closer. It introduces the idea of "developmentally appropriate" strategies.* Questions for the action researcher: *If first graders choose strategies that are not developmentally appropriate (they choose them because they are colorful for example) would this really inform your teaching? It seems like you are asking about developmentally appropriate strategies for teaching first graders mathematics. What is it you really want to find out about these?*
How can I use developmentally appropriate math assessments in my first grade classroom to guide mathematical instruction?	*Now the question is focused. It is within the sphere of influence for the student teacher/researcher; it benefits students and supports the development of the student teacher becoming a teacher; the results will bring the student teacher/ researcher satisfaction.*

→ TABLE 2.6: Evolution of a Critical Question: Secondary

How can high school chemistry students learn to study more?	*The question is too broad.* Questions for the action researcher: *How would you define study skills? How do you want your high school students to study? Why do you want them to study more? For what purpose?*
Will teaching my high school chemistry students study skills enrich their understanding of the content area?	*This is getting closer. The question now includes a purpose for using the study skills.* Questions for the action researcher: *Study skills is a broad area that has different meanings for different people. What specific study skills do you want to use? What would be most appropriate for your high school chemistry students? What strategies would provide you with data for intervention and supporting student learning?*
Will the use of graphic organizers, quick draw chalkboards, and review games influence my high school chemistry students' content knowledge and understanding?	*The question is now more focused. Specific study skills are identified for use in the classroom. The purpose is clear: to increase students' content knowledge. The student teacher's own practice will be improved through the study. It may remain to more clearly define what is meant by "understanding."*

📓 Okay—give it a try! Draft a critical question.

Your question may resemble those in the first row of Tables 2.5 and 2.6 in that they will need to evolve. Go back and draft your question in two or three forms. Draft one for several areas of interests. Read the question aloud; how does it sound?

We suggest that you begin the process of refining your question right away by reviewing Table 2.4. Share your question with a colleague and your mentor-teacher(s). Try it on for a few days and see if you like it. As you observe and work in your classroom, ask yourself, "Is this a meaningful question for me as a student teacher and for the students in this classroom?" Be honest about what your colleagues and your intutition are telling you: don't fall in love with a first-draft question!

Finally, a reminder: you are not trying to "prove" anything with your critical question. If you find "proving" language—such as, "Will guided reading or sustained silent reading most promote reading comprehension?"—revise your question. Student teacher action research is attempting to discover something meaningful to you; lessons you can carry with you as a professional educator that will make you a wiser, smarter, more creative, joyful teacher!

After drafting your initial critical question, share it with your critical colleague and your mentor-teacher(s). Continue to allow the question(s) to evolve as you are informed by your setting, coursework, and distant colleagues.

Sharpening Your Critical Question

In Chapter 3 you will design an action research study to better understand your critical question. But first, consider what type of action research approach is best suited to your critical question. In Chapter 1, we presented an overview of research methodology and designs; you may want to review this section before continuing. Four kinds of action research were presented: *design research, self-study, ethnography,* and *curriculum analysis* (see Table 2.7).

→ TABLE 2.7: Action Research Design Possibilities

Design Research	Self-Study	Ethnography	Curriculum Analysis
To specifically "try out" a teaching method, practice, or approach in order address a concern or to improve student learning, attitude, or motivation	*To deliberately trace the process of becoming a teacher*	*To better understand the issues of students and schooling*	*To analyze curriculum, based upon the literature in the area, to ascertain strengths, weaknesses to address as a teacher*

We used a chart to categorize these kinds of action research, but a better visual may be a Venn diagram of overlapping circles, as shown in Figure 2.2. This diagram demonstrates how elements of design research, self-study, ethnography, and curriculum analysis are ultimately pieces of any action research project. To better understand how these approaches overlap, consider the questions posed in Figure 2.3 based on a study involving teaching math. Note how the action research question changes the methodology.

→ FIGURE 2.2: Venn Diagram/Action Research

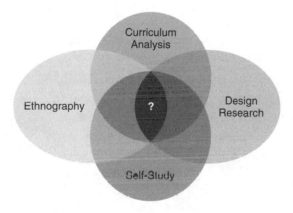

→ FIGURE 2.3: Action Research Designs and Questions

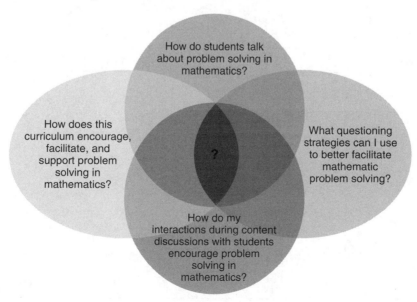

In seeking answers to any one of these questions an action researcher analyzes, to some degree or another, the other questions. Choosing the actual approach has more to do with where you will focus your inquiry: on *self*, *students*, *curriculum*, or *ethnographic interactions*.

An Additional Illustration

Note how the question changes in each of the following examples, depending on the focus of the study. Using your own area of interest, complete the chart in Table 2.9 to see how each approach to action research can alter the possible focus of your study. Write a different critical question for each approach using the model given earlier in Table 2.8.

Which of the above approaches best gets at your primary area of interest? Take some time to dialogue with critical colleagues, mentor-teacher(s) and instructor(s) to further narrow your action research. Revise your critical question(s) accordingly.

➔ TABLE 2.8: Literature Conversations

Design Research	Self-Study	Ethnography	Curriculum Analysis
How can I effectively use literature conversations to increase reading comprehension?	*How can I improve my questioning strategies to improve the quality of literature conversations and scaffold reading comprehension?*	*How do the ethnically diverse learners in my classroom talk about literature and how does this inform my assessment of reading comprehension?*	*In what ways is the adopted reading curriculum effective or not effective in scaffolding and encouraging literature conversations that increase reading comprehension?*

➔ TABLE 2.9: Choosing a Research Focus

Area of Interest _____

Design Research	Self-Study	Ethnography	Curriculum Analysis

Dissecting Your Critical Question

At this point you are likely still unsure about your critical question. As we said before, your critical question should remain somewhat fluid as you progress through your project; the critical question you have now will likely change as you collect and analyze data. Still, many of our students find themselves with a critical question that seems too broad, too vague, or too lacking in direction. Often, initial critical questions don't seem to add clarity, momentum or impetus to taking the next steps in an action research project. This final activity may help you 1) identify areas of your current critical question that are problematic, 2) make changes to your critical question that bring your project into clearer focus, and 3) help you visualize how your research will actually look in practice. You may work through this activity using your own critical question, or you may practice by using one of the sample questions included in Appendix D.

Activity: Dissecting and Re-Formulating Your Critical Question

You may find it valuable to do this activity with your critical colleague, in small group, or even as a whole class.

1. Begin with a blank piece of paper, chart paper, white board, or mind-mapping software such as *Inspiration* (www.inspiration.com).

2. Write your current critical question in the middle of the page or workspace.

   Example: "What impact does collaborative learning have on elementary school students' conflict resolution skills?"

3. Identify one or more words or terms you use in your critical question that seem ill-defined, vague, too broad, or simply "problematic" for any reason. Circle these words, phrases, or terms.

   Example: The critical question "What impact does collaborative learning have on elementary school students' conflict resolution skills?" has a number of ill-defined terms, including "conflict resolution skills," and "collaborative learning." Also, the term "elementary school students" may be too broad given the teacher's sphere of influence.

4. Start with one of the problematic words or phrases. Draw a line away from the word or phrase, extending into an empty part of the paper, giving yourself plenty of room to write. In the space, brainstorm about the term or idea, seeking to clarify what you believe the term or idea to mean. This is great time to gather input from your critical colleague or others. If the term seems too vague, seek to clarify it. If the idea seems too broad, seek to narrow it.

   Example: In the above example critical question, we circled "conflict resolution skills." A key question for the researcher to ask is "What do good conflict resolution skills look like in my classroom?" Look back to your literature review materials; how do your "distant colleagues" define conflict resolution? If you were observing a classroom to study the conflict resolution skills of its students, what behaviors would you be looking for? Brainstorm a list of what constitutes good conflict resolution skills.

5. Examine your work. How can you use the ideas from your brainstorming to re-write or re-define the problematic phrase or idea? It may be that your idea is too broad to work with, and so you must work with a smaller subset of the idea. It may be that the idea simply means many different things, and you need to choose the one thing that it will mean to you for the purposes of your project.

    Example: After brainstorming, it become obvious that "Conflict resolution skills" is complex, and encompasses many different behaviors, too many to study in one project, especially during student teaching. One behavior of particular interest may be the ability of students to resolve their own conflicts without teacher mediation. One way this could be documented would be to investigate the amount of time spent by the teacher mediating student disputes throughout the class day.

6. Rewrite the problematic term or phrase. Your critical question should serve to guide and bound your project, while providing at the same time enough space and flexibility to allow changes of direction as your project progresses. Your critical colleagues will help you strike a balance between having a critical question that is too broad and vague on one hand, and too narrow and rigid on the other.

    Example: One possible re-write would be to replace "Conflict Resolution Skills" with "ability of students to solve in-class disputes without teacher intervention." While one way to document this could be "amount of time spent by the teacher resolving disputes," including this in the critical question may over-prescribe the study, unnecessarily boxing in the thinking of the teacher.

7. Repeat steps 5 and 6 with other circled terms.

    Example: The initial critical question, "What impact does collaborative learning have on elementary school students' conflict resolution skills?," could be re-written as "What impact does teaching social skills during collaborative learning activities have on the ability of my third grade students to solve disputes without teacher intervention?" Notice that "collaborative learning" has been better defined to include "what" the teacher will do, i.e., teach social skills, the context has been narrowed from the too-general "elementary school students" to the more appropriate "my third grade students," and "conflict resolution skills" has been clarified as meaning the ability to solve problems without the teachers help. While there are still some potentially vague areas of the critical question, the new critical question makes more clear what next steps need to be taken by the researcher, such as designing the teaching of social skills during collaborative learning, finding ways to document the dispute resolution processes used by students, and so on. These steps are covered in detail in Chapter 4, where you will learn how to design your study.

Summary

From this chapter you have a clearer understanding of how we research our own issues, meaningful in our current life and practice. How we pursue critical questions that resonate with our professional community and have the potential to improve teaching, learning, and life. Discovering an area of focus and developing a critical question is an act of simultaneously discovering more about your own values and biases about teaching and learning, your school community, the specific strengths and challenges of the students you will teach, and learning from distant colleagues. A strong sense of connection is one of the elements of trustworthy preservice teacher action research. Making such connections now enables you to begin thinking about research design and methodology.

Chapter 2: Content Questions

1. We began this chapter in this way, "We research our own issues, meaningful in our current life and practice. We pursue critical questions that resonate with our professional community and have the potential to improve teaching, learning, and life." Rewrite this sentence demonstrating the concept and your personal meaning-making of it.
2. In your own words, what does it mean to "problematize" and why is this important to action research?
3. How and why does context matter when conducting action research?
4. What are characteristics of a workable critical question? Why do critical questions often change during action research?

Chapter 2: Process Questions

1. What do you know about your school/classroom community where you will be conducting your action research project? How does context matter to your action research study?
2. What have you discovered about your research topic from distant colleagues? How will their expertise guide your study? In what areas do you still need to find out more information? Where will you look for this information?
3. What does your choice of topic, draft question(s), and choice of distant colleagues say about your own values and beliefs about teaching and learning?

Self-Study 2.1: Images of Self as Student Teacher-Researcher

In this activity you will examine yourself, as you are becoming a teacher-action researcher within your school setting. Consider these words by Lampert (2000):

For every inquiry into one's own practice, there are many possible stories to tell. For every story that is told, there are many possible meanings to interpret. Stories about practice are not mirrors of experience: like all texts, they are constructed by the author with certain intentions in mind. (p. 68)

This activity is designed for you to "hear" some of the stories you are telling about your student teaching placement and assist you in "locating" that story in your own experience, intentions and paradigm. Doing this activity so allows you to practice *reflexivity* in your research. Complete this activity after you have spent some time in your student-teaching position.

While this activity may be completed individually, as with all research, collaboration will add depth through additional perceptions. Use the synthesis statements you write at the end of this activity as a starting point for dialogue with a critical colleague.

Another variation is as follows: Assume the position of interviewer and use the questions to interview a critical colleague. Become the researcher, and based upon the information from the interview, complete the analysis, synthesis, and deconstruction. Return this analysis to your critical colleague: does she agree with your analysis? What does she "see" and "hear" in the interview that you did not? How have your own paradigms influenced the process? Using this variation will better mirror the research process.

Complete the following statements in a phrase or at most a sentence or two. Afterward you will analyze, synthesize, and deconstruct your responses.

Connections

1. My mentor-teacher reminds me of . . .
2. While in my mentor-teacher's classroom, I observed the following incident that reminded me of when I was a student . . .
3. If I were a student in this classroom, what I would enjoy most is . . .
4. If I were a student in this classroom, what I would not have enjoyed is . . .
5. If I were a student in this class, how I would honestly respond to the question "What are you learning in school?" is . . . (Note: content or skills are not always what are learned.)

Questions

6. The procedures and/or processes that I question most about this classroom are . . .
7. The strategy I observed being used in this classroom that I'd like to know more about is . . .
8. I find it interesting that my mentor teacher made this choice. What I would like to ask about this is . . .

continues ➜

Surprises

9. What surprises me most about the student(s) is . . .

10. What surprises me most about this classroom is . . .

11. I just never thought that . . .

Anticipation

12. I can't wait to go back to this classroom because . . .

Fear

13. I am concerned about going back to this classroom because . . .

Analysis, Synthesis, and Deconstruction

You can do this activity alone, but we think it would be more useful to make this a collaborative effort. Interview your critical colleague, using these questions as conversation starters; if you need to wander to make discoveries, feel free to do so!

Connections

Step away from your answers. What do your responses tell you about your assumptions of school, teaching, and learning? What do your responses tell you about how you might define a "good teacher"? How might these assumptions both open up possibilities and limit learning in your own classroom?

Questions

Is there any pattern to your responses in this section? Is there a general area where questions seem to form? Are some responses more meaningful to you than others? How do these questions—or how could they—relate to the critical question for your action research project?

Surprises, Anticipation, Fear

Analyze these three areas together. How do these responses inform you of your values concerning a "good" education/teacher? What are useful and dangerous about these responses?

Synthesis

In no more than three sentences, describe yourself as a student teacher in your current classroom based upon the data produced in this activity. Is there any information here that might be useful in considering an action research topic and project?

Cultural Context 2.1: Getting to Know Your Classroom Culture

Critical questions for action research can often be found embedded in issues and needs at the school setting where teachers teach and live their professional lives. Frank (1999) writes, "classrooms are *particular* social settings, mini-cultures in themselves that are *not* universal. Events are different in classrooms because teachers and students are different, establishing and creating their own rights and obligations, roles and relationships, and norms and expectations" (p. 7; emphasis added). Knowing the school and classroom culture where you will be student-teaching will give you insight into how to make your lessons relevant, what kind of assessments to use, possible action research topics, and what kinds of actions will be valued by the school and classroom community.

To gather data about the classroom where you will be teaching, you will be using both formal and informal techniques. Practice listening well to the language that is allowed (and not allowed) in the classroom by both the teacher and the students, note the behaviors that are affirmed and condoned, and observe the structures for learning most often used and those structures least used.

Classroom Data Collection Activity 1: The Classroom Map

1. Draw a map of the classroom. Include all physical details, including where desks and/or tables and other furniture is arranged. Note items on the wall and other artifacts that lend ambience to the room. Include computers, sandboxes, rug areas, or libraries. Attend to as much details as you can in your map.

2. Visit with your mentor-teacher about the environmental setup of the room. Ask her/his rationale for arranging the room in such a way. Be curious; avoid being judgmental.

3. Analyze the items on the map by considering the following questions:

   - How does the classroom represent a "typical" classroom for you?
   - What might be missing from this classroom?
   - What does the environmental setup of the classroom suggest about the teacher's philosophy for teaching and learning? How does it *not* seem to support the teacher's philosophy for teaching and learning?
   - How does the environmental setup of the room support the developmental needs of the children or adolescents in this classroom?
   - How does or doesn't the classroom represent the gender and ethnicity of students in the classroom?
   - Note where the teacher's desk is: how does this position the teacher?
   - If there are posted rules, slogans, or inspirational phrases, how might they be categorized? Who and what do they represent?

Write several synthesis statements about what the data might suggest about the classroom culture. Do these synthesis statements suggest possible action research project topics for you? If so, what

continues →

are they? "Test" these synthesis statements as you continue to be present in the classroom. Revise them as necessary as your insights continue to expand.

Classroom Data Collection Activity 2: Mentor-Teacher Interview

Mentor-Teacher Interview: The suggested questions may be downloaded in document form from the *BTAR* companion website.

One of the most important things you can do as a student teacher is to carefully interview your mentor-teacher about various aspects of the classroom. It is much better to ask rather than to assume through uninformed judgments. Having written this, we realize that mentor-teachers are busy people; they may not have the time to sit down and answer questions over coffee. However, you can have a list of questions ready and ask them throughout the day. Just make sure your mentor-teacher knows that you are doing this and understands the reason you are asking such questions.

Here are some suggested interview questions:

- How is a typical class period and or day structured?
- What kinds of things interfere with this structure?
- Are any students regularly pulled out of the classroom? For what reasons?
- How is the teacher creating an inclusive classroom for all students?
- What routines are established and regularly used?
- What does the teacher consider to be some of the most effective teaching-learning strategies for her students?
- What are some of the factors the teacher believes most influence her decisions concerning teaching?
- What are the rules, policies, and/or consequences of the classroom? Why have these been established?
- How does the teacher generally believe students, administration, community, and government mandates influence her teaching?
- What issues, concerns, or dilemmas does the teacher currently have regarding her practice?

Include other questions that reflect your own areas of interests.

Analyze the data generated from this interview by grouping the data under general categories such as: *Teaching and Learning Philosophy*; *Beliefs About Students*; *Structures of Classrooms*. Revise or create new categories as needed. As you were categorizing the data, did you notice any particular key words or phrases the teacher used more than once during the interview?

Draft synthesis statements from the data you have collected and analyzed. How do these synthesized statements inform you as a student teacher? How do you see yourself "fitting in" to this culture? Did the interview generate any possible action research topics?

Classroom Data Collection Activity 3: Observe

Spend at least 30 minutes observing a class session. Divide a paper into two columns: *What the Teacher Said/Did* and *What the Students Said/Did*. Record the phrases and behaviors accordingly. Attempt to

continues →

do this without using biased or descriptive phrases. For example, rather than writing, "student sighs as if bored," write, "student sighs." This note-taking is described further in Chapter 3: *Action Research Methodology*.

After note-taking, make notes about the observation on the right side of your paper. Pose questions, theorize, jot down additional influences. In this column you might write—opposite of the observation, "student sighs"—"Is the student bored, tired, lacking understanding . . . or just being 16?"

Now analyze the observations for patterns. What language was repeated during the session? How would you categorize "teacher talk" in this classroom? What is acceptable "student talk"? How would you categorize "teacher–student talk"? What kind of student talk was overheard? What might the teacher's behavior (actual physical actions) suggest about his view of "the teacher" and "the student"? What kind of behavior was acceptable for students? Not acceptable for students? Who was engaged most, or least, in the lesson? What does this data suggest about teaching and learning in this classroom?

Synthesize

Review all the data from this activity. What patterns emerge across these data sets? For example, what language was used by the mentor-teacher across the data sets (the interview and the classroom observation)? What about the physical classroom appears to be consistent with the mentor-teacher's passions, concerns, and interactions with students? How does or doesn't the physical aspects of the classroom support student learning in the observations? What "norms" of the classroom can you identify? What inconsistencies appear to exist?

Deconstruct

Consider how your own assumptions, beliefs, and framework for teaching and learning influence your interpretation of the above data. In what ways do you find yourself intrigued by this classroom culture? In what ways do you find yourself frustrated or challenged by this classroom culture? How is this classroom the way you *think* education should be? How is it not what you think education should be?

Cultural Context 2.2: Analyzing School Documents

To conduct this analysis, you will need to collect documents produced by the school and/or district where you are student teaching. (One official document will work; more than one allows for comparison.) The goal of your analysis is to ascertain what the official stance of the school is toward teaching and learning. This official stance more often than not represents the "sacred story" of the school (return to the previous Cultural Context side road if necessary). Documents that work well for this analysis include any school publication specifically written for the community, school and/or district such as school handbooks, websites, or newsletters. An interesting extension to this analysis is to collect recently published community newspapers about the school and/or district and to compare/contrast what is said about the school in the news to the "official documents" of the school.

Analyze the Documents

1. Read through each document carefully. Note specifically any mission statements or school or district goals and objectives. Highlight specific language that addresses the following: academic expectations, behavioral expectations, parent/community expectations, and teacher expectations.
2. Create a chart and categorize the language from the documents into the areas listed above. Add an additional category for words and phrases that seem to "jump out" but don't fit any of the above categories.
3. At the bottom of each chart, summarize what is said in the documents concerning these areas.

Synthesize

1. Synthesize by looking across the categories and summaries you have made from the document study. Interpret what you think is being said about the teaching/learning process. Who are the "ideal" students, teachers, and/or parents as presented in these documents? What is the "ideal" school?
2. Consider what this means to you as a student teacher-researcher. Write down possibilities but avoid conclusions.

Deconstruct

1. Consider the assumptions the documents make about students, teachers, parents, and systems for learning. What do the documents assume such groups want to hear? From where might these assumptions come?
2. Deconstruct certain words or phrases that may be commonly used among educators and are used more than once in the documents. For example, the word "*excellent*" is often used in such documents. "*Safety*" is another commonly used word. How are these words used? In what context? Are the words specifically defined? How are they defined? What are the multiple possible messages such words convey?

continues →

3. Consider your own assumptions in the interpretations you have made. What values and beliefs about education do these represent? For example, if you find yourself support or disagreeing with statements made, consider why you hold this position and what it says about you, as a future teacher/researcher.

Knowing Your Community of Practice

Getting to know your placement, your "community of practice," is about more than just gathering demographic information about the school. Coming to know your community of practice is about listening, interacting, and being aware of *how* you are listening and interacting. As you review the data and your interpretations, what do you want to remember as a student teacher? How have these activities informed your areas of interest for action research? Does the information open up possibilities for a critical question?

CHAPTER 3
ACTION RESEARCH METHODOLOGY

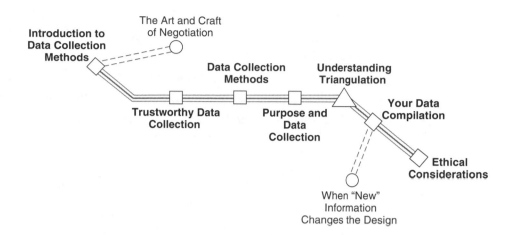

Science states meanings; art expresses them. . . . The poetic as distanced from the prosaic, esthetic art as distinct from scientific, expression as distinct from statement, does something different from leading to an experience. It constitutes one.

—John Dewey, *Later Works*

Research (and good teaching) is both the science and art of gathering trustworthy data to inform practice. Chapter 3 describes principles of data collection methodology. The data collection process may appear fairly straightforward; however, the side roads of Chapter 3 touch on issues of cultural context and how this influences decisions about methodology. As you read the chapter, ask: what methodologies best support my inquiry and critical question? How can I collect purposeful data? How can I plan for trustworthiness?

Introduction to Data Collection Methods

One cannot have an action research project without data. Data becomes the evidence of hunches, a confirmation of theory, and the source of paradigm shifts. Data is the evidence you will use to respond to your critical question(s) and develop further questions around your research interest. Data underlies the trustworthiness of your project, measuring its depth and defining its usefulness, determining the richness of your experience. Deliberate data collection is the extended eyes, ears, and soul of the teacher; it is the way we come to know our students, change our practice, and grow our teaching identity.

Data collection and interpretation share much with good classroom assessment. We know that assessment drives instruction. As teachers, we assess our student knowledge, skills, and/or conceptual development in any given area using multiple means so that we can make wise instructional choices. This is the same process in action research: we collect data (forms of assessment) so that we can make wise instructional choices. We circle back to the concept that we are *teacher-researchers*, and our continual and ongoing research question is, "How can we better facilitate learning for our students?"

What does action research data look like? Consider Lisa, a student teacher investigating the critical question, "How can I improve student math achievement by increasing on-task behavior during math time in my first grade classroom?" Her mentor-teacher, Mrs. James, collected on- and off-task data while Lisa monitored math time. The students, sitting around rectangular tables, are labeled A–H on the chart. Every three minutes, from 9:00 to 9:15, Mrs. James performed a "sweep" observation of the students, recording whether each was on-task or off-task. The chart she made is shown in Figure 3.1.

→ **FIGURE 3.1: Observation Data 1: On-Task/Off-Task Behavior for Students A–H**

First Grade: Ms. Reynolds   Observation: October 26, 2003   Conducted by: Mrs. James, CT   Lesson: Math

Activity: Independent Choice Work Time

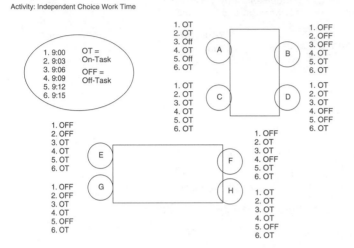

In your notebook or journal, respond to the following questions:

- What information does Figure 3.1 contain about on-task behavior? What information is provided about student achievement?

- Lisa recorded in her research journal the results of math journal entries completed by the children before going outside to recess after the math lesson. Her notes indicated that all six students were successful in learning the math concepts in the lesson. What important information did Lisa's notes contain that the behavior chart did not?

- During recess, Lisa and Mrs. James shared their information side-by-side. What questions/issues arise when looking at Mrs. James' chart and Lisa's notes together?

- While looking over the chart and notes, Lisa and Mrs. James both saw the same contradiction: If some students were largely off-task during the lesson, why didn't this result in those same students not understanding the concept? They realized that more information was needed. (Lisa jotted down a record of this meeting as data to include in her research notebook.)

The following day during math time, Mrs. James did another observation session, modified to reflect what was discovered the day before. What added information is in the second observation chart (Figure 3.2)? How does this information help answer Lisa and Mrs. James' questions? What other information do you think would be helpful in analyzing Lisa's original question about on-task behavior and math achievement?

In this short example, the observation charts, math journal entries, and Lisa's notes about her meeting with Mrs. James are all different pieces of action research *data*, providing important information that will help Lisa better understand, and ultimately answer, her research question. Other sources of data related to this episode could include Lisa's lesson plans, handouts and other curriculum used, photos of the classroom arrangement, student demographic information such as gender and first language, and so on. In addition, Lisa might interview her students to confirm her hunches. Lisa's data collection methods are associated with qualitative inquiry.

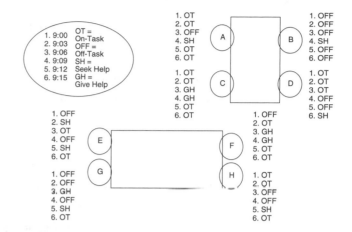

→ FIGURE 3.2: Observation Data 2: On-Task/Off-Task Behavior for Students A–H

First Grade: Ms. Reynoids   Observation: October 28, 2003   Conducted by: Mrs. James, CT   Lesson: Math
Activity: Independent Choice Work Time

Throughout the rest of this chapter, we emphasize three broad types of action research data often associated with qualitative inquiry (see Chapter 1 for more on being a student teacher-researcher): 1) *observations*, 2) *interviews*, and 3) *artifacts/documents*. A complete *data set* consists of specific data representing all three data types. The purpose of this section is to help you design specific data-collection methodologies that will provide a rich research compilation with which to provide insight and meaning around your critical question.

Why These Data Collection Strategies?

Qualitative research is a rich and varied field, often contested and resisting standardization (Denzin & Lincoln, 2003a; Lather, 2004; Lincoln & Guba, 2003; Smith, 1993). Denzin and Lincoln chronicle the historical field of qualitative research across seven different "moments" or periods since the early 1900s. "Qualitative research means different things in each of these moments," they note (2003b, p. 4); each moment is constructed by historical, cultural, economic, and political thought or paradigm.

This does not mean that student teachers do not use quantitative data—they do and often should. Teachers use all kinds of tallies, test score data, and school or community statistical data. For teacher-researchers with small sample sizes (their classroom population) and more qualitative designs, quantitative data is one kind of data used to create a more complete picture of classroom experience. We will address how to use this data and later how to interpret this data.

We focus in this book on specific research methodologies and methods that seem most appropriate for student teachers. In making these choices we:

- acknowledge the role of language in constructing and limiting our understanding; therefore, the meanings we construct are partial (Britzman, 2003; Gore, 1993; Lather, 1991; Weedon, 1987);

- recognize the powerful influences of culture on ourselves and our interpretations (Butler, 1997; Foucault, 1972; Lather, 1991; Spivak, 1993; Weedon, 1987);

- acknowledge how the material, non-human entities, intra-act with teachers and students to create each learning event as unique and full of possibilities (Barad, 2007; Deleuze & Guattari, 1987; Lenz Taguchi, 2010; Phillips & Larson, 2012);

- see classrooms as places where meaning (but not always the meaning we intend) is actively constructed (Britzman, 2003; Crotty, 1998; Ellsworth, 1997);

- embrace the complexities of these classrooms as the element that brings surprise, joy, and heartache to those of us who teach (Bullough, 1992; Dudley-Marling, 1997; Hargreaves, 1999).

With the above assumptions in mind, reconsider the example with which we opened this section—that of Lisa and her mentor-teacher working to understand on- and off-task behavior. We see in even this short example a layered complexity of meaning, demanding a variety of data-collection strategies as suggested in the qualitative research literature.

Data and Assessment

Action research data collection and instructional assessment share basic principles (see Table 3.1).

→ TABLE 3.1: Shared Principles of Research Data and Instructional Assessment

Data collection and assessment are purpose driven.	*What do I want to find out?*
Paring the research and/or assessment goal with a complementary data collection and/or assessment strategy is critical.	*How does this data collection and/or assessment tool reflect what I want to know? Does the task and/or tool match my overall research/teaching goals?*
Both research and assessment data require some kind of criteria and/or standard in order to be evaluated.	*How will I interpret the research and/or assessment data? What criteria will I apply? Whose standard and for what purpose will these standards be used?*
Research and assessment data can be isolated and useless without interpretation and action.	*How will I use the results of the research and/or assessment data?*

Teachers "do" research every day in their classrooms. When teachers give a test, collect drawings, review student portfolios, listen to children read, evaluate speeches, observe behavior, or evaluate lab reports, they are collecting data. These activities may be done by an individual teacher, or as part of a collegial group or professional learning community. Once the data is interpreted, it will inform them of the effectiveness of their instructional choices and direct them in planning their next teaching steps. Seeing research data collection and instructional assessment as integrated concepts gives meaning and purpose to both. The separation of the two is often more a matter of language, than of concept. We will use the language of research through out this text, such as *data, data set, research compilation,* but behind and through these words is the idea of *assessment.*

Travel the side road Cultural Context 3.1: *The Art and Craft of Negotiation* found at the end of the chapter on p. 97. If you are student-teaching, making methodology decisions is a collaborative endeavor with your mentor-teacher. This side road will provide you with some suggestions.

The Art and Craft of Data Collection

Understanding the relationship between research data and assessment is just part of seeing data collection as both art and craft. There is art and craft in choosing the data collection strategies, getting the data collected, organizing the data, and interpreting the data.

Here are some general guidelines for the craft of data collection:

- collect generously; organize diligently;

- be deliberate, even ritualistic in data collection, but in your deliberateness, be willing to alter the plan as the data informs you;

- collect from multiple and complimentary sources.

Remember that data is lifeless without purpose, ongoing analysis and interpretation. (See Chapters 5 and 6 for more on these topics.)

Here are some useful questions for the art of data collection:

- Is the data collected meaningful to you? Is it enriching your understanding of teaching and learning?

- Is your data gathering manageable as part of everyday teaching?

- Does the data provide "Aha!" moments of clarity, help you see something you might have ignored, challenge your thinking or confirm a long-held hunch?

- Is the data assisting you in constructing meaningful responses to your critical question(s) and/or facilitating needed changes in your critical question(s)?

Here is some advice: you won't often know what you are looking for until after you've collected it and it is too late to return and gather more data; therefore, collect, analyze, and revise your design—*often*. (Again, see Chapters 5 and 6.) Remind yourself regularly that this action research project is not about "proving" something to be true or false: this is about becoming a teacher *through* action research, about making discoveries in context about teaching and learning processes.

Trustworthy Data Collection

We previously introduced five elements central to trustworthy action research (see the Introduction). It is now time to revisit these elements in more depth. Why now? *Trustworthiness* is the lens we use in choosing, evaluating, and implementing data collection strategies in our research.

Evidence of Becoming

Central to trustworthy student teacher action research is evidence of the transformation from student to teacher. The re-telling of your journey through the collection and interpretation of data ought to demonstrate self-reflexivity and a growing awareness of the complex role of "teacher" and the relationship of this role to the many participants in a school community. Reason and Bradbury (2001) write, "Since action research starts with everyday experience and is concerned with the development of living knowledge, in many ways the process of inquiry is as important as specific outcomes" (p. 2). As you plan for data collection, consider how the data you collect will allow your thinking to be transparent. How will you record and document your thoughts and ideas for later use? What data can you collect that will move your teaching and learning into new spaces? Will the data you collect provide evidence of your *becoming* a teacher?

Self-Reflexivity

Inherent in making transparent the transformation between student and teacher is a strong sense of self-reflexivity. When practicing self-reflexivity, "the investigator relinquishes the 'God's-eye view' and reveals his or her work as historically, culturally, and personally situated" (Gergen & Gergen, 2003). Practicing self-reflexivity as a student teacher-action researcher means describing your values and belief systems, what is important to you, your past experiences, what you know, what you think you know, and what you want to know about teaching because "*How* we know is intimately bound up with *what* we know, where we learned it, and what we have experienced" (Lincoln & Denzin, 2003, p. 631). This is a kind of self-interrogation, recognizing your personal, biased role in choosing methodology and methods, curriculum, and making interpretation and evaluation. Self-reflexivity keeps paradigms, theories, assumptions, judgments, biases, and the transformation of thought transparent throughout the research process. Self-reflexivity results in and makes clear your changes in thinking, your moments of transformation, and your continued evolution as a teacher. Self-reflexivity is yet another piece in constructing credible qualitative research (Arminio & Hultgren, 2002; Gergen & Gergen, 2003; Johnson, 1997; Lather, 1991; McCotter, 2001; Moore, 1999). Your research journal is the most important place where you can practice self-reflexivity. How can you plan to journal in a way that works for you?

Multiple Perspectives

Multiple perspectives are foundational in creating trustworthiness (Gergen & Gergen, 2003). Seeking multiple perspectives, insights, or "voices" provides for layers of interpretation the teacher-researcher could not apply in isolation. Without multiple perspectives, interpretation of data can become dangerously close to relying on our own personal belief systems. Seek and listen to the voices of colleagues, mentor-teachers, participants (students), parents and advisors, as well as those "distant colleagues" in the literature. What data collection strategies are most appropriate for seeking multiple perspectives? Which ones are most appropriate to your action research project?

Strong Sense of Connection

Trustworthy student teacher action research should include a strong sense of connection between your emerging identity as "teacher," the context and culture of the classroom where you are teaching, the project design and lessons you teach, and the literature base or expertise of distant colleagues. Place your action research within the company of experts, those "distant colleagues" who have published in the literature (Eisner, 1998; Hubbard & Power, 2003; Johnson, 1997; McCotter, 2001; Patton, 2002). How are the data collection tools you plan to use particularly suited to the context of your action research project? How are you using the literature to inform your data collection? How do you expect the various kinds of data collected to "talk to one another"? How will each data inform another piece of data? What kinds of connections across the data collection plan will be made?

Meaningful Results

Finally, when you have completed your research project, you will ask yourself "How does the knowledge and meaning derived from my action research project make me more insightful and wise as a teacher?" (adapted from Kincheloe, 2003). To have meaningful results, you need to collect data that that will allow you to seek to multiple perspectives, practice self-reflexivity and make strong connections. How will your data collection do this?

As you work through this chapter selecting data collection strategies and drafting your action research design, keep asking yourself, "How can I plan for trustworthy teacher action research?" How can I collect data that will document my thinking, wondering, theorizing, guessing, and actions – my *becoming* a teacher? How can I organize data so I can reference it at a later date and make trustworthy analysis and interpretations?

Data Collection Methods

Within this trustworthy framework, teacher action research data is collected via three broad methods: *observation*, *interview*, and *artifact/document*. A complete *data set* contains data from each of these three categories. For example, if you are focusing on a single lesson, you may take notes while students are working (*observation*), have several informal conversations with students (*interview*), and collect submitted student work (*artifact*). Each data type provides a different way of seeing the critical question.

Observations

To *observe* as a student teacher-researcher is to *critically and deliberately watch*, as a participant in the classroom. The act of observing recognizes that "live action" provides powerful insights for teacher-researchers. It can be useful to digitally record sessions and then observe the recording.

Interviews

To *interview* as a student teacher-researcher is to *inquire*, to *ask questions of, and listen* to, students, colleagues, supervisors, mentor-teachers and others connected with your project in order to hear another side, version, or angle of the story. Note that while observation data takes on the voice and viewpoint of the observer, interview data takes on the voice and viewpoint of the person being interviewed. In interview data, the researcher asks the questions or gives the prompts, and the participant answers. Interviews may be conducted either verbally or on paper, and may be conducted individually or in groups.

Artifacts

An *artifact* is any kind of physical documentation that sheds additional perspective on your research question and topic. Artifacts are pieces of physical evidence, such as student work, tallies of student behavior or test score results.

Observations, interviews and artifacts are basic data collection strategies that are applicable to any of the research designs introduced in Chapter 2. However, the strategies can look and feel differently depending on how they applied in the design. For example, in a design research project, data collection is usually spread more equally across the three areas of observation, interview and artifact. Self-study may rely more heavily on the researcher's journal and artifacts. Ethnography often uses audio and video-recordings and artifacts more than interviews. Curriculum analysis leans heavily on the literature when developing data collection tools. Research design will be discussed in greater depth later in this chapter. For now, as you read and work through the scenarios of data collection, consider how the genre of action research you have chosen (design, ethnographic, self study, or curriculum analysis) to implement might influence the kind of data that is collected.

There are many ways of gathering interview, observation, and artifact data; see Table 3.2 for a few examples. Some forms of data may fit into more than one category depending on how they are implemented.

→ TABLE 3.2: Data Collection Tools

Observation	Interview	Artifact
Note-taking	Survey	Student work
Anecdotal records	Questionnaire	Internet postings
Logs	Attitude rating	Portfolios
Checklists	Formal interview	Student self-assessments
Mapping	Informal interview	Test scores
Shadowing	Focus group	Attendance records
Digital photography	Sociogram	
Digital video and audio	Multiple intelligence approaches	

These data collection strategies are further described with examples in Appendix E. We highlight a few of these methodologies here but we highly recommend that you review the whole of Appendix E before continuing in this chapter.

One challenge of planning for data collection is to choose methods you can carry out while teaching. If you are a student teacher-researcher, you may elicit assistance from your mentor-teacher, perhaps a teacher's aide, your student teaching supervisors and action research faculty. If you are not yet student-teaching, you may have a different kind of access to the site where you are conducting your research. And if you are an in-service teacher, you will need to choose strategies carefully, keeping in mind what you can manage while teaching full days in the classroom.

Observation data collected by teachers often take the form of anecdotal notes written down after, rather than during, a teaching session (see Appendix E2). Anecdotal notes are a way of capturing critical observations and recording them in the midst of busy classrooms. Anecdotal notes are also an effective way to collect data concerning specific students, small groups of students, or for use in a self-study. When taking anecdotal notes, write down quick descriptions or quotes and then come back to them later the same day to add more detail. You can take anecdotal notes on sticky notes, in a traditional composition notebook, with a clipboard, or by using an iPad or other tablet device. Some record anecdotal notes using audio devices. An advantage of an electronic device is that it can be password protected and the data backed up remotely. On the other hand, if you are observing for specific kinds of behaviors, language, or actions, then you may be able to devise a checklist that will work efficiently in "real time' as you teach (see Appendixes E3 and E4). Our students find that video or audio-recording students at work or themselves teaching is extremely useful. Audio and video-recordings provide an opportunity for a second and deeper look into the classroom.

Much of the data collected in the classroom reflects class work done during the everyday process of teaching and learning through the collection of student assignments. These assignments become artifacts, or documentation of student work and thinking. Assignment artifacts are often complemented by accompanying lesson plans or other data that will give them context. Photos or quick videos taken with a smart phone or tablet are easy ways to not only record student assignments, but also collect classroom moments that are otherwise left to memory. What we have learned alongside our students is the importance of noting these photos and videos in a notebook or electronic device. All too often, our students come back to photos and cannot remember the date or time of the photos or even what made the event so memorable at the time!

Interviews can informally be done through the school day. Think of these as quick but intentional conversations with the students. What turns such an interview into data is when it is documented. This can be as simple as writing "results" on a sticky note, writing notes in a small notebook, or using an iPad or tablet to record the conversation. Interviews can also be more formal, such as writing and distributing a questionnaire or survey (Appendix E6).

Purpose and Data Collection

While we have discussed the types of data as belonging to these three categories, there are times when there are overlaps and a single piece of data may serve more than one purpose. Do not be overly concerned whether a video-recording is an observation or an artifact (it may be both); that said, it is important to determine the *purpose* for the video-recording. Consider, for example, a student teacher-action researcher who video-records a team of high school students discussing plans to restore a streambed. What will the researcher do with this video-recording? Why is he making this recording? What does he hope to learn from it when he later views the recording?

The purpose served by a given form of data is determined by returning to the critical question. In this scenario, the critical question is, "How do students think like engineers during STEM (Science, Technology, Engineering, Math) projects?

If this is the critical question, how might the action researcher use the video-recording? What would the *purpose* be?

For the video to be useful as data, the action researcher will need to determine what "thinking like an engineer" sounds like during a student discussion. How might high school students talk if they are thinking in this way? Let's assume the high school students have recently returned from a visit to the streambed and are brainstorming possible approaches for restoration. The action researcher could focus on how students are approaching the problem. Are students working to identifying and prioritize threats to the streambed first? Are they working on designs for restoration without identify and prioritizing threats to the streambed? Are they using academic vocabulary related to streambed restoration? Any of these questions could lead the action researcher to sharpen the critical question as discussed in Chapter 2.

If approached from this angle, then the video-recording is an observation, since the action researcher is *critically and deliberately watching* students as they process and talk about streambed restoration. (It could also be classified as an artifact since the recording will be physical evidence of students at work.)

Let's think now about how this artifact generated during the above brainstorming session might further support this action researcher's data set. The teacher-action researcher requires the team to document their initial site visit to the streambed by creating drawings and taking measurements as necessary. He asks the students to return to this document and add to it during the video-recorded discussion. These notes are artifacts, *physical evidence of student work*. Again, it is important to consider purpose.

Why would the student teacher-action researcher collect these notes? What would he expect to learn from them? How would this artifact complement the video-recording/observation?

Returning to the critical question, the teacher-action researcher might evaluate the artifact, the document created by students, for use of the engineering cycle in identifying problems and designing solutions. In a nearly perfect teaching and learning scenario, the artifact would mirror much of the later discussion by students. What if, however, the document the students create amounts to unreadable scribbles while the discussion is focused and animated? Or perhaps just the opposite is true. Or perhaps both the artifacts and the discussion records aren't particularly helpful; there is little evidence the students are seriously thinking about streambed restoration because they are neither talking nor writing about it!

In all of these possible scenarios, the teacher-action researcher could decide to follow up with an *interview*.

⬛ What might be the *purpose* of conducting an interview with these students? How would an interview complement the observational and artifact data he already has? How would interview data help the teacher-action researcher determine the next step in his planning? What questions might the teacher-action researcher ask to fulfill the purpose of his interview? Would the teacher-action researcher interview all the students or just a few or one of the students? What might guide this decision?

There are many possibilities, yes? Here are a few:

- The teacher-action researcher may notice that two of the team members seem to be doing most of the talking and writing. He could decide to conduct an informal interview with the other two members. The purpose of this interview would be to check for content understanding.

- If the artifact, the notes the team is required to take, is scribbled, then perhaps the teacher-action researcher might meet with the team and ask process questions that will scaffold their learning, "Draw for me what you are thinking. How does this drawing support your thinking?" Now the purpose of the interview is to teach.

- Alternatively, if the team is not focused, the teacher-action researcher may interview students individually to determine what problems the team may be encountering. (Are they not interested? Is it a lack of content knowledge? Do they not understand the learning goal?) The purpose of this interview is problem solving.

This scenario illustrates how in selecting data to collect, we consider *purpose*. Purpose is determined by the critical question and previous analyzed data. (The purpose of the interview in the above scenario is determined after analyzing the observational and artifact data.) In addition, the scenario illustrates how data from each of the categories (observation, interview, and artifact) allows a teacher-action researcher to see their critical question and topic from three distinct perspectives. This is *data triangulation* in qualitative research (see Figure 3.3).

➜ FIGURE 3.3: Seeing Your Critical Question From Three Perspectives

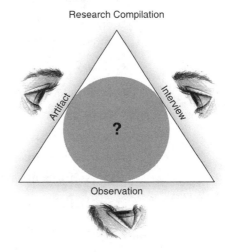

Understanding Triangulation

Because triangulation is such an important concept in action research, let's consider its meaning before proceeding further. We will provide a metaphor for triangulation and a scenario in which triangulation is used, and then allow you space to create your own meaning around this concept.

Using Triangulation to Find Your Way in the Wilderness

Global position systems (GPSs) have changed the way the authors of this text do our wilderness treks. With a GPS, we can have an accurate way of knowing exactly where we are in the world, specified as the intersection of lines of latitude, longitude, and altitude. GPS systems rely on triangulation in order to do this. If you are standing in the middle of the wilderness not knowing where to turn next, you can turn on your GPS unit and it will search for satellites positioned in space. You can watch your unit "lock" into the satellites. Constructing the geometry of latitude, longitude, and altitude requires readings from three different observers. In this case, the observers are satellites, and at least three satellites are required. If you only lock into one satellite, your location cannot be determined. With two satellites you may be able to get a rough idea of where you are but one of the three parameters—longitude, latitude, or altitude—will be impossible to determine. The unit needs to lock into *at least three* satellites; when it does, it will give you the minimum necessary data to somewhat accurately describe your location. Your location becomes even more accurate as more satellites "lock in," becoming accurate within a few feet of your true location. However, even with this data, you will need a map; the map gives the GPS data context. The GPS data, with a map, gives you a location.

How is doing research like a trek in the wilderness? How is the triangulation of data like receiving GPS signals from three (or more) different satellites? And how is the research design and critical question like the map?

A Teacher Finds Her Way Through the Classroom with Triangulation

In attempting to see if simulations are increasing eighth grade students' understanding and appreciation of current events and issues, Mara collects the following data set:

- She videos her students as they role-play within small groups a debate about the future of a rainforest (her video-record is *observation* data). The purpose of these videos is to listen for students' ability to identify issues of deforestation.

- She provides each small group with a list of questions about the deforestation issues raised in the role-playing exercise. Students discuss the questions within their small groups, and the conversation is audio-taped directly after the role-playing exercise (the recorded student responses to her questions are *interview* data). The purpose of this interview data is to assess students' content knowledge of the deforestation issues.

- That evening, Mara writes a journal entry about the role-playing exercise. She mentions everything, from funny things she heard, to her worries about management, how room set-up seemed to hamper movement and thus the role-play, and to what she would do differently next time. In addition, she includes a copy of her lesson plan. The purpose of the journal is to give the observation and interview data context.

- The next day, Mara assigns students to write an essay about one of the issues facing the rainforest (*artifact*). In brainstorming ideas for the essay, Mara draws upon the role play from the previous day. Students have time to draft, revise, and polish the essay over the next two weeks, using multiple resources. The purpose of the artifact is to assess final content knowledge.

📖 Will this data set help Mara know whether her use of simulations encouraged students' critical thinking about current events and issues? What might she be looking for across the data that might confirm that stimulations do encourage critical thinking? What data might be missing from this data set? If Mara reflexively analyzes the role-play and critically watches the digital video, and concludes that while students were having a good time they were not really debating the issues with much depth, what might she need to do next? What kind of outside literature might best support Mara's interpretation of this data set?

Limitations of Triangulation

Triangulation does have limits by suggesting that three views provided by three data types will provide a complete or whole view or "the" problem and therefore of "the" answer. Our understandings are always partial; we collect multiple perspectives to better piece together our seeing, and raise further questions that moves our teaching and learning into other critical spaces of learning (Ellsworth, 1997; Haraway, 1996; Lather, 1991; Richardson, 2003). In the above scenario, Mara will need additional perspectives, perhaps even additional data, in order to process the use of stimulations in her classroom. For this reason, Richardson (2003) suggests the metaphor of a crystal may be better suited than that of triangulation. Crystals come in many shapes, change under varying context. They "grow, change, alter, but are not amorphous" (p. 517). We use triangulation in action research since it is an established concept in qualitative research. However, overlaying the concept of triangulation with the metaphor of a crystal enriches the concept and honors the complexities of teaching and learning.

Problematizing Practice: Practice Data Selection

A student teacher-action researcher plans to collect purposeful triangulated data. He/she will analyze this data to better understand his/her critical question. It can be challenging to imagine the kind of data that is necessary to collect. Through the following scenario, work to better understand the principles of data collection, triangulation, and trustworthiness.

Jay's school has placed a new emphasis on the importance of reading nonfiction books. As a result, children in Jay's fifth grade classroom are required to read more nonfiction texts. The fact is that while the children do read, and like to read, they rarely choose to read or express any desire to read nonfiction. Jay and his mentor-teacher theorize that in part this is due to a lack of exposure to "good" nonfiction material. But what is "good" nonfiction according to fifth grade students? Jay has reviewed the work of distant colleagues. He knows the criteria as described by experts, and while this helps him focus his search for engaging nonfiction books for fifth grade students, it doesn't specifically help him find the "right" nonfiction for his students. He wants to engage the students' expertise in identifying criteria for "good" nonfiction texts. He plans to secure approximately 30 nonfiction texts recommended by experts in children's literature. He wants children to be involved in evaluating the texts, reading the texts, and writing about the texts. His critical question is, "How, why and when do fifth graders select nonfiction text?"

Assist Jay in planning his research and his teaching. Begin by studying Table 3.3, which outlines his plans for a beginning interview.

➔ TABLE 3.3: Jay's Data Set Plan

Activity	Data Type	Research/Teaching Purpose	How this Data Might Move the Research/ Teaching Forward
Arrange books around the classroom. Allow time for children to pursue books. Each child rates books using a signed sticky note and a numbering system: 1—This book looks really good! I would check it out! 2—This book looks interesting; I might check it out. 3—I would not check this book out.	Interview: an inquiry into the thinking of the students.	Research: an inquiry into how children choose books; what entices them to follow-up with a book. Teaching: to engage children with nonfiction texts.	Jay can evaluate the books that receive the most #1 ratings: what do the books seem to have in common?

Jay plans to have children discuss their top two choices of books in small groups. He is going to audio-record these discussions. Assist Jay by completing the remaining columns of Table 3.4.

➔ TABLE 3.4: Purpose for Jay's Data Collection

Activity	Data Type	Research/ Teaching Purpose	How this Data Might Move the Research/Teaching Forward; How It Connects to the Interview Data Above
Cluster students according to their number 1 and number 2 book selections. Ask students, "Why did you select these books as your first choices? Ask students to determine their top criteria for choosing these books. Have them create a chart showing and illustrating their reasons.	Interview: an inquiry into why certain books were selected. Artifact: the chart children will create about their selections.	*Complete the column:*	*Complete this column:*

Assist Jay in planning for his project by considering how an observation might further develop this data set and thus his research and teaching. Complete Table 3.5 and discuss possibilities with your colleagues.

→ TABLE 3.5: Complete Jay's Data Set Plan: Observation

Activity	Data Type	Research/Teaching Purpose	How this Data Might Move the Research/ Teaching Forward; How It Connects to the Interview Data Above
	Observation		

Imagine sitting down to analyze this data set with Jay. Do you think this will be enough documentation to better understand how the fifth grade students are selecting nonfiction text? What might the strengths and weakness be of this data set? How do you imagine this data set moving Jay's research forward? How will this data plan ensure a trustworthy action research project? Is there anything Jay might add to make it more trustworthy?

Connecting to Your Study

Brainstorm your own action research topic and question using Table 3.6. What kinds of data from each category might you collect to best inquire about your action research question?

→ TABLE 3.6: Data Category Brainstorms

Observation	Interview	Artifact

Bringing It All Together: Your Research Data Compilation

While *triangulation* is one of the primary ways we make sure our research is trustworthy, even data collected via triangulation can be isolated and taken out of context. One way a teacher-researcher can provide context for data is through an entire *research data compilation*. A research data compilation speaks to the whole of multiple data sets and includes journal entries, sketches/photography/videos, and lesson plans and/or unit overviews, as well as ongoing data analysis.

The research compilation is also a place to organize contextual information: a list of students in the participating classes, information about those students (often this includes initial surveys or questionnaires related to the research topic), school demographics and policies, and other contextual information that may shed light upon the data collected. This is critical: context matters in data analysis and interpretation. *The research data compilation is confidential*; it should not be kept in a public place like a classroom or a place that could become public, like the backseat of your car! While your research data compilation may be partially or even mostly electronic, be very careful about backing up your work and information—you have no research without data! Also make sure any computer-stored data is password protected. We suggest that student teacher-researchers take a smaller composition book or iPad or other tablet to class with them to record anecdotal notes; later, place these notes in the research data compilation. The research data compilation is the mind, heart, and soul of the teacher-researcher chronicling their own reactions to data collected, **analytic memos**, and interpretation.

A Closer Look at the Researcher's Journal and Its Place in the Research Data Compilation

We use the term "journal" here to refer to any kind of active reflection that provides context for the data collected. The journal acknowledges that you, the student teacher-action researcher, are a participant in the study. It is the place to record the questions, wonderings, emotional reactions to, around, behind, and over the data you collect. The researcher's journal may take many forms from a computer file, a traditional composition notebook, to a collection of sticky notes, later organized and further explored through writing or a voice recorded memo. The journal could be a series of drawings or sketches. It not so much the form the researcher's journal takes as the function of the journal: to provide context for the data collected. The quality of these journals often determines the quality of the ongoing data analysis and final data interpretation that can be accomplished.

Consider the following two excerpts from journal entries:

Excerpt 1: Today was a great day! Had fun conferencing with Salvador. He is such a kick! He had a good poem idea (Christmas) and so I just helped him brainstorm some additional details. I more or less followed the conference protocol. It was easy since Salvador wants to do his work. Since he had a poem written by the time I left the conference, I am considering this one a success!

Excerpt 2: I conducted a writing conference with Gil today. I've been noticing how he is really too small for his chair. In order to write, he has to sit up on one leg to reach the tabletop. This seems to make him squirm and at first I thought he wasn't paying attention. He has trouble holding the pencil. I wonder if this makes writing a chore for him. Sometimes he is so slow writing, I get anxious, I start thinking about how much time the conference is taking and wonder if I should leave and come back. Gil had a good idea for a poem today. He wanted to write about soccer; specifically about a time he scored a goal. Armando was sitting beside him and helped with ideas, "You should add a word like 'zoomed,' like you "zoomed" by the guard." The conference was interrupted twice when Heath kicked the end desk and made everyone's desk shutter. Each time, I had to refocus Gil, "Okay—let's not worry about the kicked chair—let's focus on that soccer kick!" Gil had all the prewriting squares filled in with ideas. What he didn't seem to know how to do was put these into a poem format. I decided this would be my teaching point.

Imagine the journal entries along with the other data collected for the above study: teacher's record sheet of writing conference (short antidotal notes written during the conference); student daily writing folders; and, final pieces of student writing. While the first journal entry works as a daily record, it is easy to see how the second journal entry will be more meaningful when the student teacher-action researcher begins the tasks of reading across the data to complete ongoing data analysis and final data interpretation.

Organizing the Research Data Compilation: The Alternative to Data Scatter

It is critical that the research compilation is well organized. There are numerous ways our students use to organize data. Some use a single system, others a combination:

- Notebook: a large three-ring binder with dividers works best.

- Crates or file boxes (with lids): hanging files work well.

- Electronic files; use a scanner or digital camera for student artifacts. Create a special folder with files for all other data.

Here are some of the ways our students arrange their notebooks, crates, file boxes and/or electronic files:

- Chronologically: all data are combined together according to the chronological order of teaching experiences and other settings in which data were collected.

- By data sets or **data collection period**: For example, a lesson plan is kept with corresponding observational data and student work. Ongoing analysis is also included (described in Chapter 4).

- By data type: all observation/interview data is organized together. All student work is kept in another place, and lesson plans in another, and so on.

Work with whatever seems logical to you, but make sure you are deliberate about keeping your data organized. *Make sure you date and label all data at the time it is collected.* A word of warning: those teacher-researchers who do not attend to details of organization can find themselves mired in distracting and sometimes harmful professional and personal circumstances. So while it may seem mundane, be deliberate in these areas and plan prior to the first data collection period how you will organize, date, and label your research process.

It is too easy to collect data from "everywhere" since "everything" seems important; use your critical question to purposeful plan data selection.

How Much Data Is Enough Data?

"How many data sets do I have to collect?" The easy response is this: *the more data, the more trustworthy the research.* Recall that time constraints, guest status, context constraints, multiple uncontrollable factors, and the transformation factor all influence the action research process (see in Chapter 1: *Critical Considerations for being a Student Teacher-Action Researcher*). The amount of time you are in your placement, your access to the mentor-teacher and students, records, and other artifacts all influence the amount of data you will collect.

Ultimately the question, "How many data sets do I need?" may be answered by your action research advisor and/or professor given your individual circumstances. However, it is important that you keep in mind at all times the restrictions on data collection imposed by your position as a student teacher or guest in the classroom and that you make these limitations clear in any presentation of your action research.

Is This Enough Data? (Is It Focused, Purposeful Data?)

Table 3.7 shows a complete list of Cindy's data sets for her action research project. The focus of Cindy's project was building community among fifth grade students. Cindy collected data from November through March. She began data collection while a part-time student teacher and continued data collection throughout her full-time student teaching. As the table shows, Cindy collected items like students' drawings and descriptions of an ideal community; pictures and descriptions of team inventions; and student's journals about working together. These *artifacts* allowed her to follow the depictions of community development generated by her fifth grade students. Cindy also recruited her university supervisor to conduct specific observations during group work time; she added her own observations to these. These observations provided an opportunity for Cindy to see if what children were writing and drawing about community matched their behavior while *in* community. Through observations, Cindy was able to theorize whether or not her lessons and community building were affecting change in children's behavior. Cindy conducted focus group interviews and had children complete a sociogram both at the beginning of her research and at the end of the project. These interviews were important because Cindy did not want to rely upon children's ability to write and draw alone to communicate how they were growing as members of the classroom community. Finally, Cindy kept a researcher's journal throughout the project.

Cindy's data collection planned for trustworthy research. She relied upon literature to decide what kind of community building lessons to teach and to define attributes of "community." She collected multiple perspectives from children, her mentor-teacher and her university supervisor to determine the effectiveness of her lessons. She practiced self-reflexivity by regularly writing in her journal and conducting ongoing analysis. The data she collected acted as a crystal—each piece reflecting off another piece, so that she could create strong connections across the data. Together, this data collection illustrates Cindy *becoming* a teacher.

→ TABLE 3.7: Cindy's Collected Data

Data Set	Date of Action	Action Implemented	Data Collected
#1	11/7	Conducted a sociogram recording top 3 students each child would prefer to work with on a class project.	• Sociogram identifying stars and isolates within the class.
	11/12 through 11/25	Colonization Unit: Students worked in groups on a colonial region project. CT and I observed group interaction during group work time.	• Artifact #1(A#1) – Students listed characteristics of an ideal community. • A#2 - Journal entries from group projects; • Informal interviews with group leads
	12/5	Students draw and describe their ideal community	• A#3 – Student pictures and descriptions of ideal communities
#2	1/5	**Spanish immersion experience**: 30 minutes solid instruction in Spanish with class meeting to follow (no clues were given in English).	• Field notes by CT • Notes taken from student responses in class discussion • Student journal on reflections and feelings during immersion experience and what they learned about their classmates • Researcher's journal entry
	1/16	Each team created and named a **team mascot** then wrote a description of mascot's diet, hobbies, and a strange thing the mascot could do. This mascot became their team name.	• Field notes on group interaction • Researcher's journal • A# - Team mascot posters
	1/23	Teams imagined they were a team of **famous scientists**. They had to draw and describe an invention that would make the world a better place.	• A# - Picture/description of team inventions • Researcher's journal • Field notes on group interaction during teambuilding activity • Field notes on group interaction during cooperative science activity • Student journals on group inclusion of all members
	1/30	Team **word creation game**: Two-part experience where students first listed as many words as they could find inside of a phrase, without the help of classmates. Then the second round they worked as a team to do the same and discovered they did much better working as a team than on their own.	• Focus group interview of students from each group (tape recorded) • Field notes on group interaction in word creation game • Field notes by university supervisor on group interaction during math problem solving activity • Student journals on what they like best about working in their groups
#3	2/11	**Silent Castle Building**: Teams had a stack of scratch paper and roll of masking tape and were given 10 minutes to construct a freestanding castle without the aid of any other materials or the use of written or spoken language of any kind.	• Researcher's journal • Field notes on group interaction by CT and myself • Notes on group discussion responses • Student self-reflections on who they do/don't work well with and what they can personally do to make their group function better • Anecdotal notes on group interaction during M&M math lesson (2/5/04)
	2/20	**Take a Good Look Game:** Teams were given one minute to memorize a picture on the overhead, then the picture was taken away and the teams listed as many things as they could remember from the picture.	• Students lists of picture observations • Field notes by university supervisor on group interaction during game • Time interval field notes by university supervisor during math partner work • Researcher's journal • Time interval field notes by cohort leader on group interaction and inclusion during group work time on math worksheet (2/17/04)
	3/3	**Star Share:** Within individual teams, each student draws a card and shares with his/her group who/what they would be and why, based on the card they drew (card says "movie star" – student shares which movie star they would be and why).	• Student journals on what they've learned about each group member and what worked/didn't work in their groups • Individual interviews with unofficial group leaders • Individual interviews with bilingual students • Researcher's journal • Interview with CT sharing preliminary results of research and seeking her feedback on those results
#4	3/4	Conducted final sociogram recording top 3 students each child would prefer to work with on a class project.	• Sociogram identifying new stars and isolates within the class.

Is This Enough Data?

If Cindy was writing a Ph.D. dissertation, or if her research was expected to be published as "groundbreaking" and be replicated in multiple sites, then the answer is "no." It was, however, enough data for Cindy to learn critical and trustworthy lessons about becoming a teacher. She learned about how to use data as assessment to drive instruction, and about how to facilitate community among children from diverse backgrounds, language groups, and social classes. Combined with her literature review, she could be fairly certain that what she was learning was consistent with what other researchers have discovered with more in-depth studies taking much more time. Cindy kept a researcher's journal and this journal further recorded insights and daily happenings that might have or did influence the data. The journal gave context and meaning to Cindy's data. While Cindy's study is smaller than a major research study, her experience in making these discoveries was *personal*—her action research project is *her* story of becoming a teacher; she has *personally constructed* the resulting insights, meanings and questions. This action research project provides a place of beginning, a first chapter in Cindy's professional development.

Is This Focused, Purposeful Data?

This question is as critical as asking, "Is this enough data?" Scattered data or data that does not complement itself or create strong connections is not useful data even if there is a great deal of it. Focused quality data keeps the critical question front and center; it relies upon the insights of distant colleagues to create a background; it is context-specific and dependent.

Here are three questions to evaluate your data collection plan:

- "How does this data answer my critical question? Given this data collection plan, what might I be missing?" If you find the data you have collected sparsely answers your critical question, than you need more *connected and focused* data.

- "How do the literature support both my data collection and the results of my data collection?" Making strong connections between data collected and the literature is one criterion for trustworthiness in action research. *Connect the data you collect to your literature*!

- "Will this data collection result in trustworthy action research? How?" These are critical questions to ask throughout data collection.

Perhaps you are still struggling with the question, "Will I have enough data?" You may be saying; "I don't even have as much time as Cindy!" You can still follow the plan for developing a research design and collecting data as outlined in this book, even if you only have time to collect one complete (triangulated) data set. You can still learn about the skills of data collection (assessment) and interpretation. You must, however, recognize and state clearly the limits of your findings or results. Do not attempt to generalize based upon a limited data collection or make unfounded research claims. In such instances where you are only able to collect a single data set, focus your results on what you have learned about the collection of data and interpreting data and how you intend to use this in your future teaching career. Your "results" may well be additional and more informed critical questions.

> Travel the side road Self-Study 3.1: Personal Perspective and Reading the Classroom found on p. 95 to analyze how our personal paradigms matter.

Problematizing Practice: Applying the Key Concepts of Data Collection

The following research scenarios are designed to problematize the act of data collection, to further develop your understanding of data collection, and to support you as you develop your own action research plan.

Research Scenario 1

Loren and Matthew were co-student teachers working together in a kindergarten classroom. They were conducting ethnographic action research and their critical question was, "How can technology support meaning-making for kindergartners?" Three weeks into the action research project, they had collected the following data:

- *Observation*: 30 pictures of children using digital cameras during nature walks and engaging in free play primarily with Lego. The pictures at this time were still on the memory card of the two digital cameras being used by the action researchers.

- *Interviews*: Informal conversations with five children. These consisted of asking children, "What are you taking a picture of and why?" The results of these interviews were sparse; each action researcher had written down some notes but had not completed any analysis of these notes.

- *Artifacts*: None.

Matthew had written one journal entry about a lesson involving the cameras and a nature walk. Loren had not yet completed any journal entries. Their research compilation included the lesson plan from the nature walk day; the lesson plan was saved on Mathew's computer.

In your notebook or journal, theorize why Loren and Mathew felt discouraged about their project after the first three weeks. Provide specific advice to them: what kind of data do you recommend they collect and why? (Check out Appendix E if you haven't already!) What other actions might support their research project? How might they use their review of literature to assist them? What else can they do to make sure they are collecting trustworthy data?

Problematizing Practice: Research Scenario 2

Lalia and Eli are not yet student-teaching but they are conducting an action research project by request of a local elementary school principal and classroom teachers. Their project can be considered a curriculum analysis; the critical question guiding their project is, "How do grade 3–5 classroom libraries represent diversity?" Lalia and Eli data collection plan is as follows:

- Tally the number of books representing diversity in each classroom.

- Take a sample of the books representing diversity and evaluate them for quality.

- Conduct focus group interviews with children about which books representing diversity are most appealing to them.

What tools will Lalia and Eli need to develop in order to complete their data collection? How will their literature review guide their data collection? How might personal belief systems influence data collection and subsequent data analysis? What can they do to avoid this kind of influence or at least make it transparent? In what ways does or doesn't this data collection plan represent trustworthy action research? Provide advice as necessary.

Problematizing Practice: Research Scenario 3

Adrianna is student-teaching and completing an integrated action research project in a sophomore mathematics classroom. The majority of the students are English Language Learners. Her critical question is, "How can inquiry be used in developing academic language in mathematics?" For her first lesson, students were given an authentic data set with which to work. The data set showed the location, date, and magnitude of earthquake activity for the last 50 years in the area where students lived. Students did not know that the data showed earthquake activity. They were instructed to make sense of the data by charting and graphing the data in any way they could think of, and to hypothesize what data might show. During this lesson, Adrianna collected the following:

- *Observations*: Each group was given an audio-recorder to record their group discussions.

- *Artifacts*: Each group produced additional charts used during their inquiry. Each group presented their charts to their peers, describing their thinking and arguing for their hypothesis. Adrianna took observational notes during this time.

- *Interviews*: After completing the activity, students completed a questionnaire asking 1) What mathematical thinking did you use during your data inquiry? 2) What was most helpful in the process of the inquiry? 3) What questions do you still have about the earthquake data set?

Adrianna completed a researcher's journal entry during her preparation period immediately following the class session.

If Adrianna continues to collect data similar to this, will she have enough data to adequately theorize about her critical question? Why or why not? How is (or isn't) her data collection focused? (And what more do you need to know to answer this question?) What information would you suggest she include in her journal writing? Adrianna recorded the small group interactions. What kind of literature might assist her most in collecting and analyzing her data? What might Adrianna look for in her data when she begins analyzing it? Does this appear to be a trustworthy data collection plan?

Read back through the above scenarios and consider these three questions:

- Earlier in this chapter we said that data collection strategies are closely aligned with assessment. How do the data collection strategies described above also act as instructional assessment?

- Triangulation or crystallization is the way data reinforces itself to partially answer a critical question. Do the above scenarios represent triangulation or crystallization of data? We also said earlier that data collection must be focused. Reading across the scenarios, which project appears to have the most focus? Why? What other factors may influence the outcome of these action research projects?

- "Careful planning of data collection is attentive to criteria for trustworthy action research." How is this statement true? How does it work?

> Travel the side road Cultural Context 3.2: *When "New" Information Changes the Design*, on p. 99. We plan carefully for data collection, but life in classrooms is not a scripted affair. Sometimes new information changes the design, even the question of the action research project. CC 3.2 explores this very real possibility.

Ethical Considerations for Action Research: Gaining Permissions

Before going further, we need to consider what it means to do ethical data collection and action research. This includes gaining permission from participants and the participants' parents and/or guardians if they are going to be included in a research study. While there are strict guidelines for gaining permission from participants in research studies, the kind of action research done by student teachers is categorized somewhat differently, with a relaxing of some of the restrictions.

The genre of action research we have advocated throughout this text is one that is embedded in the teaching and learning process. It represents the cycle of teaching (plan, implement, and assess). The results of such a project should be a teacher with improved understanding and/or skills, and an improved, more just education for students. Because this process is embedded within the teaching and learning process, as a teacher you would not need to gain permission if the research was not formal and you did not plan on making the research public.

Imagine, however, that as a student you found out after the fact that a story was written about you and presented to a group of people you didn't even know. You would have reason to feel deceived. The same is true for participants in the student teacher-researcher's project.

Table 3.8 presents a checklist to determine the level of **informed consent** (the term researchers give to gaining permission from participants) that may be needed for your project. Answer each of the four questions to determine whether or not you will need to seek permission.

→ TABLE 3.8: Guidelines for Gaining Permissions

Question 1: *Will your research project be made public?* (Will it have an audience larger than your professor and your peers? Will it be made into a poster? Will the paper be posted at a website? Will there be a presentation?)

Yes	No
You must gain written permission from parents and verbal permission from students. University and/or school district policies may apply; check with your advisor.	*If the project is embedded within the teaching-learning project, you may not need to gain permissions. Check with your advisor. Getting permission is always preferred.*

Question 2: *Does your research project include participants who may be more vulnerable than others or have protected status under law?* For example, do you have students in your study who are designated as "learning disabled," or have some other "special" classification? Do you have students who speak English as a second language or do not speak English at all?

Yes	No
Check with your advisor, mentor-teacher, school specialist, and building administrator. Permission is critical. Make sure that any letters sent home can be read and understood by parents.	*Please refer to the general guidelines in this section.*

Question 3: *Is there any possibility the data collected from your research project would be harmful to participants (emotionally, physically?)* Remember, the goal of action research is to make the education of all, and for all students, more just and more equitable.

Yes	No
Re-think and revise your project. The goal of action research is to make education a better place for students! Anything harmful, even potentially harmful, should not be included in your project. This includes any opportunities for other students to taunt or tease students, "put downs," or any practices that might harm a student's sense of self-worth. Grades should never be tied to participation in action research.	*Excellent! Continue to the next question.*

Question 4: *Do you plan to audio-tape, video-tape, or take pictures of students?* Do you plan to make any of these public during a presentation?

Yes	No
Many times schools have policies surrounding video-taping and/or taking pictures of students, even if they are not going to be made public. Check with your mentor-teacher. If you plan to include any of the above in a public presentation of any kind, include this in your letter asking for permission. Specific permission must be sought for any images to be placed on a web page.	*Are you sure? Often times, audio-tapes, video-tapes, and/or pictures provide good data for triangulation and placing the data in context.*

The process of obtaining informed consent, or gaining permission, from participants involves written permission from parents and verbal permission from students. Exact guidelines are determined by the university's informed-consent policy and the policy of the school district in which you are student teaching. We offer these general guidelines:

- Check with your university advisor and find out what expectations exist for informed consent; do not begin collecting data until this is known.

- Write a letter seeking permission from parents to use data generated by their students in your projects. ⊕ You may download a template for this letter from the companion website. Make sure your university advisor, mentor-teacher, and the administrator of your school approve your permission letter. Check with the school specialist if you are collecting data from those students who may have protected legal status.

- Do not use the data from any student where parental permission is not provided. Confidentiality is the critical issue; make sure you protect all student and school identities by using pseudonyms.

- Students who participate in your study should not receive special rewards; nor should your study be in anyway related to student grades.

The letter sent home to parents to gain written permission should include:

- the topic of the project;
- the objective of the project;
- strategies that will be implemented;
- data to be collected;
- a timeline of the project;
- how the project will be made public;
- why video-taping or picture-taking will occur (if applicable);
- request to use any pictures or videos for presentations (if applicable);
- how confidentiality will be maintained;
- any potential risk to students, or the absence of risk to students;
- a return slip to be signed by the parent.

The best guideline for gaining permissions is to be open about your study. Discuss it not only with your mentor-teacher, but also with your students. Let them know you are doing this study to become a better teacher. If possible, allow students to assist you in interpreting the data; this will make your work more trustworthy.

All universities have an International Review Board (IRB). If you are required according to your university policy to seek IRB approval for your project, then check out the companion web resource, "A Guide to Completing an IRB." ⊕

Synthesizing the Act of Data Collection

We have covered critical principles of data collection methodology. Let's take a moment to synthesize across this chapter.

- Data collected fall into three broad and often overlapping categories: observation, artifact, and interview. Data from each category are referred to as a data set.

- Data are triangulated so that the critical question is seen from at least three different angles.

- A data compilation includes not only multiple data sets but also documents and journals that will provide context for the data.

- Careful selection of data collection methodologies is done with purpose, focused around the critical question, and is a critical piece of conducting trustworthy action research.

- Organized data is the framework for later meaningful data analysis and interpretation since data can be easily retrieved and recalled according to context.

- Ethical treatment of data equates ethical and respectful treatment of participants and of yourself as the action researcher.

Here's the question: *How will data work for your action research project?* This is what you must begin to imagine as you move into the action research design phase. Apply the principles above as you continue through your journey of becoming at teacher through action research.

Chapter 3: Content Questions

1. Describe or draw triangulation, as you understand it. Now compare this to the concept of crystallization. How do the concepts of triangulation and crystallization work with the criteria for trustworthiness?
2. Synthesize how purpose, focus, and trustworthiness work together when selecting data collection methodology and designing an action research plan.
3. Summarize ethical considerations of doing action research by writing your own slogan or "golden rule" for research.

Chapter 3: Process Questions

1. What might be the limitations of even a trustworthy research design? What might be done about these limitations?
2. How do you see the context of your action research project influencing the research design?
3. What does it mean to your student that you are both the action researcher and a participant?
4. What do you anticipate will be most challenging about collecting data? What is your plan for dealing with these challenges?

Self-Study 3.1: Personal Perspective and Reading the Classroom

Our own positionality—our values, beliefs, gender, and all the labels that socially construct who we are—follow us as researcher, whether we are doing qualitative or quantitative research. To explore this further, work through the following teacher–student writing conference. But first, respond to the following questions:

- Do you like writing?
- What is your best memory of a writing teacher?
- Do you have a bad memory of a writing teacher?
- How do you think writing should be taught in the elementary school? Should writing be taught in middle and high school content areas? If so, how?

Analyze your responses—they reflect your paradigm about "good" writing instruction. As a teacher-researcher, this paradigm influences the way you evaluate writing instruction. Keeping this in mind, read through the following teacher-student writing conference and evaluate it for its effectiveness. *(Note: this activity works best when completed with a critical colleague. Share your evaluations and trace their origins together.)*

Student: Then, this—then . . . . Hey, [name of student] do you have a pencil I can borrow? Wait—I need to find a pencil . . .

Teacher: You need to be prepared for writing. We have been in writing workshop for 15 minutes and you still do not have a pencil? You need to be responsible. You can use my pencil. We need to get started. Settle down here. [to other student, No he doesn't need to borrow a pencil.] Are we ready now? Okay, what are you working on today? 'Cause I know we met yesterday, right, or the day before?

Student: [still fidgeting, working with notebook] Yesterday, I think.

Teacher: And I asked you to go back and fix some specific things in your writing. Did you do this? What did you do?

Student: Ummm . . . I was suppose to make it better?

Teacher: What did I ask you to do last time? Check your notebook.

Student: [looks through notebook.] I can't find it—where it is.

Teacher: Here, let me look. Okay, here are our notes from the last conference. Right here [points].

Student: To talk about the green spots in the water.

Teacher: Right. Did you do this?

Pause and analyze your reaction to the writing conference so far. From your perspective, how is the conference going? Would you have done things the same or differently? Why? Would you have used

continues ➔

the same language as this teacher? Why or why not? Listen to yourself: what values do your responses reflect about "good teaching"?

Student: Yeah, see, right here. [student reads from paper]. *Back in the water, I noticed the lake spots that look like giant space ships. There's also shadows in the water making it look like a darker green. And when I touched the water, it makes me shiver.*

Teacher: Oh, yeah. [looking at picture student is describing] They look like space ships to me. Okay, I want to hear that part. I want to hear just the part that you edited.

Student: Oh, *back in the water, I noticed the lake spots that look like giant space ships. Oh, there's also shadows in the water making it look like a darker green. And when I touched the water, it makes me shiver and I breathe and I smell all the trees and water.* Oh, that's what—this is—that is the part I fixed!

Teacher: What do you mean you fixed that part? What did you do? Did you move it down here? [points to paper; student nods] Okay. So, now, what's this part? From looking at the bushes, they seem to be trying to hide behind the trees. That's personification right there, the bushes are hiding. Did you mean to do that?

Student: Yeah.

Teacher: Good.

Pause again in your reading. How is the conference going? Is the teacher doing a "good job" in this section of the conference? Why or why not? What are your responses saying about your definition of "good teaching"?

Continue reading through the transcript:

Student: Hey—I know, it is like an elephant trying to hide behind a pencil.

Teacher: Now that is very creative! How do you feel about your writing now as a writer, after you've added in that part and revised a little bit?

Student: It seems like I made it better.

Teacher: Are you proud of yourself? You should be!

What do you think of the way the teacher ends this conference? What experiences and education inform your thinking? What sources of information do you need to make your thoughts on this conference an analysis rather than an opinion?

Our personal perspectives form the lens through which we read classroom experiences. They also influence our choices in data methodology. It isn't that personal perspectives are good or bad or that we should somehow try to be "neutral." Rather, we need to acknowledge these perspectives, listen to others, and become a collector of perspectives outside our own as teachers and researchers. Think of designing your action research project as self-study and a collaborative act—and in doing so, build the trustworthiness of your work.

Cultural Context 3.1: The Art and Craft of Negotiation

Sometimes our students come back to us and say, "I can't do my action research project; my mentor-teacher doesn't believe in the teaching strategy I want to try." In certain situations, this may be true and the student teacher will need to change the entire topic of her action research project. However, other times we find the approach the student teacher takes in introducing the action research topics has a great deal to do with how a mentor-teacher responds to the idea.

Here are a few suggestions:

- Whenever possible, connect the action research topics to the identified needs of the students, the mission of the school, or concerns your mentor-teacher has shared with you.
- Share with the mentor-teacher your own goals for learning. Share your interest, passion, and maybe even your personal story of why this topic is important to you.
- Avoid being judgmental and/or "the expert"; in other words, avoid implying a deficit in the classroom that you can somehow "fix" as a student teacher.
- Appreciate that even if your mentor-teacher has a different style or approach to teaching, he does have expertise to share with you.

Here are some "lead lines" that our students have found to be successful in negotiating a research topic with a mentor-teacher:

- I have an idea for an action research project, what do you think of this? How do you think this might work in your classroom?
- I've noticed the last couple of weeks that the students in this class don't seem to _____. I've been learning about _____ in my teacher education program. What if we . . . ?
- My methods teacher introduced this pretty radical idea in class last week. Here's the concept as she explained it. What do you think? I'd love to try this as an action research project!
- Most of my school life, I've struggled with _____. I would really like to assist other students who have this difficulty in school. What approaches have you successfully used?
- I am having difficulties coming up with an action research project that is meaningful. When you consider your classroom and your students, do you have any questions that might be meaningful for us both to pursue while I am student teaching here?

Co-teaching

Another possibility you may wish to consider in negotiating your practicum placement is co-teaching. Co-teaching has been described as the act of "learning at the elbow of another" while planning and implementing instruction (Roth & Tobin, 2002, p. xi). Whenever two or more teachers work together simultaneously before a group of students, they are co-teaching. Co-teaching is different from being

continues ➜

coached or supervised from the back of the room, or observed and evaluated from the perspective of a "fly on the wall." While co-teaching, partners experience classroom moves, actions, and reactions in "real time," without the space for considered reflection and analysis. Co-teaching partners experience teaching events and episodes from a common perspective (in front of the class working with students); subsequent conversations and debriefing sessions are between partners who have each "walked the walk" in the classroom under consideration. These are powerful opportunities for learning to teach, not only for you, but also for your co-teaching partner.

You have (or will) likely do some co-teaching with your mentor-teacher as you begin to assume increased responsibility for instruction. You may also co-teach at the elbows of "outsiders" such as a university supervisor, methods instructor, or other mentor. This experience can be extremely valuable connecting the ideas of university methods courses and supervisors to the reality of your classroom.

Consider inviting your mentor-teacher, supervisor, or other trusted colleague to co-teach at your elbow during your action research work. By co-teaching at your elbow, your colleague will gain vital understanding of not only your teaching setting and context, but the nature of your critical research question and data collection as well. By inviting others to "walk the walk" alongside you, you will both benefit from a new level of collegiality and understanding of the work of becoming a teacher.

Cultural Context 3.2: When "New" Information Changes the Design

As a student teacher, it is impossible to know everything about a school community when you enter as a guest for the first time. In some instances, there is very little time between when a student teacher arrives at the school site and when he begins the action research project. It is particularly important that student teachers keep their senses attuned to the environment to learn information that may change the design or even the question of their research. Read through the two following scenarios and suggest changes in the design based upon the "new" information each student teacher obtains.

Scenario 1: Holly

Holly, a student teacher at a high school, is exploring reasons students are disenfranchised at school. She makes a correlation between students in her classes who are involved in after-school activities and those who are not. She begins to assume that students involved in after school activities are more motivated than those who are not.

Then, she discovers the fee structure (per student) for various activities and resources at the high school:

- $40 for student body;
- $225 for sports (not to exceed $900 per family);
- $125 for dance or cheerleading (per semester);
- $95 for any other after-school club (drama, chess, etc.);
- $50 for the yearbook;
- $250 for parking;
- $15–$30 for art, photography, or technology;
- $10–$20 for foreign-language resources;
- $15 for life skills studies;
- $50 for family and consumer science studies;
- $50 textbook deposit;
- $12 for the science lab.

How might this data provide context for Holly's study? How might it redirect where and how she looks at issues of socioeconomic class, attitudes, motivation, and students being disengaged in school?

Scenario 2: Martin

Martin is not from the small rural community where he is student-teaching in a federally funded program specifically for preschool children of migrant families. The town where he is teaching has grown by 1,600

continues →

in the last decade to a population of 5,178. Latino immigration/migration has contributed to three-fifths of this growth and now represents 35% of the population. Of this population, many are seasonal agricultural workers, although the community is also growing its nonagricultural employment base. The staff at the preschool has been anxiously awaiting a decision from the city council concerning a land use permit in order to build a new and larger facility.

Martin senses a number of community tensions play out in daily life between school and community, and somehow he knows that this is important not only to his teaching, but to his action research project on building and maintaining parent involvement in his classroom via parent groups.

Martin attends the city council meeting with his mentor-teacher. The meeting is tense. Opponents focus on a number of issues. Some cite potential traffic congestion. Others question whether a low-income migrant program belongs in a white middle- and upper-class residential neighborhood. Still others question if there is even a need for such a program. Someone states that property values will be diminished if such a center is constructed. Martin's mentor-teacher testifies that the program now serves around 300 migrant families, but someone else in the group questions the notion of *migrant*, claiming the definition is too broad. Monitoring the meeting is a federal civil rights officer. A local advocacy group had contacted the federal agency earlier, questioning whether the denial of the land use permit was a civil rights issue. One of those testifying is clear in pointing out that this "is not a race or class issue, but a land use decision only." Someone else testifies, "Somebody always has to play the race card and this isn't about race."

The end of the meeting is hardly the end: everyone knows this decision will most likely be settled in the courts. Martin is left wondering how this context is important to his action research design and his research topic on building a supportive parent group and network at the school.

📖 How do you think this context matters? In what ways does this new information influence Martin's action research project?

CHAPTER 4
ACTION RESEARCH DESIGN

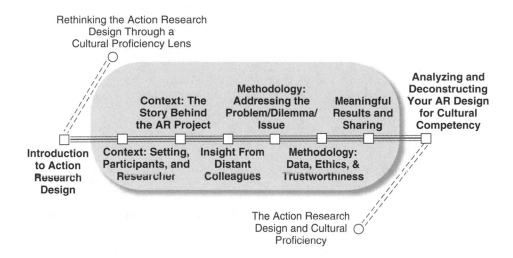

Chapter 4 guides you through the formal process of writing an action research design. There are (at least) three ways to approach this chapter: Now that you have determined the kind of research you want to do (design research, curriculum analysis, ethnography, or self-study) and refined your critical question, you are ready to apply principles of data collection as you develop your research design. Alternatively, you may find it useful to merely skim this chapter at this point and continue with Chapter 5 *Ongoing Data Analysis* and Chapter 6 *Final Data Interpretation* to gain a better picture of the whole action research journey. After doing so, you could return to this chapter and complete the action research design. Or you might work through this chapter, completing most of the design, and continue reading the next chapters and revising your draft action research design as you proceed. Whatever route you choose, this chapter will provide the scaffold for you to plan the implementation of your action research project.

Introduction to Action Research Design

We begin this section on action research design with a true story to emphasize that research context includes *you*—you are not outside of the school and community where you conduct action research. You are the "participant observer" (Atkinson & Hammersley, 1994; Patton, 2002); you are the "human instrument" (Lincoln & Guba, 2003). As an active participant in the research study, your own paradigm and resulting attitudes for seeing and doing in the classroom influence the outcome of the study; furthermore, you become part of the population to be "analyzed" in the study (McCotter, 2001; Weiler, 1988).

The story is of one mentor-teacher, Ms. Buckman, and two student teachers, Liz and Jodi. The first student teacher was placed with Ms. Buckman the first half the year; the student teachers were to trade placements the last half of the year. Liz reported:

My mentor-teacher uses a scripted, prepackaged literacy program. I can't implement any of the literacy strategies I've learned in my teacher-education program.

Because of this, Liz changed the focus of her action research project.

Midway through the year, Liz went to a different placement, and Jodi joined Ms. Buckman. Jodi had implemented literature circles as her action research project in the first half of her placement. After one day in Ms. Buckman's classroom, she reported,

I am so excited! Today I talked with Ms. Buckman about introducing literature circles. She was really supportive. She told me she had wanted to do this but wasn't quite sure how to go about it! I am so fortunate to be able to share with her what I've learned, and to have her expertise about the children and reading instruction to guide the rest of my action research project!

What made the difference? Attitude, approach, and a student teacher's comfort level with both the content and the teaching and learning strategy are just a few factors that make a difference in action research process. Consider yourself as you design, implement, and interpret your action research.

> Travel the side road Self-Study 4.1: *Rethinking Your Action Research Design Through a Cultural Proficiency Lens* found at the end of this chapter on p. 111. Doing this side road now will better prepare you to draft the action research design.

The Action Research Design

The research design is a map to the action research project. Research designs include four main sections: *The Context of the Study; Insights from Distant Colleagues (Literature Review); Methodology;* and *Meaningful Results and Publication.* Each of these sections is described below. Designs are tailored to the specific kind of research you intend to do (design research, self-study, ethnography, or curriculum analysis). If you have not yet made this decision, review Chapters 1 and 2. There is a general purpose template for an action research design included in Appendix F.

The generic template and additional research design templates tailored to specific kinds of research design, along with completed designs, can be found on the companion website.

You may find it helpful to download the research design of your choice and take notes on it as you read the next section.

> Take the side road Cultural Context 4.1: *Context Matters* found at the end of this chapter on p. 116 to better analyze your own action research context.

The Context of the Study: Setting, Participants, and Researcher

The research design begins with a description of the setting. This includes the participants, and yourself as the researcher. Concisely describe:

- The community and school. Include defining information that specifically matters to the context of your study. Show how the school reflects the community or certain sections of the community. Demographic data is usually important, for example rural or urban, student access to the school, mission and values of the school, wealth descriptions of families, and labels applied to the school such as *Title I.*

- Students or participants of the action research project. Include specific demographics: gender, ethnicities, languages spoken, and other pertinent information.

- The physical classroom where the action research project will take place. Be precise in your details. Choose information that matters to the study. For example, if there is little room for students to move around and you are planning to implement drama as a learning strategy, how will you allow enough space? Consider a scanned drawing with annotation. Additionally, consider what messages are conveyed through posters and other artifacts in the room. How does the mentor-teacher's philosophy as told through room design influence your research project?

- Describe yourself as the action researcher. Include connections and comfort level to the setting and the participants. Include concerns or affirmations. Deconstruct your description; be wary of familiarity. "This feels just like the school I attended!" While this is important information, it is only useful if deconstructed. For example, what is useful and dangerous about familiarity? *Note:* if you are doing this project as a collaborative study, each action researcher completes this piece. Additionally, include information on why you are working as a team.

- *How this information matters to the action research project.* This is the connection piece. The data described above is isolated and without meaning if direct connections cannot be made back to the critical question. How is the critical question, intervention, analysis or self-study connected and meaningful to this setting, the participants, and yourself as the action researcher? A careful writing of this section is the practice of critical self-reflexivity and provides transparency, both criteria of trustworthiness, to the action research design.

The Context of the Study: The Story Behind the Action Research Project

Describe how the critical question and research project was conceptualized. Concisely describe:

- The critical question(s) and research project and how it evolved.

- The intervention to be tried and redesigned; the curriculum to be analyzed; the phenomenon of the ethnography to be studied; or the dilemma or hunch behind the self-study.

- Why you have an interest in this area.

- How your own beliefs, values, and sense of what is "good teaching" are represented in this action research project. *Note*: if you are working as a collaborative team, each member completes this and the previous bullet piece.

- *How this information matters to the study.* This is the connection piece: practice deconstructing and critical self-reflexivity in connecting all of the above information. This information should also connect to the first section of "context." A reader of the design should be able to see how this critical question and action research is a "good fit" with the context of the study.

Insight From Distant Colleagues (Literature Review)

Review Chapter 2 and the section on the Literature Review as needed to complete this portion of the research design. In this section, list synthesis statements from your literature review, followed by specific references that support the synthesis statement. Here is an example:

Synthesis statement: *Teacher talk is critical in creating an environment where students will take risks as readers and writers.*

Calkins, L. (2006). *A Guide to the Writing Workshop: Grades 3–6.* Portsmouth, NH: Heinemann.

Johnston, P. H. (2004). *Choice Words: How Our Language Affects Children's Learning.* Portland, ME: Stenhouse Publishers.

Johnston, P. H., & Powers, B. M. (2012). *Opening Minds: Using Language to Change Lives.* Portland, ME: Stenhouse Publishers.

The purpose of synthesis statements and citations is to provide the framework surrounding the critical question, data collection, ongoing data analysis, and final data interpretation. It should be clear to a reader of the design how these align. Recall that this is a way of creating trustworthiness into the design, by relying upon the perspectives of distant colleagues and making strong connections in this area. A reader should be able to understand why *this* literature, supports the critical question, designed for the specific school-context of the particular action research project.

Methodology: How the Problem, Dilemma, and/or Issue Will Be Addressed

The next major section of the research design is methodology: how the problem, dilemma, and/or issue of the project that forms the critical question, will be addressed.

Methodology: Data Compilation

Begin by describing the data you will collect. Include additional documentation you will collect that will give the data context. Also include how and when you will use your researcher's journal. Table 4.1 shows the beginnings of a data compilation plan.

→ TABLE 4.1: Methodology: Data Compilation

Kind of Data to be Collected Be specific: *observe small groups during math work.*	Purpose What you hope to learn from collecting this data: *I hope to learn how middle school students engage with iPad technologies during math. My theory is that engaged students will better learn.*	How Data Triangulates with Other Data *I will compare the observations to the actual work students do on the iPad (artifact). I will also compare this to test data (artifact), and interview data.*
Observation		
Interview		
Artifacts		
Additional context Documentation		
Researcher's journal: How will be kept; when you will write in it; how you will use it.		

Next, describe how you will organize the research data compilation:

- Where will data be collected (files, crates, electronically, etc.)?

- How will data be organized?

- Where will journal entries be kept?

- How will classroom observations and notes be taken and stored?

- How will this data be kept safe and confidential?

Methodology: Calendar for the Action Research Project

Build a calendar for the action research project. To complete this and the next sections, you might find it helpful to skip ahead to Chapter 5 *Ongoing Data Analysis* to learn about the shared principles of ongoing data analysis and final data interpretation, along with the cycles of data collection. Alternatively, you may find it useful to read the expectation for these sections of the design as outlined in this chapter, draft ideas, and then return to it after studying Chapter 5. In Chapter 5, we suggest collecting data for a two to three week period, pausing to complete formal ongoing data analysis, and then repeating this cycle two more times. This cycle will change depending upon the parameters of your study; adjust as necessary.

The calendar includes:

- Dates for specific data collection and related classroom activities (e.g. if you are teaching, include the curricula elements that are related to data collection).

- Dates for formal ongoing analysis.

Include a draft of your calendar here. The reader of the design should be able to imagine how the action research project will unfold in the classroom.

Methodology: Ongoing Data Analysis and Interpretation

Continue the methodology section by outlining how you will complete data interpretation. Jump ahead and skim the beginning of the section in Chapter 5 entitled *Shared Concepts of Ongoing Data Analysis and Final Data Interpretation*. Then you will be able to define the terms

- analyze

- synthesize

- deconstruct

- contextualize

and generally apply them to your project. You can return to this section after reading Chapters 5 and 6 more carefully and develop your ideas.

Methodology: Trustworthiness

A critical question of methodology is, "How is this design trustworthy? Refer back to Chapter 3 as needed for review. Complete Table 4.2 to make transparent how your research design is trustworthy.

→ TABLE 4.2: Methodology: Trustworthiness

Describe how your research design plans for each criterion. Be specific about what data collected best supports the criterion.	
How and where will you practice self-reflexivity?	
How will you seek multiple perspectives? (Whose perspectives will you seek?)	
How does your design have a strong sense of connection to the literature, the data to be collected, the context of the study, or your plans for analyzing and interpreting the data?	
Evidence of Becoming a Teacher Taken together, how will the data you collect and the analysis and interpretation you do provide evidence of your own transformation throughout this action research project?	

Methodology: Ethical Considerations of Action Research and Gaining Permissions

Describe here how you are conducting ethical research. Include what permissions you are or are not pursuing and the rationale for each decision. Answer how you are keeping students' identity confidential. If you are sending an informed consent letter home, include it in this section of the action research design. A sample template for a Gaining Permissions Letter is included in Appendix G.

Meaningful Results and Sharing

In this final section of the action research design, describe what actions you expect or hope to be as the result of your action research project. How do you hope your project is beneficial to students and their teacher(s)? How do you expect your project to make a difference? How are you positioning yourself as a student teacher-action researcher to be open to the unexpected? What is it about this design that both guides and allows for critical diversions as necessary that might lead to meaningful results? How will this design support you in becoming a teacher?

Finally, how do you plan to share your journey of action research? Chapter 7 has some ideas on how you might present your work. (Read ahead if you like!) Remember, if you are "going public" you need to attend to issues of confidentiality and permissions.

Upon completion of your draft action research design, evaluate your work using the following:

- Connection and alignment between the critical question and insight from distant colleagues, the plan to be implemented, methodology, and desired results: do these all support one another?

- Triangulation of data within each data set. How will the data you plan to gather support one another, provide a "crystallized" view of the dilemma, problem, or question of the action research?

- Design manageability. Can you actually implement this design? Is it do-able? Why or why not?

Continue to evaluate, analyze, and deconstruct the action research design by working through the following section.

> Travel the side road Self-Study 4.2: *The Action Research Design and Cultural Proficiency* found at the end of the chapter on p. 113. Prior to analyzing and deconstructing your action research design, pause to work through Mark's action research design using the lens of cultural proficiency.

Analyzing and Deconstructing the Action Research Design for Cultural Competency

Complete this section once you have completed a draft of the action research design. This section will guide you in deconstructing your design and practicing self-reflexivity, thus demonstrating attentiveness to issues of trustworthiness.

It is much easier to make the connections between culture and action research when analyzing someone else's work. We are so close to our own sense of culture that we take these daily acts of living and the paradigm behind them for granted. With your draft action research design beside you, work through the following questions, marking places in the design to revise at a later date. Discuss your analysis with your critical colleague.

Read again through the Context sections of the action research design and ask the following questions.

Question 1: How does this context matter to my action research project?

- Given your description, do you think the majority of the community would support your action research topic and believe it is useful? Why or why not *or* do you not know? Give a reason for your response.

- Given your description, do you think those considered the "minority" of the community would support your action research topic and believe that it is useful? Why or why not *or* do you not know? Give a reason for your response.

- How are teaching, learning, and doing research supported or not supported by this context? (This is an important question to consider.)

- Consider the community demographics as you have presented them. What do you suppose this community wants from their schools? On what do you base your answer?

Question 2: What is my comfort level within this community/school context?

In the space below, create a Venn diagram. Label one circle as "My School Community" and the other circle, "Me, as a Teacher-Researcher." Using the demographic and descriptive information from your action research design, explore how you are different from and/or the same as the community where you are teaching. The first time, complete the Venn diagram based upon the dominant population and the second time do it based upon other populations within the school:

Review the story behind your action research project and ask the next question.

Question 3: How does this information matter to my action research project?

- If you met the families of students in your classroom at a social event, what kind of event would this most likely be? A) Family-sponsored event; B) Neighborhood block party; C) Church sponsored event; D) An open house at a local art gallery; E) Civic event; F) Potluck at a neighborhood center. Would you be comfortable in this setting?

- Do you think you could become friends with all or part of the families represented in your classroom if you met them in another setting? Expand on your answer.

- Do you believe the majority of the families in your classroom would agree with your description of "good teaching"? Why or why not?

- Which families in your classroom would agree with your perception of "poor classroom behavior"? Why?

Question 4: How does the strategic intervention, innovation to be implemented, evaluation to be conducted, and/or other action to be applied in your study support learning for and by all children and/or adolescents in your classroom?

- How does your action research design and specific action support differentiated learning (learning for all students)?

- How does your action research design recognize and support diversity?

- How does your action research design plan for multiple viewpoints?

- How do organizational and/or school systems provide possibilities and barriers to your research?

- How does your action research design deal with conflict?

Next, review your plan's trustworthiness and for ongoing data analysis and final data interpretation, ask Question 5.

Question 5: How does your design account for cultural proficiency *when interpreting data?*

- Where in the data interpretation might you need to be aware of cultural knowledge when interpreting behaviors personal interactions? Who might be a good resource for this kind of knowledge if you feel you are lacking in this area?

- If there appear to be conflicting "results" in your data interpretation, how do you plan to resolve and/or represent these conflicts?

- What stereotypes and/or prejudices might influence the data interpretation?

- What kinds of distrust might exist within the school context that could influence your data interpretation?

- What kinds of systems, organization, and/or structures exist that may need to be questioned for their influence upon your data interpretation? What do you assume about these systems, organization, and/or structures?

Having worked through these questions, return to your action research design and read your critical question. *How is your critical question reflective of your own cultural context? Do you need to make any revisions here?*

Summary

Plan well for your research journey. Just as in teaching, design a calendar for implementation, organize necessary systems; be cognizant of ethical considerations. Take time developing your design to make it trustworthy: analyze and deconstruct it. And then—leave the door open for change. You are not designing a wall of defense for your project. You are designing an open space, a space that can be adapted as data informs and transforms the process. This is the act of critically learning, teaching, and researching. Anticipate the process!

Chapter 4: Content Questions

1. Consider for a moment curriculum design: we align unit goals to specific instruction and align this with assessment. How is the same principle applied to an action research design?
2. How is alignment between the critical question and the action research plan creating a "strong sense of connection"?

Chapter 4: Process Questions

1. How will you balance the demands of learning to teach and the act of conducting research? How is teaching and research the same, different?
2. Describe your action research design in one brief concise paragraph. Now read it to someone who is not as familiar with your project. Have them summarize what they hear. What questions do they have for you? Do they understand the goals of your action research? Is there anything you need to revise based upon their comments and/or questions?

Self-Study 4.1: Rethinking Your Action Research Design Through a Cultural Proficiency Lens

Making sense of a situation is always in part an act of self-understanding on the part of the researcher. How one chooses to approach a research situation is shaped by the researcher's subjectivity, his or her place in the web of reality—Joe Kincheloe (2003), Teachers as Researchers: Qualitative Inquiry as a Path to Empowerment

In this activity, you will evaluate yourself in terms of *cultural proficiency*. Being a culturally proficient educator is critical in any educational setting in which the goal is to teach all students. Culturally proficient teachers know how to create a environment in which students of all cultural backgrounds and life histories have a place for powerful learning and growth.

You may have preconceived notions about what cultural proficiency means and how it applies to you and your setting. This activity will help you define cultural proficiency in a way that applies to you, regardless of your setting. Then you will examine and rethink your action research design through a lens of cultural proficiency.

What Does It Mean to Be a "Culturally Proficient" Teacher-Action Researcher?

In your notebook or journal, write out the definition of *culturally proficient* as you have come to understand it in your teacher-education program. How do you think this definition does or does not apply to you as you become a teacher? What are the specific ways you might be a culturally astute teacher-action researcher?

Your comfort and ease in responding to these two questions may serve to inform you about your evolution as a culturally proficient teacher-action researcher. *Evolution* is a word that acknowledges that there is no arrival at cultural proficiency—we keep developing, reinventing, and revisiting our paradigm, our pedagogy, and our approaches to solving cultural issues and conflict in our classrooms and lives.

Writers have adopted multiple orientations toward the concept of teacher development of cultural proficiency. For example, Howard's (1999) white identity orientation includes "modalities of growth" that illustrate white identity transformations in the areas of *thinking, feeling,* and *acting.* He describes a developing and ongoing transformation in thinking, moving from a linear, fear-driven, and autocratic position to a dynamic, self-reflective, holistic mode of thought. Such transformation means moving from a "my way is right" perspective on culture to one that is characteristic of empathy, respect, transparency, and openness to change. He describes a movement from monoculturalism and "treating all students the same" toward a place of advocacy and active learning from other cultures as Eurocentric perspectives are challenged.

Lindsey, Robins, and Terrill (2003) note, "The transformation to cultural proficiency requires time to think, reflect, assess, decide, and change" (p. 40). They focus on the *transformation of behaviors.* An educator who acts with cultural proficiency would exercise these "essential elements" of cultural proficiency (Figure 4.1).

This transformation requires deliberate action on each individual's part. It isn't easy to deconstruct what seems "normal" in our way of life. Throughout the present volume, we've attempted to create a

continues ➜

→ FIGURE 4.1: Essential Elements of Cultural Proficiency (source: Lindsey, R. B, Robins, K. N., & Terrell, R. D. (2003). *Cultural Proficiency: A Manual for School Leaders* (2nd ed.). Thousand Oaks, CA: Corwin Press, Inc.)

Assess Culture: *Name the Differences*
- Recognize how your culture affects the culture of others.
- Describe your own culture and the cultural norms of your organization.
- Understand how the culture of your organization affects those with different cultures.

Value Diversity: *Claim Your Differences*
- Celebrate and encourage the presence of a variety of people in all activities.
- Recognize differences as diversity rather than as inappropriate responses to the environment.
- Accept that each culture finds some values and behaviors more important than others.

Manage the Dynamics of Difference: *Frame the Conflicts Caused by Differences*
- Learn effective strategies for resolving conflict, particularly among people whose cultural backgrounds and values differ.
- Understand the effect that historic distrust has on present-day interactions.
- Realize that you may misjudge others' actions based on learned expectations.

Adapt to Diversity: *Change to Make a Difference*
- Change the way things are done to acknowledge the differences that are present in the staff, clients, and community.
- Develop skills for intercultural communication.
- Institutionalize cultural interventions for conflicts and confusion caused by the dynamics of difference.

Institutionalize Cultural Knowledge: *Train About Differences*
- Incorporate cultural knowledge into the mainstream of the organization.
- Teach the origins of stereotypes and prejudices
- For staff development and education, integrate into your systems information and skills that enable all to interact effectively in a variety of intercultural situations.

scaffold around your ability to do this Through various activities. We have said repeatedly that "context matters." This is because we recognize that none of us can escape being influenced by our personal culture, for culture is "everything you believe and everything you do that enables you to identify with people who are like you and that distinguishes you from people who differ from you. . . . Culture provides parameters for daily living" (Lindsey et al., 2003, p. 41).

Viewing Your Research Design Through a Cultural Proficiency Lens

What, then, does all of this have to do with your action research design? At this point, you've most likely successfully drafted the design, so why bring up cultural proficiency now? The answer: We want to be deliberate in taking time to assess our own cultural biases and to be cognizant of how these biases may influence our design. We understand, with Banks (1997), that,

[e]ducators communicate their perspectives, values, and attitudes towards ethnic groups to students primarily through unwitting actions and words. Consequently, it is important for educators to examine not only the knowledge that underlies their curriculum and methods but also their own values and perspectives to determine the extent to which they promote equity and justice for all students. (p. 50)

What we learn from writers such as Banks is that we have to be purposeful to affect change. It doesn't just "naturally" happen out of our own good intentions.

Self-Study 4.2: The Action Research Design and Cultural Proficiency

The *BTAR* companion website includes a downloadable template for this activity.

Read the following example from an action research design. As you read, ask yourself: How does Mark's personal culture matter? How does Mark's cultural identity influence his action research topic, design, and data interpretation?

Example: Mark

Mark is an upper elementary/middle school preservice teacher. His action research question is: *Will using homework as an enhancement exercise rather than an extension exercise increase the quality of students' schoolwork and improve their attitude toward homework?*

Mark describes his interest in researching homework as follows:

I am interested in researching homework because I think that students often rush through their class work to avoid having homework. I think that allowing ample time for work to be completed during class will increase the quality of the work turned in by the students and improve students' attitudes about homework. After observing the sixth grade students in my class rush through their work in an attempt to finish it, I became curious about studying this. If homework is taken out of the equation—it's already assigned—and students are motivated by turning in quality work instead of finishing quickly I expect them to perform better. The motivation and expectation should be the same—QUALITY. Furthermore, if homework assignments are geared toward enhancing or enriching lessons rather than extending class work time, I expect that attitudes toward homework will improve and completion rates will increase.

He describes some of his own values:

I grew up in an upper-middle class neighborhood. As a white male with a secure family background I always had familial support and even pressure to perform academically. I know that I always could get help from my parents and would get regular reminders from them to complete my homework. While I did not rely on teachers to provide academic motivation, I believe that an important part of good teaching is being able to motivate your students to do their best. A teacher cannot be solely responsible for motivating students, but they do play an important role. There are several factors that go into a teacher's motivation of their students. One of the most important factors has to be meaningful class work. If students are rushing through work to get it done, the work is obviously not meaningful. There are different things that can be done to give work meaning and one of them is to give the work meaningful class time. If it's important enough to do, it should be important enough to dedicate class time toward doing it. Homework should be meaningful as well. I believe that homework should be dedicated to enhancing a day's lesson or preparing for an upcoming lesson.

Mark describes his own experiences with motivation in the work world and identifies why motivation and expectation are important to him:

continues →

It is difficult to remember what my experiences with homework were, especially when I think about sixth grade in 1978–79. However, the following example from my most recent job should give you some idea of why I feel strongly about motivation and expectations being the same. During my last job, before entering my teacher-education program, the salespeople of the company I worked for were expected to close as many deals as possible during the week. Each week—sometimes daily—statistics were posted publicly showing each salesperson's numbers from the previous week. Ironically, salespeople weren't paid commission based on sales volume. They were paid based on profit margin. In fact, sales below a certain profit margin were deducted from pay. The salesperson's motivation is pay based on profit margin. However, they're being asked to produce as much revenue as possible. The motivation and expectation contradict each other. Similarly, students are expected to turn in quality work, but their motivation is finishing quickly eliminating or limiting homework. Again, the motivation and expectation contradict each other.

In the next segment, Mark talks about his own beliefs about his students and what he assumes about their values:

I think that kids want to do well and want to please other people like their parents or their teachers. If given ample class time and meaningful homework, I believe that students' work will improve. I also believe that all students have enough time at home to complete the homework which they will be assigned. It is my impression that many of the students I am working with have limited parental involvement at home with regards to academics. If I can help create the motivation in my students to turn in quality work by providing them with time to complete assignments and meaningful homework that they are eager to complete on their own, I expect the quality of their work to improve—their motivation and my expectations will correlate.

Analyzing and Deconstructing the Example

Read through the above example one more time to answer the following questions. Using different colors of pen/pencil, underline portions of the text that might answer the questions; color code for the question/ evidence in the text. Read for both explicit statements and for the innuendoes of the text.

- According to Mark, why is motivation important in and out of school?
- Who is responsible for a student's motivation to do well?

Read through the text again and attempt to answer the following questions with evidence from the text. Once again, underline portions of the text that might answer the questions; color code for the question/evidence in the text. Read for both explicit statements and for the innuendoes of the text.

- How might Mark's choice of an action research question reflect his own cultural context?
- How might this context influence Mark's data interpretation? For example if students do not do any better with his intervention strategies to improve homework quality, what kinds of conclusions might Mark come to if he does not take into account his own context?

Now, consider the context where Mark is teaching. Here are the details as he provides them:

continues ➜

Walker Elementary School is located 20 miles from a downtown urban area. It is one of the largest suburbs of this city with a population of nearly 80,000 people. Walker Elementary reflects the suburb in that it consists of students representing a wide variety of ethnicities and socio-economic backgrounds. Forty-three percent of Walker's students receive free or reduced lunch while others are the sons and daughters of a major computer manufacture's managers and executives. Approximately one-third of Walker's students represent a race other than Caucasian. The majority of those are Hispanic.

Twelve of the 29 students (41%) in my classroom represent persons of color. One of the students is on an Individual Educational Program and two of the students are taking English as a Second Language courses although they both seem functionally fluent in English. Fifteen of the students are male and 14 are female. Only two of the 28 students achieved "exceeded standards" for fifth grade benchmarks on standardized testing.

Overall, I would say that the class is very average academically and the students have a difficult time expressing themselves through writing. They have shown limited vocabularies and poor study habits. On average, less than half of the students will turn in all of their assignments during a given week. With few exceptions, the students seem to accept poor academic work and are apparently more motivated to get work turned in rather than turn in quality work. Is this because the students are trying to avoid homework, or is this because students simply don't care or are not capable of better? I think these students are capable of more and that the quality of their work is related to avoiding homework. This action research project will serve to help me answer this question.

Read through the above text again and attempt to answer the following questions with evidence from the text. Once again, underline portions of the text that might answer the questions; color code for the question/evidence in the text. Read for both explicit statements and for the innuendoes of the text.

- How is Mark's background similar and different than those of his students?
- How do Mark's background and values influence his description of his students?
- How might Mark's background and values blindside the questions he asks? What additional questions might he consider?

In the space below, explain the connections between Mark's personal context, his choice of action research question, his values and beliefs as evidenced here, and the context of his school. You may find that sketching a diagram or chart is a helpful way of conceptualizing these connections. Demonstrate areas where Mark might want to be particularly wary while conducting his action research project. The introduction of this section and review of Lindsey et al.'s (2003) of *Cultural Proficiency: A Manual for School Leaders* may provide you with useful information for this activity.

Cultural Context 4.1: Context Matters

Context matters. Work through the following scenarios and think about what you might do in each of these different contexts. Then, return to your own ideas for an action research design and re-consider *context* and how it matters to your research project.

Edward wants to introduce computer-based simulations into his engineering course for his action research project. He has 23 students in the class. The dilemma: computers are limited at his school. The media center has one computer lab, which is always booked during the time he will be teaching. There are three laptops available for use in his classroom.

- Does this mean Edward cannot complete his project? Should he abandon it altogether? How might he go ahead with his project?
- If you have thought of a way for Edward to continue with his project, how will this context (23 students; three computers) make a difference in the project? How will this influence his research design decisions?

Margie wants to introduce theatrical elements as learning strategies for the students in her fourth grade math class. She imagines them acting out fractions, using their bodies to create fraction lines and to learn to add and subtract fractions. However, she is teaching in a module, which has limited space. There are 33 students, 33 desks, and very little room for maneuvering.

- Be specific in listing the context considerations Margie might encounter.
- Given this list, should Margie continue with this research idea? Why or why not? If you think she should continue, what are her options?

Julia is enthusiastic about blogs—she personally loves to blog and she thinks that inviting her otherwise not so enthusiastic ninth grade students to blog about poetry might be just the ticket. She is, however, a bit worried about her action research project. To date, despite her enthusiasm for teaching and her well-planned lessons, students seem apathetic. Julia isn't sure if she should give this project a go or not. Her university supervisor suggested that given that fact students rarely turn in their homework, it might be better if she instituted a program to encourage homework completion.

- How might Julia evaluate the strength of her possible blog action research project?
- How might she learn more about her students and their apparent "apathy"?
- Do you see other ways she might negotiate between her own action research goals and her university supervisor's suggestion?

CHAPTER 5
ONGOING DATA ANALYSIS

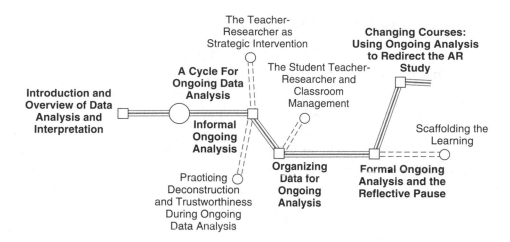

It is time to begin the research! You have an action research plan and perhaps some of you will now be beginning the journey of gathering data, most likely while teaching and completing ongoing data analysis. This is not small task! Learning to be organized, deliberate, and thoughtful when so much is happening is learning to live the teaching practice of action research. You will find that ongoing data analysis is critical in transforming your teaching practices and thinking and guiding next steps of research and teaching. This chapter will provide you with strategies for making this happen.

Introduction and Overview of Data Analysis and Interpretation

You have defined action research, formulated and articulated a critical question, and designed a well-triangulated and trustworthy action research study. Now it is time to begin the research, to collect data and complete ongoing data analysis. Ongoing data analysis is a process that continues throughout data collection. This step may feel like moving into a dark, foggy forest of unknowns. Maybe you have never before analyzed real, messy data—at least not the kinds of data you are collecting in your action research. You may be unexpectedly haunted at this point by the fact that your data doesn't seem objective or even particularly clear or organized. You may wonder if you have enough data to draw any conclusions from at all. All of these are legitimate and important questions. The purpose of this chapter is to consider these questions and to guide you through the process of making sense of your data in a way that not only provides insights into your critical question, but leads to additional questions and perhaps other ways of thinking about your critical question.

Ongoing data analysis is what happens *during* the data collection process and is the topic of this chapter. Final data interpretation is what happens *after* you have completed data collection and is the topic of Chapter 6. Both ongoing data analysis and final data interpretation share common principles of *analysis, synthesis, deconstruction,* and *contextualization,* located within a trustworthy framework. We will explore these critical concepts before continuing with strategies for ongoing data analysis.

Shared Concepts of Ongoing Data Analysis and Final Data Interpretation

To illustrate analysis, synthesis, deconstruction, and contextualization, we use a series of pictures of a flower in a mountain jungle.

Analysis

To *analyze* means to take apart, to break down or dissect. We divide the data into categories, columns, or other regularized spaces. We separate pieces of the data, making it simpler to study. To analyze is to narrow our gaze; it is pulling in the subjects, problems and questions with the micro lens of inquiry.

Key questions for analysis include:

- What seems to be happening in this data? What is *not* happening in this data?

- What is repeated in this data (words, behaviors, attitudes, occurrences)?

- What is surprising, perplexing, disturbing in the data?

- What information seems to be missing from the data?

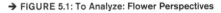

→ FIGURE 5.1: To Analyze: Flower Perspectives

Synthesis

→ FIGURE 5.2: To Synthesize: Flower in Context

To *synthesize* is the act of putting back together again, of creating wholeness, or integrating pieces to form a sense of harmony or unity. To synthesize the data means pulling away from the parts (analysis) and seeing the data set as a whole. When we synthesize data, we change the lens of inquiry to wide angle and see the data with all of its pieces, as an entire photo.

Key questions for synthesis include:

- What patterns emerge across the landscape of the data?

- Where are the contradictions, paradoxes, and dilemmas in the data? What does not seem to fit in the landscape?

- What are the emotional and intellectual reactions to this data?

- What confirms and disaffirms what is thought about the research question?

Deconstruction

To *deconstruct* is to check assumptions, to consider what personal and social context frames our analysis and synthesis. To deconstruct data is to check under, around, behind, and over our conclusions. When we deconstruct data, we put the camera of inquiry down, walk back up the hill and look behind us to see what view we've been missing.

Key questions for deconstruction include:

→ FIGURE 5.3: To Deconstruct: Peruvian Mountain

- Where have categories of either/or interpretations been made? How can these either/or conclusions be reconstructed using a different lens?

- What are the limitations of the analysis and synthesis? What do you not know and what can you *not* know?

- What assumptions are being made in the analysis and synthesis? What values and beliefs do these assumptions rely upon?

- What would students, parents, a mentor-teacher, an advisor, or authors in the literature say about the analysis and synthesis?

- What is useful and dangerous about the analysis and synthesis?

Contextualization

If you have traveled the "Cultural Context" side roads so far in this book, you have made discoveries of the importance of context in studying our practice as teachers. The cultural, social, and political context of who we are as teacher-researchers creates the lens through which we interpret our data. We like the idea of "situated knowledge" (Haraway, 1996). Situated knowledge means that knowledge (and thus our interpretations of data) is related to specific location, historical, and sociopolitical context. It matters who you are as a teacher-researchers. Where we've grown up, our ethnic identification, our social class, all matter. Our religious beliefs, our values based on gender, our understanding of "good" and "bad" teachers all matter. The physical attributes of the classroom and strategies we employ as teachers, matters. Consider who *you* are in taking this "photo" of data (Figure 5.4). Ask the question, "Why is this subject/scene one I desire to photograph or one I have chosen to focus on in my data?"

→ FIGURE 5.4: Context of Flower

Key questions in considering context include:

- How does your role as a student teacher influence the data and the analysis and interpretation of data?

- How are your own developing identity and abilities as a teacher influencing the data and the outcomes you see in the data?

- In what ways is the action research project "concluding" in the way you as the teacher-researcher wanted? How does this reflect your own beliefs/values?

- How do your data analysis and interpretations reflect your beliefs/values of what "good teaching" is, "good students" are, and "good curriculum" should be?

- How do your analysis and interpretations align with the stated school and community values and beliefs where the project was conducted? Does it really matter?

- How does the physical classroom or other non-human entities of the classroom influence the data?

- How does the context, the unique setting of the school where you are researching and teaching, influence the data and the analysis and interpretation?

Finally, ongoing data analysis and final data interpretation are always done in the company of trustworthiness. Throughout the process of ongoing data analysis and final data interpretation, ask yourself: Does my data . . .

- Provide evidence of *becoming*?

- Demonstrate self-reflexivity?

- Seek multiple perspectives?

- Develop a strong sense of connection?

- Acknowledge limitations?

- Avoid generalizations?

- Represent ethical and professional standards for research?

- Result in meaningful actions?

A Cycle for Ongoing Data Analysis

While every action research project and setting is different, it will be useful to examine the way analysis might work in practice. In this section, we will assume that there is time and space to conduct data for three distinct periods. Each data collection period builds on the one before, incorporating changes and adjustments as you analyze and interpret your ongoing work. A general pattern of data collection for three data collection periods might include the following activities and adjustments to the study:

Data Collection Period One

Data is collected and analyzed. The data may seem somewhat disconnected, lacking in clear patterns or themes. Through critical reflexivity and analysis, the teacher-researcher 1) refines his/her critical question; 2) discovers gaps in the data, determines what data are most useful, and what data is needed, and as a result 3) refines data collection strategies, and 4) adapts teaching and lesson planning.

Data Collection Period Two

Following analysis, the data is likely more focused, showing patterns and themes more clearly. Through critical reflexivity and analysis, the teacher-researcher 1) may further refine his/her critical question, 2) connects the data more closely to the literature, 3) is able to identify emerging themes and questions, 4) further refines data collection strategies focusing on emerging themes and questions, 5) further refines teaching and lesson planning, and 6) begins to seek multiple perspectives such as those of the mentor-teacher, students, or other context and content experts.

Data Collection Period Three

The data is now richer and deeper; connections across the data sets and literature are now clear. The teacher-researcher 1) may further refine his/her critical question, 2) interfaces the data with the literature more completely, 3) identifies, enriches, and expands themes and questions, and 4) continues to refine teaching and lesson planning.

There is nothing magical about having "three" data collection periods. Engaging in even more data collection periods may deepen your research; however, as illustrated, three data collection periods usually allow the necessary time for an action research project to develop. The number of data collection periods you are able to work through is often limited based upon the length of time you are in the classroom as a student teacher-researcher. Even if you only have time and space for one thorough data collection period, you will likely uncover significant questions and areas for further study and consideration.

Our cycle of ongoing data analysis is divided between informal ongoing analysis and formal "reflective pauses" that occur between the data collection periods. Let's begin with a look at informal ongoing analysis and the relationship between the research collection and the theorizing and questioning of analysis.

Informal Ongoing Analysis

Informal ongoing data analysis occurs continuously, in "real time," as well as when you pause to reflect and write; in this sense, it is as much a habit of mind as it is a specific and practiced task. Informal analysis is often documented in note-taking/note-making and journal entries, spaces where you think aloud about what is happening in your classroom: the responses of students, the results of data collection, informal observations and comments by students and other professionals in the classroom, critical incidents, how students demonstrated (or didn't demonstrate) their learning on assessments and/or any other stories of your practice. Informal ongoing data analysis may take the form of sticky notes on a clipboard, notes alongside a lesson plan or quick writes after a day of teaching and researching. Informal ongoing analysis is the daily practice of self-reflexivity, a staying aware of your surroundings. Informal ongoing analysis is supported by the whole of the research data collection: lesson plans, schedules, artifacts, and note-taking/note-making or other anecdotal notes, and the researcher's journal.

> Self-Study 5.1 *The Teacher-Researcher as Strategic Intervention* found at the end of this chapter on p. 145. How you define "good teaching" matters to ongoing data analysis. Check out this side road to learn more.

How it Works: Illustration of Informal Ongoing Analysis

Note-taking/note-making is a strategy for ongoing data analysis and is adaptable for many uses as a student teacher-action researcher. Picture a page divided into two columns. The left column is where raw data is recorded. The right column is for thinking about, asking questions of, and contextualizing the data. The two columns merge at the bottom of the page; this space is reserved for further analysis (theorizing, questioning, and wondering) (see Figure 5.5).

→ FIGURE 5.5: Note-Taking/Note-Making

Note-Taking/Note-Making	
Who: What: When: Why:	Time:
Summary	

A student teacher-action researcher may carry the note-taking/note-making form on her clipboard, jotting down notes in the left column while teaching. She may collect anecdotal notes on sticky notes and later attach these in the left column. Or, a teaching and learning session may be audio or video-recorded. Later, as the student teacher-action researcher listens or views the recording, she can complete the note-taking column. A mentor-teacher or supervisor or other observer might make observations or take anecdotal notes using this same form. In all scenarios, raw data is entered into the left column.

After the raw data is entered into the left column, the student teacher-action researcher takes time to think, question, contextualize, and theorize the data in the right column. This could be completed collaboratively, particularly if someone other than the teacher-researcher collected the data. It is most beneficial if the right column is completed near to the time of the original note-taking.

Figure 5.6 shows an excerpt of a note-taking/note-making event. The teacher-action researcher, Rylie, was collecting data from literature circles in his sixth grade classroom. The action research project was an inquiry into how literature discussions might be structured to support a sense of community among students while improving reading comprehension. Rylie audio-recorded the literature circle and after class while listening to the recording, completed the note-taking portion of the chart.

After recording the note-taking, Rylie made notes in the right column. His notes provide contexualization (where students were sitting, how Elena handles the directions) and raises questions about the data ("How can I encourage these two to invite the others into the conversation?") The bottom section of the note-taking/note-making form shows his thinking and how he is planning to use the data to make his next instructional move. Rylie did this thinking on the same day the literature circles were held. This kind of ongoing analysis keeps the data from piling up and becoming overwhelming. It also makes data useful in real time—a teacher can adapt instruction based upon the data immmediately instead of waiting for a week to pass and finding out perhaps too late, modifications may have benefitted student learning.

Rylie included in his research collection the lesson plan for the literature circles, which included the questions he wrote to prompt discussion for the literature circle. He also collected student self-assessments after the discussion. These served as artifacts. Finally, Rylie wrote

→ FIGURE 5.6: Excerpt of a Note-Taking/Note-Making Event

Note-Taking/Note-Making	
Who: 6th Grade Literature Circle: Elena, Richard, Moses, Catherine **What:** Discussion: Bridge to Terabithia **When:** February 14 **Why:** How are students interacting? Are the lit conversations supporting reading comprehension?	11-11:30 (Based upon audio-recording of group & sticky notes (antidotal notes) taken during class).
Students get into circle on the floor.	Students chose to sit in the back corner of the room on the rug. This seems like a good choice; they are somewhat isolated from the other lit discussions in the classroom.
C: I hated the way this story ended. Didn't you? How come they always make people die? (Talks with hands; leans into group.)	C. really gets into reading. She just finished PIG – maybe she is reading too many books about death? Maybe I should check on this.
R: I didn't like her anyways.	Not a great conversation starter but R. has certainly read & comprehended the book. He doesn't have to like Leslie.
C. That's rude. I like – liked Leslie a lot.	
R: I thought she was a snob – being from the city and everything. Hey, why did they cremate her? Do you think that is weird? (Directs talk to C. only.)	How can I encourage these two to invite the others into the conversation? This has happened before – they get off into their own world.
E: Aren't we supposed to start with the questions on this list? (She has been looking down until now.) (M. is just sitting and listening.) C: Mmm … I don't know. Is that what Ms. Ryan said? (C. directs this to R.)	Is this E.'s way of getting into the conversation or is she really concerned about following directions? She physically placed the questions in the middle of the group. Impossible to ignore her actions. How do my questions get in the way of the conversation? They are supposed to be a scaffold …are they?
E: We are supposed to answer these questions. R: Okay, so what are the questions?	Curious she insists on answering the questions but doesn't offer a response herself. I was watching at this moment and she drew herself up with authority here.

E: (reads) How did you feel when you first learned that Leslie had drowned?	This question seems ineffective hearing it here. It is what students were already talking about
C: I felt really sad. No, I think I was mad. Different than, like, when my Grandfather died because he was old and sick and that was really sad but it wasn't like just having someone like Leslie drown.	C. makes text to life connections here. She comprehends at a high level. Is this empathy? Understanding what it might be like to have a young person, the age of herself, die?
R: But Leslie isn't even real. I didn't like her.	Is this a way of dealing with grief? I wonder how to talk about this with kids?
C: Yeah, but it is like somebody real died.	
E: Do you want to go to the next question?	E. stops the conversation here, a really good conversation! Just realized, M. still isn't in the conversation.
(Note-taking continues…)	(Note-making continues…)

There seems to be a lot happening in this discussion. Catherine and Richard do not need my questions to discuss the book. The book draws out the conversation. This seems to reflect what I've been reading about social imagination and reading engagement. This is great for Richard and Catherine but Moses never says anything! How can Moses be included in the conversation? And what do I do about Elena with her insistence on following the directions? This is the second audio recording and basically this same pattern of interaction occurs in both. I am wondering about doing a conference with Richard and Catherine, asking them to be leaders in asking Moses and Elena what they think about the reading. I wonder if this might be an effective way to get the others engaged? I also think I should check in with Moses. I wonder if he is reading the book? Just checked – his reading log is blank for the week. Here's another thought: maybe this group doesn't need my questions any more? Maybe I should just let them discuss next time, ask Richard and Catherine to lead a discussion?

journal entries at the end of each week of his project. In the journal entries, he critical reflected *across* the collected data. He begins his journal with a kind of venting of emotion and detail:

I am finishing the first week of literature discussion in my 6th grade classroom. Some days, they are brilliant, like when Catherine and Richard were discussing Leslie's death or the group insisting that they needed on the Internet to see climbing routes up Everest better before continuing to read *The Climb*. Other days, they are a nightmare, like when Katy and Ian spent the entire time arguing or when Matt wouldn't stop pestering Jayme, who was in another literature circle. Oh, and then there was the day of the fire drill. That pretty much destroyed the lesson entirely.

Then, his journal entries transition to the work of problematizing the practice of literature discussions, raising questions, and challenging assumptions and theories:

It doesn't come as too big of a surprise that the students most enjoying the literature circles (and learning the most from them) are those that are most engaged. I read through all the student self-assessments and most kids are pretty honest . . . one question emerging is about engagement: what engages kids on a day-to-day basis? The story? The other kids? Why is it that some days kids argue and the next day they forget the pettiness of the day before and have an amazing conversation? Or maybe calling the disagreements "petty" is just my own adult perspective . . . .

Rylie continues to problematize and now strategize in his journal:

Here's the thing: I have different books for different readers, but the instructions for all the groups are the same. I talked this over with my mentor-teacher: we need to start differentiating the strategy of literature discussions according to the needs of each group . . . maybe this will help with "engagement"?

Finally, Rylie practices self-reflexivity:

I am so learning how my own assumptions about what kids will like and how they will behave are based upon my own learning experiences. I think I expect them to be like me.

The ongoing analysis Rylie completes allows him to refinine his teaching and research. In the next weeks of his action research, he implemented different kinds of literature circle structures based upon the needs of the students in each group as defined by data. This is what informal ongoing data analysis ought to do: *move the teaching and research forward*. It should provide direction for a "next step" in the action research and teaching processes.

Sometimes student teacher-action researchers collect lots of data; just collecting data isn't doing research. There has to be ongoing analysis, the thinking *about* and *with* data. It is overwhelming to face an entire data collection at the end of a three week period or end of a research project to "do" analysis. Ongoing analysis is, as we have said, *a habit of mind* and a *practice of teaching*. It is the daily "checking in," the using of data to inform our practice.

Cultural Context 5.1: *Practicing Deconstsruction and Trustworthiness During Ongoing Data Analysis* found at the end of this chapter on p. 151. In this example, see the significance of seeking mutliple perspectives as a check against bias during note-taking/note-making.

Part of the practice of researching and teaching includes organizing data so as an action researcher you can "see it" to analyze it. There are a variety of ways data is organized; the following section will guide you through the possibilities.

Organizing Data for Ongoing Analysis

As a teacher-researcher, you will have data from a variety of sources. Finding ways to organize this data to make sense from it is another critical step in the research process. One way is to create a chart for recording sample data in order to "see it" as more of a whole (see Table 5.1).

→ TABLE 5.1: Sample Data Collection Table

Planned Data Collection			Actual Data Collection		
Date	Data Collection	Purpose	Date	Data Collection	Purpose: Why changed
9/14	Lab reports	How are students processing information	9/14	As planned	
9/15	Individual journal writes	Does the writing reflect learning from yesterday?	9/15	Exit slips	Not enough time for journal writing; changed to exit slips
9/18	Lab team meetings (audio recorded)	Discussions of content: Are concepts being learned?	9/18–9/22	Lab team meetings	Re-organized to have one group per day
9/25	Lab team: scenario problems	Can students transfer information?	9/25	Quiz	No time for the longer scenarios

For example, Emerson planned a curriculum study of the literacy program at her kindergarten student teaching placement. She read deeply in the area of early childhood literacy. One piece by Brian Cambourne (1995) became her "anchor text" (see Chapter 2) because it seemed to provide a way for her not only to organize her data but to firmly place it within a literature framework which would better scaffold her analysis. She set up a chart with Cambourne's *Conditions for Literacy Learning* (1997) listed on the left-hand column and then she created subsequent columns labeled: "classroom observations," "classroom examples," "discontinuities," "questions," and "supporting literature" across the top of the chart (see Table 5.2). Emerson recorded samples of the data in the chart as a way to "see it as a whole."

Emerson's peers created similar charts. Neikla wanted to explore how young children engaged with, and how they could be supported in, story-making in different settings. She organized a chart according to the kinds of story-making where she anticipated collecting data (see Table 5.3) As she collected the data, she entered data samples into her chart. Yet another peer, Robert, conducted research on the use of podcasting to increase reading fluency. His chart is organized by the kind of data he collected (see Table 5.4).

Reading Across the Data

Creating charts such as these can be a way of organizing and analyzing qualitative data. The charts are filled with sample data; the remaining data, the teacher-researcher's journal and

→ TABLE 5.2: Emerson's Data Collection Chart

Sample Data Collection Chart Organizing Based Upon Work By Distant Colleagues	
Condition of learning	*Immersion* Being saturated in what is being learned.
Classroom observations	Map of the classroom (shows the literacy and the literacy opportunities around them). Morning meetings, interactions with classmates and teachers, words and writing displayed around the classroom. Constant "talk" about books, authors, and writing. "Literacy" throughout the day – for example reading strategies reinforced when reading in science.
Examples from the classroom	Here is an example of the morning message. *Good Children! Today is Monday April 6, 2009. We will prepare for student led conferences this week. Get ready to "wow" your family. This morning we will reflect on citizenship and stewardship. How have you grown? We will finish the day by celebrating Sarah's birthday! Sincerely, Ms. Edwards.* Additional questions are asked of children to prepare them for writer's workshop.
Additional research	Cambourne (2002) Rushton (2003) Ford (2002) Christie (1999)
Classroom examples that do or do not align with the distant colleagues	In one article, I read that children who are immersed in learning literature often self-correct their mistakes. I observed students self-correcting during word sort activities. For example, I was partner reading with a child today who after originally spelling "shave" as "save," returned to the word after continuing his reading and seeing the word again, and put the "h" correctly into the word without any direct instruction from me.
Questions	Am I looking in all the right corners to see "immersion"? What happens during play time?

→ TABLE 5.3: Neikla's Data Collection Chart

Sample Data Collection Chart – Organizing By Data Collection Event						
Date	**Child**	**Story-Making Event** *(location, context and initiation)*	**Genre**	**Actions** *What child says/does*	**Actions** *What other children say/do*	**Actions** *What adult says/does*
3/11	Josey and Roberto	Playground Children initiate story	Personal story	J: "We are digging a hole to China. Yep we are getting pretty close. I think I see China."	R: "If we dig over there we will end up in Egypt."	Teacher: "Where would you end up if you were to dig over there?" R: "I don't know. Let's go find out!"

→ TABLE 5.4: Robert's Data Collection Chart

Sample Data Collection Chart—Organizing by Data Type						
Student	**Post-Multidimensional Fluency Scale**	**Survey Responses**	**Self-Evaluation: Fluency Rubric Podcast**	**Post-Self-Evaluation Fluency Rubric Podcast**	**Post-Survey Podcast**	**Anecdotal Notes**
A	Not administered yet	Says she is a reader some of the time but only when reading by herself. Recognizes different kinds of readers in the class. Doesn't like to read aloud.	G, G, O, O, G, G	O, D, O NW, NW, O	Not completed yet	Chose a rhyming book for the podcast because, "This will sound good."

additional contextual data found in the research collection can be cross-referenced and used to support data in the charts. There is, however, a danger in organizing data in this way: data that makes it into the charts or "fits" the charts can become the only data that is considered. Furthermore, just "fitting" data into premade charts is not analyzing or critically thinking *about* and *with* the data. In all of the instances above, the student teacher-action researcher needs to complete the next step of thinking *across the data*, across the categories, asking questions, comparing data to the literature, theorizing about what the data does and does not "say."

Here is an illustration from an action research project being completed by Thomas and Macy (see Table 5.5). They were completing an ethnography prior to full-time student teaching, collecting and analyzing data about how a kindergarten classroom created community. They planned to use this data to create their own unit of instruction when they later began teaching

→ TABLE 5.5: Thomas and Macy's Ongoing Data Analysis

Morning Sign-in: How Does the Ritual Work?	Daily Letter: How Does the Ritual Work?
Engages parent and child. Fosters the parent/child relationship through learning. Teaches children their name has value (and therefore, that they have value). Writing one's name is an act of developing identity. Allows parent to be "teacher." Works as a transition between home and school: parent hands off the baton to teachers at school. Values parents as teachers, a member of school community. There is a scaffold (tracing) so that a child is going to be successful at the name writing.	Engages all children. Every child is working individually but they are also working together and with the teacher to complete the sentence on the SmartBoard. Children help each other; are encouraged to help each other. Children are learning academics even as they are building community. Each child gets to be the "leader" at some point. An incorrect answer is not seen as a bad thing—effort is rewarded, process is honored. Everyone interacts!
Theorizing	
This ritual builds community by including the parent as a valued member in the learning. It isn't like the teacher is the only one who "teaches." It builds a child's identity as a learner. It is engaging and interactive. Child can take risk in writing because there is a scaffold (tracing).	Children are not afraid of taking risks, of being "wrong." Incorrect answers are not considered "failure" so children are free to try. Everyone is valued for his or her effort. The SmartBoard acts as a scaffold. They are all engaged in learning.
Cross-Data Theorizing and Thinking	
In both rituals, there are adults who are mentors. Children are willing to take risks, it seems, because taking the risk is valued (effort is more important than a "right" answer), so doesn't that equate to more learning? It also makes for a safe environment. While the activities build community, they also build individual child identity. Both activities provide some kind of scaffold. Children are highly engaged; the activities are both interactive, involving the "whole" child.	
Tentative Synthesis	
A condition for building community could be the use of low stress, scaffolded interactive activities that foster collaboration, learning, and positive individual identity. Key conditions: deliberate planning, deliberate teacher talk, adult mentors. Continue to collect data on other rituals and traditions. Does this synthesis statement hold true? Can there be learning without community? How does community create the conditions for learning?	

in this same classroom. Thomas and Macy synthesized the literature they reviewed into several categories, identifying, among others, the importance of rituals and traditions in building classroom community. As part of their ongoing analysis, they routinely placed data from note-taking/note-making into the categories from the literature. Weekly, they paused to look across the data collected in each category. For example, they both observed two "rituals" of the kindergarten classroom: morning sign-in and the daily interactive letter. They read through the data they had collected from these two rituals and asked the question, "How does the ritual work?" They quickly made a list. Next, they engaged in "theorizing" why each of the rituals worked. In the next step, they engaged in "cross-data theorizing and thinking," or reading across the data. They asked, "What conditions are similar in both data sets?" Finally, they wrote a tentative synthesis statement based upon their data. Based upon their synthesis, they determined to collect more data on rituals and traditions to see how their tentative synthesis statement might evolve. In this way, the ongoing analysis directed the movement of future research.

> This is a good time to do Self-Study 5.2: *The Student Teacher-Researcher and Classroom Management*, found at the end of this chapter on p. 147. How will you handle the challenges of management and research?

Organizing Quantitative Data for Analysis

Many data sources are quantitative; examples include surveys with "closed" multiple choice or Likert-scale questions, checklists, test scores, and attendance records. One way to approach such data is to calculate numerical measures of central tendency such as mean, median, and mode. While these may be useful ways of analyzing some of your data, these simple statistics often leave out critical patterns and trends, and can even lead you to untrustworthy interpretations. On the other hand, more powerful statistics such as *t*-scores and correlation coefficients are only suited to experimental and **quasi-experimental designs**, large sample sizes, and control groups. With these limitations in mind, it may seem that quantitative data is not suitable for teacher research. We disagree. Any data type may be useful in your work; however, it is critical that the data is analyzed and interpreted in a way that aligns with the nature of teacher research.

To explore quantitative data often collected in the classroom, we suggest the data be plotted or represented graphically in order to observe possible patterns, trends, and relationships. This process is often creative and invokes a sense of exploration as the researcher becomes more familiar with structure of the numerical themselves. Graphical data representations can be created by hand, or by using data visualization software such as *InspireData* (www.inspiration.com) or *Fathom* (www.keycurriculum.com/products/fathom).

In the following, a student teacher-researcher explores her quantitative data, finding some clues about what is happening in her classroom. Notice that the researcher resists the temptation to let the quantitative data represent the final or absolute answer to her questions. Rather, she uses the quantitative data as a tool to generate hunches and possibilities that remain to be triangulated and verified by examining her other data sources.

An example: Stephanie, a high school physics student teacher, was interested in the way various labs and activities implemented in her classroom impacted certain concepts of force and motion held by students. Her first data set, collected over a two week period, consisted of lesson plans, observations of class sessions, student journals, and scores on quiz items taken from the "Force and Motion Concept Inventory" (FCI), a standardized test often used in physics education research. She gave different versions of the same quiz after each of five class periods. During a pause in her research, she compiled the data into a table as shown in Table 5.6.

→ TABLE 5.6: Compiling Quantitative Data

Student	FCI scores by lesson					
	1	2	3	4	5	Gain
1	0	1	2	3	5	+5
2	1	1	1	2	3	+2
3	3	3	3	4	3	0
4	1	2	3	4	5	+4
5	2	4	Absent	5	5	+3
6	4	2	3	4	4	+0
7	1	4	5	5	5	+4
8	0	2	3	4	5	+4
9	1	0	1	2	1	0
10	1	3	3	4	4	+3
11	2	2	2	3	5	+3
12	0	Absent	2	3	4	+4
Average	1.3	2.2	2.5	3.6	4.1	+2.7

Stephanie noted that the average FCI gain of +2.7 seems "pretty good," but is concerned about students who only gained 0 or 1 point. In order to explore this further, she created a visual plot showing all of the student scores after each lesson, and labeling the data points according to student number (see Figure 5.7).

→ FIGURE 5.7: Exploring Complex Data

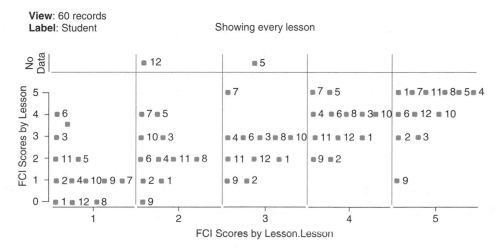

While examining her plot, Stephanie makes some observations she records in her researchers notebook as "interesting." For example, she notices that Students 6, 3, and 9 had FCI gains of 0, yet scored "all over the map" after Lesson 1 (4, 3 and 1 respectively). She also noticed that, at least visually, the scores seemed to increase more after lessons 2 and 3. In order to explore this possible pattern further she created a second plot by joining the lines between each student, showing the trend in scores for each student over time (Figure 5.8).

→ FIGURE 5.8: Visualizing Patterns in Complex Data

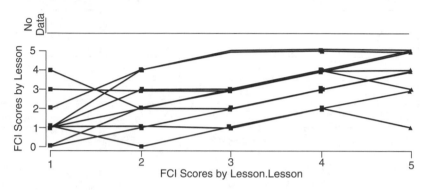

Stephanie observed that the upward trend in scores seems most clear after Lessons 2 and 3, and not so clear after Lessons 1 and 4. She writes in her notebook that perhaps Lessons 2 and 3 were somehow "better" than her other lessons. In order to follow up this hunch she returns to her lesson plan and observation data in order to explore what may have been unique about those lessons. She decides in her next data set to collect more careful data about what the students believed worked best for them about each lesson.

The illustrations of ongoing data analysis for both qualitative and quantitative kinds of data speak to the goal of moving the teaching and research forward based upon the data. We repeat this critical concept again to underscore its importance. It is not just about collecting and organizing data (although these are necessary prerequisites); it is thinking about and *with* the data, analyzing, deconstructing, contextualizing, synthesizing, and practicing self-reflexivity along the way, that determines the "next step" in the teaching/learning/researching process. This is what it means to have data inform teaching. Most action researchers find it helpful to schedule time for this kind of ongoing analysis, usually completing some form of note-making or journaling close to the time data is collected. Everyone's action research project is unique so the scheduling will need to fit the specific project and process—the point here is: *be deliberate in completing ongoing data analysis.*

Practicing Ongoing Data Analysis

Would you like to practice doing ongoing data analysis? Appendix H includes a complete data set with instructions for ongoing analysis. Take a break and give this a try.

Additional data sets for practicing ongoing data analysis can be found on the companion website.

Formal Ongoing Analysis and the Reflective Pause

Formal ongoing analysis uses a deliberate pause between data collection periods to analyze, synthesize, and deconstruct data. Rather than waiting until all data is collected, action researchers conduct ongoing formal analysis during the data collection process. Some reasons for doing this are:

- to modify the action research design; through ongoing analysis, action researchers may realize the data they are collecting doesn't adequately address the question, and in these cases, data collection methods need to be modified;

- to recheck and possibly modify the critical question; through ongoing analysis, action researchers may discover the question, itself, has changed;

- to change the course of practice; ongoing data analysis can show us as teachers that some of our practices, choices, or decisions are not the best for our students, and this may be the best reason to do ongoing analysis—to alter the course of our teaching to make our classrooms better places for learning.

Formal ongoing analysis ought to occur several times over a period of data collection time; this is the way the action research project makes transparent the process of becoming a teacher, central to creating trustworthiness in student teacher action research.

The Analytic Memo as a Formal Space for Reflective Pause

Informal ongoing analysis is continuous throughout the action research project. Along the way, the action researcher also takes time for a formal "**reflective pause**" to analyze the data more closely. The *analytic memo* is a tool used by researchers to scaffold the process of formal ongoing analysis. Analytic memos can take many forms, some of which will be introduced in this section. Sometimes we think of the analytic memo as a space—a space where the teacher-researcher can deliberately pause to process life in the classroom as it relates to teaching and researching. It is a space where questions, paradoxes, and contradictions can be entertained, where dialogue with a critical colleague or a mentor can occur, and where the elliptical nature of action research and teaching, of cycling back, but not necessarily to the same place, can happen (Phillips & Carr, 2007). In such a space, assumptions are challenged, self-reflexivity is practiced, and one's teaching practice emerges. It is also a space where strong connections are made between the cultural context of the classroom where the research is being conducted, advice from distant colleagues is considered and multiple perspectives are sought, not to "fix a problem," but to problematize and think deeply about systemic issues and larger questions of education. The analytic memo is a space to wander the terrain of reflexivity as a "corrective moment" (Lather, 1991, p. 13) in our teaching and researching.

Effective analytic memos share common elements regardless of the format they may follow. Effective analytic memos include:

- the use of raw data as a basis for the analysis;

- the expertise of distant colleagues;

- multiple perspectives represented by different voices (e.g. students, mentor-teachers, supervisors, critical colleagues);

- the pursuit of significant questions;

- a resistance to conclusions; an openness to discovery;

- a strong sense of connection between all of these elements.

These elements are further explored with illustrations in Table 5.7 (See also Appendix I). The goal of the analytic memo, like ongoing analysis, is to move the work forward. The difference is that the analytic memo is a more pronounced analysis, a pause in the action, that allows the action researcher time to analyze, deconstruct, contextualize, and synthesize more deliberately, thus serving to refine methods for data collection, the critical question, and the practice and processes of teaching and researching.

→ TABLE 5.7: Critical Elements of an Analytic Memo—Excerpts

Critical Element: The use of raw data as a basis for the analysis

Illustrative Passage: *During my first observation of packet work I focused on student D who is a recipient of Special Education and on an Individual Education Plan for reading, writing, and mathematics. The observation documents his repeated attempts to ask the teacher for help. She repeatedly walks up and reads the question for him while tracing it with her finger. He looks up and she walks away. After each question is read to D he looks down at his paper and looks at his neighbor's paper. He then asks the boy next to him for help but is quiet and hardly audible to the boy. He then begins twirling a pencil grip for six minutes until deciding to copy the answer of the child next to him. What I see in this data is that the packet is assessing his ability to read and write and not even touching his understanding of probability and related concepts. This type of assessment does not work for all children and certainly is not a sufficient form of assessment alone. I looked forward to assessing D through an alternative means where he was not limited by his ability to read and write. "Some students find it easier to share what they have learned through charts, role-plays, songs, models, pictures, and check lists rather than solely through paper and pencil means. All students may find multiple assessment options motivating and challenging"* (Campbell, Campbell, & Dickinson, 2004).

Critical Element: The expertise of distant colleagues

Illustrative Passage: *If we want children to flourish, says educator David Sobel (1996), we need to give them time to connect with nature and love the Earth before we ask them to save it. Sobel makes it quite clear that children needed the space and time to establish a connection with the outside world. His books became the basis for our literary study, and also a jumping off point to form our own questions. What we see in our data is what Sobel calls a "reconnecting period."* [The student teacher/researchers then continue to use raw data to illustrate this point.]

Critical Element: Multiple perspectives represented by different voices (e.g. students, mentor-teachers, supervisors, critical colleagues)

Illustrative Passage: I knew that one of the student groups were struggling during the small group activities, but I wasn't quite sure. My mentor-teacher conducted two observations. She noted that one of the students is not only off-task, but she appears to pull others in her group off-task as well. I went back to the self-evaluations from the group activity. Interesting enough, two students in this group noted that this particular student caused problems for the group. However, the student in question wrote, "nobody ever listens to my suggestions." I know the counselor has been working to develop curriculum in peer mediation. Maybe I need to visit her next.

Critical Element: The pursuit of significant questions

Illustrations: "What does it mean when high school kids say, 'It's boring?'"

"I am only seeing motivated/passionate and unmotivated/dispassionate. How else do I see this dilemma to get around it?"

"Is this the assignment, the assessment, or the nature of advance placement classes? What's the culture of such a class and how does the system support this structure?"

"Isn't it important that the reading curriculum include pictures and stories that the children in this urban school might relate to? Most of the stories and pictures reflect white middle class families with a mom, dad, 2 kids, and a dog (okay, a slight exaggeration), but doesn't this matter if this isn't 'you'?"

"I am beginning to wonder if homework even matters. Why do we have homework? For parents? Because this is just how we do school?"

Critical Element: A resistance to conclusions—openness to discovery

Illustrative Interaction:

Teacher-researcher: Other than a test or quiz, how can I measure whether the concepts are really "sticking"? I also found it interesting that such a large majority of students could answer nearly every single question correctly. Are the questions I am writing too easy? Are students simply cheating and looking to see what their classmates are answering before showing their own answer? Is my teaching so excellent that every kid gets it every time? I would say that the former are much more of a possibility than the latter.

Critical Colleague: Have you tried using an exit slip where students put everything away and write as much as they know about what you had just covered? You could allow them to write in story form, use diagrams, and explanation to see how well they were following you. I have been pleasantly surprised by this method.

Teacher-researcher: Hmmm . . . this is an interesting idea. I'll definitely try this out during my next data set! I'm going to be doing acids and bases, so this might be a great review tool especially since they are going to be getting so much information!

Critical Element: A strong sense of connection between all of these elements

Illustrative Passage: This data set does feel like more of a success to me then the last. It was unfair and inaccurate to grade the students on fluency when they had little practice and understand of the script. This time the students became more familiar with the play and how to read it. They practiced with their groups. They also did activities that helped them comprehend the plays. One example of this was that the students created dioramas of a specific scene in their play. They had to discuss the play with their partner. Then they had to decide on the best scene to make a display. The students used clay to represent what was happening in that scene and had to be able to explain it to others. They did not have this kind of understanding during the first recording of the play. They only had time to read through the script twice as a group and then we did the recording of the podcast. This time the students had more time to practice the play and discuss what was happening in each scene. They also had to go through the play and tell me where to put sound effects and why they chose that sound effect. This was another kind of assessment of their comprehension of the play. If they chose appropriate music to be in the background it demonstrated that they understood the mood or events of that scene. As Routman (2003) says, "The National Reading Panel defines fluency as 'the ability to read a text quickly, accurately, and with proper expression.' I find this definition inadequate, because fluency without comprehension is not reading; it is calling words" (p. 128). Comprehending the play was important for my students. One student told me, "We can record. We get it now." I believe that comprehension of the story made the students' reading fluency better. How are they to display expression and emotion in a play they do not understand? I feel that the activities we did to help their reading, understanding of scripts, and comprehension made a world of difference for their fluency.

Illustration of the "Reflective Pause" and the Process of Analytic Memo-ing

Leilani was student-teaching in a school that is 60% African American; 24% Hispanic; 10% white, with the remaining 6% "of multiple ethnicities," according to data provided by the school. The students in the first grade classroom where she was co-teaching with her mentor-teacher reflected this demographic profile. The critical question for her action research project had two parts; her project was both a curriculum analysis and ethnography: "How does the scripted reading curriculum represent race, socio-economic, and family structure, and how might this influence teaching and learning in my urban school?" During the first phase of her data collection, Leilani's goal was to "explore what and who the [scripted] curriculum represents."

In her first analytic memo, Leilani describes her data collection and ongoing analysis:

I began by creating a table that defines several possible racial groups, socio-economic statuses, and family structures that could be represented within the curriculum and its materials. I used this table to calculate and clearly illustrate who is being represented by the curriculum.

And then she notes, "I have quickly realized, however, the challenge in creating such a tool."

In this first analytic memo, Leilani deconstructs the very chart she created to analyze the scripted reading curriculum. She notes the challenges and dilemmas and seeks the perspectives of a critical colleague, a graduate professor, and returns to distant colleagues for advice.

Leilani continues her first memo by showing the table with the results of her analysis of the scripted reading program. She questions her own results, and her methodology. She writes, "Reviewing my data causes me to ask whether the reading curriculum portrays diverse peoples or whether my methods of data collection are inefficient or inappropriate. To explore this I will examine more of the curriculum and in a variety of ways. I believe this will add to the trustworthiness of my research."

By the end of this first refective pause, Leilani uses data and her analysis and deconstruction of that data, to plan for her second data collection: revising the data analysis chart; analyzing additional data to give the collection more depth; adding the use of a checklist for evaluating children's literature for bias; revisiting her earlier analysis; and interviewing teachers about the curriculum.

During her second data collection period, Leilani, using the redesigned chart for analyzing the scripted reading curriculum, writes, "I reviewed a month of the core scripted reading curriculum which is taught to every kindergarten student and the student population [of the school] is clearly underrepresented." She uses data to support her claim and returns to the literature to develop an argument for using curriculum that does reflect students and their lives. She also reports the data from two interviews with teachers. Of this data she writes (practicing self-reflexivity), "I have to be honest and acknowledge my surprise. I feel that both teachers support the curriculum more than I believed they would." Leilani raises questions in considering the interview data even as she acknowledges her position as a student teacher, "Perhaps, the curriculum is easy to use compared to other reading programs . . . yet . . .

[is the curriculum] worth the convenience?" Based upon her analysis of the curriculum and the interviews, Leilani was ready to move into the last period of her data collection. She revised her data collection strategies to focus on the second part of her revised question about the impact of the reading curriculum on the first graders in her school. To do this, she observed children during both the scripted reading program and during a teacher-choice reading time during breakfast. She also interviwed children. Her focus in her last data collection was to analyze how children engaged or interacted with the curriculum and with the more authentic books specifically chosen to reflect their ethnicities, family structures, and interests used during the breakfast shared reading.

In Leilani's final analytic memo, she continues using raw data, distant colleagues, and her critical colleagues and advisor to make sense of the data. She reports on all the data, raising more questions than conclusions. One child tells Leilani a story of a princess. When Leilani asks the child to describe the princess, the description fits Leilani. "I feel this comment [the description] was very kind and sweet, but it also reveals something signifcant: that her idea of what a princess is, is being white, well dressed, possibly even with blond hair and blue eyes." She places this data in the company of data collected by distant colleagues, thus making her tentative conclusions more trustworthy. She continues questioning and researching and returning to distant colleagues and her data throughout the memo. Leilani writes:

The scripted reading program may be helping children pass standardized exams, but the data I have collected and the readings I have done make me conclude that it also impacts student learning in ways that standardized tests simply do not consider. I need to spend more time with my data and the readings to further understand this. I do know this, that as a teacher within the era of scripted curricula, it will be my job to find value in my students, and to teach to their abilities, and to find ways to represent them in the curriculum, particularly when they are not represented within the curriculum.

If you would like to read Leilani's memos in their entirety, they can be found on the companion website. The excerpts as presented here are used to illustrate how the writing of an analytic memo serves as a reflective pause in ongoing analysis. This formal "stepping off the track" and getting close in to the data, the literature, and seeking multiple perspectives not only makes the action research more trustworthy, it is what moves and changes the research; it is what makes action research a living process; it is what informs teaching and learning.

Critical Dialogue and the Analytic Memo

Critical dialogue is an important piece of action research. Your analytic memo writing process may be organized to allow for dialogue that supports, raises questions, challenges assumptions and returns the teacher-researcher to the work of distant colleagues. One way of organizing the analytic memo process to support an active dialogue is as follows:

1. The teacher-researcher exchanges her analytic memo with her critical colleagues (we suggest using electronic formats for this activity).

2. The critical colleague reads and responds in the text of the memo.

3. The advisor may then read and respond in the text of the memo.

4. The teacher-researcher responds to questions, comments and suggestions by her critical colleague and the advisor. This may include the addition of data, perspectives or advice from distant colleagues.

Effective critical colleagues read carefully, with an eye for gaps or assumptions in the memo. A quality critical colleague response:

- raises significant questions, especially by asking "Why?";

- attempts to provide insight the teacher-researcher may not see;

- supports the teacher-researcher in developing and revising themes from the data;

- suggests alternative interpretation or may reference distant colleagues whose ideas may impact the analysis;

- makes suggestions about data collection methods and future data collection.

A critical colleague does not just say "good job" without specifically saying why something may reflect a good job. Vague comments do not move the work forward. For example, consider the following exchange between Loni and her critical colleague. Loni was a student teacher-researcher studying the effectiveness of an early childhood music program. In this excerpt, Loni is struggling to reconcile her vision of children and "teacher" with the realities of her classroom. Her data actually support children are engaged and learning key components about music, but Loni is having difficulties "seeing" this; she can only frame children as misbehaving:

Loni:	I have tried playing the music while the students are at their tables, at their table with their heads down, at their table while reading, on the carpet, and on the carpet with their eyes closed and the lights dimmed. In every situation the squirming and talking arises.
Critical Colleague:	Do you think it is critical for them to be quiet during this time? Could just being exposed to the music at this age be beneficial?
Advisor:	That's a great question. Maybe being still and silent at this age is over-rated? Your outcomes [as illustrated in the data] were very positive so this may be a good time to reassess your vision of what "good teaching" has to look like in this instance.

Loni continues in the memo describing "quiet children" as "children learning," tentatively concluding that she would not use the program again with primary children. Her critical colleague and professor challenge this notion:

Critical Colleague: But couldn't you still use music as an inspiration for art and storytelling?

Advisor: It seems as though you are taking an all-or-nothing approach where you are either using "the program" or you're not. Perhaps this would be a good time to really trust your instincts and review your data (excerpt adapted from Phillips & Carr, 2007).

This kind of dialogue supports and moves the research/teaching process along by challenging assumptions and providing perspectives to problematize around places where the teacher-researcher otherwise become trapped.

The Analytic Memo and Synthesis Statements

Yet another way to approach the reflective pause and the space of formal ongoing data analysis is the use of synthesis statements. Preparation for writing synthesis statements involves the same kind of reading *across* the data collection as in the approaches above. The action researcher charts, highlights, categorizes, and/or codes data to determine emerging themes in the data. From these themes, tentative synthesis statements or synthesis questions are written. Each tentative synthesis statement is followed by key data and references to distant colleagues that support the synthesis statement.

Study the following synthesis statements, each one written during three formal instances of ongoing data analysis. This is one set of synthesis statements taken over the course of three data collection cycles from Rylie's action research about literature circles (described above):

Analytic Memo #1 Synthesis Statement

There may be a "formula" or suggested way of organizing literature circles but my students don't necessarily fit this "formula." So many factors seem to figure into whether kids have a good or bad day. The weather, social interactions before they get to the literature circle, where they are reading in the chapter, if they like everyone in their group. How can I better focus students during the literature circle time?

Analytic Memo #2 Synthesis Statement

While all students have a choice of the book they will read for their literature circles, all groups have the same set of procedural directions for the literature circle. What does this assume about all groups? Could literature circles be more effective if directions were differentiated based upon each groups strengths and needs?

Analytic Memo #3 Synthesis Statement

Literature circle procedural directions and scaffolds appear to require differentiation for each unique group. What data is best used to differentiate these instructions? What has been the result of doing this for my students?

[📖] What do you notice about Rylie's synthesis statements? How would you describe them, or name the progression of thought they demonstrate? How do they represent ongoing data analysis?

Alternatives for Organizing and "Doing" Ongoing Analysis and the Analytic Memo

There are times when a teacher-researcher organizes the data he has collected and finds himself staring at the data, waiting, desiring, hoping that it will get up and dance. Instead, it remains fixed to the flat surface of the page. He knows "something is there," but that something seems illusive and remains out of sight beyond the corner. In these instances, an alternative approach to get the analytical juices flowing may be in order.

We have included alternative activities that may be useful to you. These can be found in Appendix J, "Strategies for Thinking About Data." We've borrowed and adapted two strategies from Elbow (1998) and another from Rico (2000) that we find helpful. We have also included a more structured and linear template with questions that may help guide your thinking. These may be used as 1) informal ongoing data analysis; 2) prewriting activities prior to writing an analytic memo; or 3) a formal analytic memo.

[📖] You will find examples of additional analytic memos in Appendix J, along with questions to guide your reading.

One more word on ongoing analysis: *All action research is, in one form or another, a self-study.* As you reflect on your data, *you* are learning, *you* are changing, *you* are getting better at what you do as a teacher, and *your own* assumptions are being challenged. As McNiff (1988) writes, "I join in the game. I win and I lose; I live and I learn" (p. 52). You are a participant in this action research process; you are developing your own "living theory" (Whitehead, 1993). Discovering this living theory is the deliberate act of pausing to think through what we know, how we know it, and alternative ways to frame our knowing. This is a way of practicing teaching far beyond the structure and requirement of writing an analytic memo. Learn now to perfect this practice.

Resisting Conclusions: Going with the Questions, the Dilemmas, and the Conflict

Be patient towards all that is unsolved in your heart and try to love the questions themselves like locked rooms and like books that are written in a very foreign tongue. Do not now seek the answers, which cannot be given to you because you could not live them. And the point is, live everything, live the questions now.

—Rainer Maria Rilke (1934), *Letters to a Young Poet*

The power of asking questions is that questions keep things moving. Conclusive statements shut down the conversation and therefore the possibilities. Consider these statements:

- The student is lazy and unmotivated.
- The students are not developmentally ready.

- The material is too difficult.

- The curriculum doesn't allow for that.

- This teaching strategy just doesn't work with my kids.

Each statement may hold some truth and help represent a dilemma. But if statements like this are allowed to stand alone, without debate, or turned into a question, they close down the possibilities of exploring potentially erroneous assumptions, finding solutions, or seeking other voices or perceptions.

During ongoing analysis, resist making conclusive statements. Instead, pose questions that will further your exploration of your critical question. Freewrite and let the questions flow; for example:

I want to call this student lazy and unmotivated. After all, this was a great lesson in my opinion. Am I personally offended because he/she didn't think it was a great lesson? Is it just easy to say a student is lazy and unmotivated? Why would a student be lazy and unmotivated? What do I mean about these terms? What about this lesson (content and strategy) appeals more to me than to the student? Am I trying to be the entertainer of the year or am I trying to teach? What's the difference? Is there a real learning problem here or was it just a bad day?

The same principle can be applied to dilemmas and conflicts. For example, a student may seem excited about the assignment and be very involved in class, but never turn in his homework. Don't dismiss this; *study it*; believe there is something to be learned from this situation.

Furthermore, conflicts often represent painful, if not rich, places of learning. Classroom management issues often represent such places of conflict. Again, don't ignore these instances. Ask hard questions like:

- Why does this situation make me feel like I will never be a teacher?

- Why don't I like this student? As the teacher, I thought I was supposed to like, even love each student? What's wrong with me?

- Why do I feel so hopeless?

- Why do I need control?

Kessler (2000) offers a process of creativity that may be helpful for action researchers in engaging with questions, dilemmas, and conflicts. Stages, as she warns, are rarely as sequential as they appear on paper. These steps in Figure 5.9, however, may be useful in ongoing analysis and creatively thinking out of a teaching dilemma.

→ FIGURE 5.9: Kessler's Process of Creativity

Preparation:

Focus on the problem. Apply rational and linear approaches to gather all the information possible. Work through your data. Read it again and again. Write in your journal. Read it again and again.

Incubation:

Let go of the problem. "Sleep on it." Allow the brain to consider other possibilities. Talk about the problem with others.

Illumination or Inspiration:

This is the "break through," or the "Aha" moment. This is the Idea. The idea is created. It is the next step you will plan to take towards resolving or illuminating the dilemma, question, or conflict in a different light.

Verification:

Refine the inspiration or the idea. Use the advice from the literature, your mentor-teacher, critical colleagues, and instructor. Return to preparation. Cycle back on the plan and re-create this. See where this leads you in your teaching practice now.

Self-Study 5.3: *Scaffolding the Learning*, found at the end of this chapter on p. 148. This is a good time to delve deeper into the relationship of classroom management and student teacher action research.

Getting Stuck/Getting Out: Seeking Other Voices

When you get stuck in the action research process, seek other voices—those of critical colleagues, mentor-teachers, students, parents, professors, and the literature. After seeking other voices, patterns of advice will most likely emerge. Begin creating a plan of action (adjusting the research design, teaching strategies, assessment/data collection) based upon the advice of these voices.

Changing Courses: Using Ongoing Analysis to Redirect and/or Refine the Action Research Study

Ongoing data analysis often requires that the teacher-researcher modify or outright change the way data are being collected or even rewrite the critical question. Table 5.8 describes common situations our students encounter and the kinds of response we provide them.

A Story of Change: No Science Here

Kelly believes in science education. She found it disturbing to read how many girls lose interest in science in middle school, primarily due to socialization that "science isn't girl stuff." In response to these concerns, she designed an action research project geared primarily for fifth grade girls at her school. Her idea was to instill such a love of science through project- and inquiry-based strategies that the girls would be excited about continuing in science through middle school. While the units would be taught to both boys and girls, Kelly had read the literature about how to make sure girls were more completely included in science instruction. She even planned a "field trip" to the sixth grade science classrooms in the middle school so the girls, especially, would feel like science leaders when they transitioned to the middle school.

→ TABLE 5.8: Changing Courses

This data set doesn't really answer my critical question!	Evaluate the data you have. What is missing? Change your design to collect the data that will help you better understand your question.
This data is good but in collecting it, I've discovered some completely different information about my classroom. My critical question doesn't really seem to fit any more.	Based upon the data, what do you think your questions should be? Revise your critical question. It is fluid—like your study. Document in your journal the changes you make and the critical incidents that have precipitated the changes.
I am drowning in data! I can't keep up analyzing it all!	Consider collecting data on a smaller group of students. For example, choose five students who are representative of the entire class. Collect data on those students only.
The teaching strategy I am using as the basis of my action research doesn't appear to be working all! What do I do?	Re-think assumptions: What are you assuming about yourself, your students, the context of this classroom? Check with critical others: Your mentor-teacher, your colleague and your instructor about constructing a scaffold for learning. Change strategies if you believe you can better serve students in a different way, but figure out first how the data informs the way you do change the teaching strategy.
I began with these assumptions about teaching and learning in my classroom, but now that I've analyzed this first data set, I see where I had it wrong. Now what?	Great! This is all part of the action research process. Journal about the changes then check with your mentor-teacher, critical colleague, instructor and make the changes you need to in the design and/or the critical question.

The first science unit went well. Assessments demonstrated that all students had learned the intended content and concepts, and the attitude assessments also demonstrated that the girls had responded positively to "being scientists." But after that, things changed: Kelly wasn't teaching science anymore. She asked her mentor-teacher about the delayed science units and at first the mentor-teacher assured her that she would get to teach the additional planned science units. But the teaching time never came. Kelly finally scheduled an appointment with her mentor-teacher to discuss the problem. Why wasn't science being included in the curriculum? Would she be able to teach the planned science curriculum, which was also her action research project?

The mentor-teacher explained the problem: the district was no longer focusing on science in the fifth grade. Science was not on the list of state-mandated exams for fifth graders. Therefore, the district had decided that science should be set aside to allow more time to get students ready for other subject exams. The mentor-teacher didn't like this decision and initially thought she would allow Kelly the time to teach the science units, but this was becoming impossible. There would be no more science in fifth grade, unless there was time after the exams were taken late in the spring. By that time, Kelly would no longer be a student teacher in the classroom.

Kelly was aghast at the decision to drop science. She was also seemingly without an action research project. After regrouping and talking more with her mentor-teacher and her professor, she redirected her inquiry, asking how state-mandated exams influenced curriculum and teaching practices in her classroom. The result of her project impacted decisions at her school; it also provided Kelly with lessons about the political landscape of teaching.

Most of the time, action research projects don't change this dramatically, but circumstances do require this kind of flexibility and probing of causes. Use ongoing analysis and the use of questions to continue to refine and redirect your own project as needed.

Words of Encouragement

Most of our students struggle with being confident about their ongoing analysis. Doubt can haunt the process. You will likely have moments of feeling like a novice, not an expert; a teacher, not a teacher-researcher; and most of all biased, not objective. Learn to say "no" to these self-criticisms.

Remember this wisdom from Gardner (1993):

[M]ost researchers remain open to the possibility of surprises or of new discoveries: after all, if one knew exactly what one expected to find, then the journey would hardly be worth the undertaking . . . . A degree of asynchrony is delectable. (p. 384)

A Final Word: The Importance of Getting the Data

Student-teaching is overwhelming: there are units to plan, lessons to adjust, assessments to be evaluated. There are so many expectations, so many "performances," and so many criteria to be demonstrated. So we circle back again to this critical piece of advice: *There is no research without data* and ongoing data analysis.

You must be deliberate in planning and collecting data. You must be deliberate about ongoing data analysis. You must practice direct communication with your mentor-teacher and your advisor. Take this on as a challenge of learning to live action research, as a way of practicing teaching! Then, step back – and see who you are *becoming* as a teacher.

Chapter 5: Content Questions

1. How does ongoing data analysis work? Describe this in your own words.
2. What are ways a student teacher-action researcher might organize and plan for ongoing data analysis?
3. How do data cycles, informal and formal reflective pauses, and analytic memos support trustworthy action research? How might they lead to meaningful results?

Chapter 5: Process Questions

1. What challenges of teaching, gathering data, and conducting ongoing research to you think will be most challenging for you? How do you see yourself meeting these challenges?
2. How do you think learning to teach and learning to do research simultaneously might complement one another?
3. How do you rate yourself at resisting conclusions, going with questions, dilemmas and conflicts? When is this most difficult for you and how might this influence the process of learning to teach and learning to do action research?

Self-Study 5.1: The Teacher-Researcher as Strategic Intervention

In the action research design template included in Chapter 4, you are asked to describe "How the Problem, Dilemma, and/or Issue Will Be Addressed." The "strategic interventions" you propose may appear to be merely a list of *actions* that any teacher-researcher could carry out in your setting and arrive at the same results; in this case, the appearances obscure an important truth about teacher action research: The teacher-researcher, you, *are* one of the "strategic interventions" you are trying. You don't simply perform actions, your particpation as a teacher *is* an action. You are a strategy; you are the intervention!

To consider the teacher-researcher as "intervention" returns us to earlier questions: "What is good teaching?" and "What does a good teacher look like?" The responses to such questions are many and are rooted in cultural and historical settings, promoted by those in authority, and informed by cultural values. The work of Haberman (1991) suggests that what often defines good teaching is more tradition or "ritualistic acts . . . conducted for their intrinsic value rather than to foster learning" (p. 292). Haberman notes that "good teaching" can be identified more by observing students, rather then their teachers.

Consider Haberman's "good teaching" qualities in Table 5.9. Compare and contrast your current teaching situation with his list by giving specific examples.

→ TABLE 5.9: Haberman's (1991) Good Teaching Traits

Martin Haberman (1991) "Good Teaching"	My School Site and "Good Teaching"
Whenever students are involved with issues they regard as vital concerns, good teaching is going on.	
Whenever students are involved with explanations of human differences, good teaching is going on.	
Whenever students are being helped to see major concepts, big ideas, and general principles and are not merely engaged in pursuit of isolated facts, good teaching is going on.	
Whenever students are involved in planning what they will be doing, it is likely that good teaching is going on.	
Whenever students are involved with applying ideals such as fairness, equity, or justice to their world, it is likely that good teaching is going on.	
Whenever students are actively involved, it is likely that good teaching is going on.	
Whenever students are directly involved in a real-life experience, it is likely that good teaching is going on.	
Whenever students are actively involved in heterogeneous groups, it is likely that good teaching is going on.	
Whenever students are asked to think about an idea in a way that questions common sense or widely accepted assumptions, that relates new ideas to ones learned previously, or that applies an idea to the problems of living, then there is a chance that good teaching is going on.	
Whenever teachers involve students with technology information access, good teaching is going on.	
Whenever students are involved in reflecting on their own lives and how they have come to believe and feel as they do, good teaching in going on.	

continues →

Does your own student teaching or the teaching you are observing qualify as good teaching according to Haberman? Could you list many examples of each characteristic? What are some of the reasons behind your answers? (Think about paradigms, assumptions, and structures of schooling.) Do you find yourself agreeing or disagreeing with this list? How does your reaction relate to your own paradigm for defining "good teaching"?

Haberman also argues that "good teaching" is more likely to occur in affluent schools where higher-order thinking skills are more likely to be encouraged. The pedagogy of poverty involves a different list of traits. This list is primarily associated with management and control: giving information, directions, and tests; assigning and reviewing seatwork and homework assignments; and settling conflicts within the classroom. Does this list better describe your current teaching or the teaching you are observing? Why do you think this is true? What drives these pedagogical decisions?

Self-Study 5.2: The Student Teacher-Researcher and Classroom Management

The student teachers we work with "get stuck" most often in the action research process because of "classroom management issues." At times, we receive this kind of e-mail from students:

I am going to have to change my action research project. As you know, I was going to use "literature circles" as my strategic intervention. I was hoping to see how literature circles might support reading comprehension, but after today, I know this isn't going to work. The students were terrible. Not one group really talked about the novels they are reading. Chaos ruled. My teacher says that this group just can't handle this kind of unstructured learning. I am going to have to do something different. —Leona

Our students, for the most part, agree with Haberman's (1991) list of "good teaching" characteristics. They see themselves as teachers who are student-centered. They resist notions of "teaching straight from the text." They move into the classroom with a vision of students actively "owning" and guiding the learning; they anxiously wait the day they can "take over" and implement authentic assessments, group work, and relate content to students' interests and lives. When the day finally comes, their experience may resemble Leona's experience. So what happened? Is it true that some students "just can handle" student-directed learning? Are some students "not ready"? Do some students need a teacher to tell them what to do in order to stay on-task?

Self-Study 5.3: Scaffolding the Learning

You may have decided that the "best practices" taught in your teacher-education program are not "real world" teaching strategies. After a hard day of teaching you may find yourself saying something like, "These kids just can't work with manipulatives, be trusted with a science lab, or be allowed to work with anything that has the potential to bounce." These frustrations, all of which and more we have heard from our students (and experience ourselves) stem from the dissonance between our beliefs about teaching and what happens in our practice. Whitehead (1989) calls this experiencing *living contradiction*; such contradictions encourage us to ask revised questions, seek additional voices, and rethink our teaching.

When this happens, revisit your personal paradigm and consider how you define words like *authority* and *respect*. Where do your definitions come from? Who taught you these meanings? Consider again how both your own paradigms of the "good teacher" and the "good student" and the context of your student teaching affect your teaching. Finally, think about the differences between teacher-directed learning and student-centered learning. How are these differences experienced by students?

Most often, we find student teachers enthusiastically embrace student-centered teaching; for this we are thankful. However, if students in their classes are more accustomed to a "pedagogy of poverty" (or some other pedagogy that isn't student-centered) then an abrupt change to student-centered learning can be uncomfortable. When expectations for what is "normal" in a classroom are violated, even if for reasons of higher-order thinking, fairness, and/or compassion, discomfort, resistance, and even open rebellion may be the result. Therefore, successful change requires care, thought, patience, and intentional support. In short, *change requires a scaffold*.

Consider this example. Suppose students have learned that being successful at school means completing the worksheet in a timely manner and getting the right answers. When confronted with an inquiry-based lesson in which they are asked to risk posing wrong answers, what will be the result? The lesson may not "work." Or if students are used to having all lab material supplied for them, they may be baffled that you ask them to think of a way to find the supplies on their own to conduct an experiment. If they are used to being given a study guide to memorize in review for the test, they may be confused about why you are asking them to construct their own study guide; they may see this as a waste of time, or even worse, they may think you are trying to trick them. If students have learned that "doing school" is an individual pursuit, a competition, with the best person landing the A grade, then they may not be enthusiastic about a cooperative learning assignment where they are paired with students they do not respect.

Picture a scaffold with ascending steps, as in Figure 5.10. If you are asking students to leap from teacher-directed learning to student-centered learning without the intermediate steps, you may be inviting a teaching-learning crash, as students fail in making the jump. This doesn't mean that the strategy you've tried "doesn't work" with a certain group of students; it does mean that you may need to intervene as the teacher and provide scaffolding for students, facilitating their learning and their thinking to higher cognitive and interpersonal levels. This may also mean providing scaffolding for their attitudes of respect for one another, for diverse opinion, and multiple viewpoints around conflict.

continues ➜

Don't reject a certain teaching strategy, and possibly your action research project, if you find yourself struggling with these kinds of issues. Rather, consult with your mentor-teacher, university advisor, critical colleagues and research literature. What steps do you need to take to scaffold the learning for your students? How do you need to reframe the project

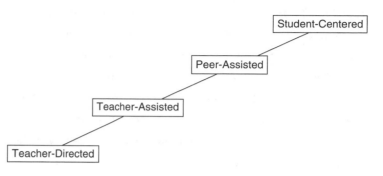

→ FIGURE 5.10: Scaffold for Student-Centered Learning

to move both students and yourself towards the kind of student-centered learning you desire? What structural changes do you need to make in the classroom? What teaching skills do you need to modify, improve, and/or reframe in order to make this happen? What are your students really telling you? Listen to context; examine your own assumptions.

Work with Table 5.10 to begin your analysis of what might need to occur in your classroom if you are experiencing this kind of challenge. Be specific with your examples.

→ TABLE 5.10: Problem Solving—Constructing a Scaffold

List How the Problem Looks, Sounds, and Feels	List How You Think the Classroom Should Look, Sound, and Feel.	Brainstorm Why You Think this Gap Exists (and what you are basing this upon)	List Steps You can Implement and How You Will Evaluate Any Success

Collect data on the outcome of your plan; conduct analysis. Record your own thoughts in your researcher's notebook. Be deliberate and tenacious in your strategic intervention. Is this starting to sound familiar? Yes, this is the action research process! This kind of action/self-study research is the kind of

continues →

research where action and evaluation occurs simultaneously with students and colleagues within context (Hamilton, 2005); therefore, the research invites and embraces change. You may find that your critical question is modified some to include, "How can I intervene and build scaffolding for student learning when using literature circles to increase reading comprehension?"

This book is all about process, not arrival. Engage in the *process* of critical analysis. Don't be "stuck" by either/or teaching based upon hard days of teaching (trust us—we all have them). Rather, use what feels like "failure" to rethink teaching and learning. Listen hard to your students; face what you want to ignore. (Maybe your own paradigm needs a corrective widening!) Be creative in coming at "the problem" from more than one way. Allow learning to *happen*.

Heidegger (1972) wrote,

Teaching is more difficult than learning because what teaching calls for is this: to let learn. The real teacher, in fact, lets nothing else be learned than—learning. . . . The teacher is ahead of his apprentices in this alone, that he has still far more to learn than they—he has to learn to let them learn. (p. 15)

And to this, Greene (2001) adds, "the teacher has to learn what it is to learn to let others learn" (p. 83). And so, we embrace contradictions, dilemmas, and challenges to do the work of such learning.

Cultural Context 5.1: Practicing Deconstruction and Trustworthiness During Ongoing Data Analysis

The student teacher-action researcher in this scenario is conducting an integrated action research project. He is studying the effects of cooperative groups on science learning.

The mentor-teacher observed one group of eighth grade male students conducting an experiment placing different model cars on a ramp. The ramp has seven pieces of different size grit sandpaper. Students test the cars on each of the different sandpapers to see how the surface conditions of the ramp (the different sandpaper grit sizes) affect the time it takes for the model car to travel the distance of the ramp. The learning goal is to teach students about friction, linear force, resistive force, static friction, kinetic friction, traction, torque, and rolling motion.

The student teacher-action researcher set up the ramp in one part of the room and collaborative teams of students rotated through this station while the rest of the students worked at other "stations" on other tasks in the room. While the mentor-teacher did the note-taking, the student teacher-action researcher completed the note-making and the ongoing analysis summary. Read through the note-taking/note-making in Table 5.11.

Deconstruct the student teacher-action researcher's comments and analysis:

- What categories of either/or analysis are made? How can these either/or conclusions be reconstructed using a different lens?
- What values and beliefs do these assumptions reflect?
- If the student teacher practices trustworthiness, how might this provide other avenues of action in his teaching then the path he is now pursuing?

Act as the student teacher's critical colleague. What questions might you ask? Do you see other possibilities in the data?

As a student teacher, it is challenging to "see" layers of analysis when there is so much emphasis placed on classroom management. It is easy to understand why the student teacher might first frame this in terms of managing K's behavior. But in focusing on behavior alone, the student teacher-action researcher misses that K is also learning, or may even even already have mastery of the science material. K is the student using the academic language of science, and is the student making the accurate prediction about which surface will produce the fastest running car.

This incident highlights the need to seek multiple perspectives as a student teacher-researcher during ongoing analysis. Imagine this student teacher-researcher continuing with his current thinking, focusing on K's behavior alone. What will his next course of action be? How will this course of action influence his thinking about cooperative learning and science? How might this, in turn, influence his "conclusions" about cooperative learning and science?

continues →

→ **TABLE 5.11: Note-Taking/Note-Making Example**

Eighth Grade Science Friction and Motion Experiment Focus on Collaborative Team	
J: Are we ready?	
K: Ready, ready, ready! (grabs car from J)	*K is a problem right from the beginning*
M: No, look, the sandpaper has a wrinkle.	*This is observant of M.*
K: (pushes M out of the way, car in hand—rolls over wrinkle). This will slow it down . . .	*K gets in the way again—I thought by putting him in a group with J & M we might cooperate better.*
M: Stop it, K. (smoothes out wrinkle)	
K still has car and is running it into J who is laughing.	*Still misbehaving here—*
J: Got it M?	
M: Yeah—roll it	
J: Give me the car K	*J & M want to do the experiment correctly but K keeps getting in the way.*
K: I wanna do it	
J: Your gonna screw it up	
K: It's gonna be fastest this time (as he bumps J out of the way; puts car on track about ¾ way up the ramp and lets it roll)	*I don't know what to do with K!*
M: We gotta start it at the top to make it right	*M tries to correct the situation. Is it too much to ask M to be in a group with K? Is it right for M to give up his learning in this way? Am I asking him to be "teacher"?*
K: Why? We already know it is gonna be faster on this one—less friction, get it? (waves car around head)	
J: Grabs car. Gotta do it right or it screws up the results.	*Now, J has to be teacher, correcting K's behavior.*
M: Grabs car. Okay—holds timer in one hand and car in other—here we go!	*Finally—I am surprised they even finished the entire experiment at this rate.*
J: Holds K who looks like he might grab the car off the ramp otherwise (all boys are laughing)	*Is K a bad influence on M & J?*
M: 3.6!	
K: I told you it would be fastest—punches (not hard) J	
J: You don't know that. We haven't done them all yet.	*Again—J is setting them all back on track.*
K: Yeah—I know—grabs car again and starts zooming it up M's back—it is "friction" and "linear force" (mimicking teacher's voice and emphasizing with a pretend pencil, as the teacher does)	*Oh, great. Now a comedian.*

CHAPTER 6
FINAL DATA INTERPRETATION

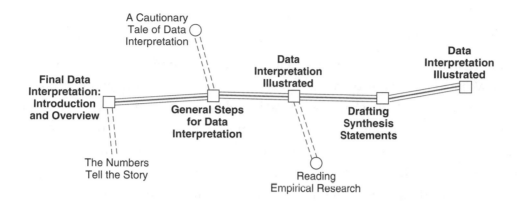

You have gathered the data for your action research project and completed ongoing data analysis: what's next? The "what's next" is the process of moving your research into different spaces that generate meaningful results. We refer to this process as *final data interpretation*. At this point in the process, the teacher-researcher has crate(s), file box(es), computer files and/or notebook(s) as organized data. Ongoing data analysis has guided the journey of action research, and now it is time to synthesize across the data and complete final data interpretation. Position yourself to be open to questions that might move you outside of your comfort zone; move in tight with your distant colleagues; seek multiple perspectives; enjoy the process!

Final Data Interpretation: Introduction and Overview

What does it mean to "interpret"?

[📓] In your notebook, take a minute to write a definition of the word *interpret*. Include several examples of the different kinds of interpretation you do in order to make sense of your own life. For example, how do you interpret a "great weekend," a "good deal," or a poem? How does the way you form interpretations reflect on your own values and personal context?

Consider this quote: "Interpretation is an art—it is knowledge treated imaginatively" (Tilden, 1957, pp. 26–27). Tilden wrote principles of interpretation to be used by curators of museums to encourage visitors to engage with museum artifacts. He wanted visitors to not simply view museum displays, but to interpret them interactively.

[📓] How might this same principle apply to the work of interpreting data generated during teaching and learning? Who is the "visitor" to your action research data? What represents the "exhibits"?

We think of data interpretation in action research as a way of making and creating understanding out of the chaos of our teaching practice. We all automatically do interpretation at different levels in our lives as teachers. We make assumptions, judgments, and inferences based upon our students' behavior, dress, and language use. We constantly make informal and ongoing interpretations to create order of our lived experiences. Such interpretations may be useful and dangerous since we often take action or make judgments based upon quick interpretations.

Barriers to Interpretation

In action research, interpretation is a deliberate action, requiring preparation and formal process. We have a collection of data and we deliberately set about interpreting this data using processes of analysis (looking at parts of data), synthesis (reading across the data), deconstruction (checking assumptions and thinking outside our habits of knowing), and contextualization (critically considering the importance of context). (These terms were introduced at the beginning of Chapter 5, *Ongoing Data Analysis*, as shared principles of ongoing data analysis and final data interpretation. If you need a review, take a moment to reread now.) The data, used with purpose and layered with meaning, becomes evidence when directed toward our question (Lincoln, 2002). The problem is that the process of interpretation often feels more messy than deliberate.

Furthermore, we often wonder what right or authority we have to make such interpretations. This question can haunt even the most experienced researcher. A lesson from interpretive methodology may allow us to reframe our ideas around interpretation. Tilden's (1957) principles, written for guiding educators at museums, are also particularly appropriate to interpreting action research data. Consider these guidelines from Tilden:

- Any interpretation that does not somehow relate to what is being displayed or described to something within the personality or experience of the visitor will be sterile.

- Information, as such, is not interpretation. Interpretation is revelation based upon information. But they are entirely different things. However, all interpretation includes information.

- The chief aim of interpretation is not instruction, but provocation.

Imagine yourself at a museum. There are scores of displays—but only a few will be meaningful to you. Most likely, the displays that you will label as your "favorites" will be those that resonate with you personally. The same is true in action research data interpretation: the data that will be most meaningful to you will most likely represent a conflict, an uncomfortable space of being or learning, or an unnerving question that relates to where you are in the process of becoming a teacher. This data may move you by affirmation, or spur you to transformation. If you find your data seems "sterile" or flat then you may want to revisit your question, your method collections, or your motivation for conducting the project. Data has the power to change practice.

In other words, the interpretations you make based on your data are personal, rooted in your individual context and self. This realization may free you from the notion that you aren't qualified to make judgments. Recall that, *"Interpretation is revelation based upon information."* *Revelation* is a word shrouded with religious fervor, meaning "an enlightening or astonishing disclosure" (*Merriam-Webster Online Dictionary*, 2005). Most of all, a revelation is personal. Your action research interpretation may not quite reach the level of "astonishing," but it should be meaningful and significant to you (Eisner, 1998). It ought to illustrate you becoming a teacher.

Interpret to Provoke, Not Instruct

Tilden suggests that "[t]he chief aim of interpretation is not instruction, but provocation." We like this concept integrated into action research interpretation particularly because it denies "conclusions" or grand statements of "truth." Partial understanding is recognized here; as action researchers we cannot ever know entirely a problem or a solution (Haraway, 1996; Kincheloe, 2003). Data interpretation should incite more questions, more hunches, more places for teacher-researchers to travel next in their professional journey. To *provoke* is to "arouse to a feeling or action" (*Merriam-Webster Online Dictionary*, 2005). Data interpretation should move teacher-researchers to *action*—interpretation simulates change as we reimagine and then restructure our practice based upon data interpretation (Bloom, 2002; Kincheloe, 2003).

The deliberate and formal act of data interpretation in action research mirrors the way effective teachers use interpretation of assessment in daily practice. Teachers who allow assessment data (not just hunches), multiple perspectives, distant colleagues, and critical self-reflexivity to drive their instructional practice, are those teachers who create spaces for children and adolescents in all contexts, from all contexts, with all kinds of diverse needs, to be successful in learning. Data interpretation is at the heart of adapting instruction for all learners.

Doubting Voices of Data Interpretation

As preservice teachers, there will be a tendency for you to lack confidence in your interpretations. We all surround ourselves with other voices to create trustworthiness in our interpretations and we acknowledge the role of context in the act of interpreting data. Most likely, you will need to refute (more than once!) the "doubting" voice that says, "You don't know enough."

→ FIGURE 6.1: Doubting Voices of Data Interpretation

"Doubting" Voices of Data Interpretation

Learn to say NO and keep thinking/writing!

"You haven't proved anything! Your research is a SHAM!"
"Yeah, where are the numbers? This is just what you think!"

Retort:
My research has never been about "proving" anything right, good, wrong, bad, or otherwise. My research is about my process of becoming a teacher.

"There isn't anything here at all. There is nothing interesting. This is really dumb. This isn't very profound. You should start over." "ppsssst! That's because you are not smart enough"

Retort:
My experience, my learning, is valuable, rich, and worth telling. There is nothing more profound then the *act* of learning to teach. I will not let this voice de-value these last intense months of my living and learning.

"You are not doing this RIGHT. You are going to FAIL."

Retort from Anne Lamott, Author & Writing Instructor (1994):
"Perfectionism is the voice of the oppressor, the enemy of the people. It will keep you cramped and insane your whole life . . . perfectionism will ruin your writing, blocking inventiveness and playfulness and life force . . . Perfectionism . . . will only drive you mad (p. 28–31)."
This isn't about doing it "right." It is about having the courage to explore my own becoming.

"Keep it secret, keep is low: what if 'they' find out you out?"

Retort:
All self-reflection requires vulnerability: the fear of "being found out" is embedded in the belief that I am not good enough. I am.

A Final Retort from T.H White (1958), The Once and Future King:
Learn why the world wags and what wags it. That is the only thing which the mind can never exhaust, never alienate, never be tortured by, never fear or distrust, and never dream of regretting. Learning is the thing for you (p. 186).

Data interpretation in student teacher action research is "personal meaning making." In the company of friends and colleagues you interpret, assume, ignore, embrace, and question the results of your work. Borrowing again from museum specialists, we learn to be skeptical of orthodoxy, including our own.

None of us really "know enough" when it comes to teaching or researching. Our meaning making is always partial and influenced by our own values and beliefs. Our "conclusions," then, are tentative and surrounded by self-analysis and reflexivity (Arminio & Hultgren, 2002; Gergen & Gergen, 2003; McCotter, 2001).

Data interpretation is hard work. Despite the feeling that it may be a "leap of faith," some magical ability to gaze into a crystal ball, or simply "touchy-feely," it ultimately requires tenacity to critically read, think, analyze, synthesize, and deconstruct. Even statistical analyses based strictly on numerical data don't simply speak "truth" on their own. Someone, a subjective person, has to interpret the results. But while all interpretation is subjective, there are methodologies that make interpretation personal without falling into the untrustworthy trap of self-centered babble. In the next section, you will practice and apply some of these methodologies.

Finally, a reminder: as you embark upon final data interpretation (is there a drum roll?): *stay open*—there may be an "astonishing disclosure" sitting right next to you.

> Travel the side road Cultural Context 6.1: *The Numbers Tell the Story*, found at the end of this chapter on p. 175.

General Steps for Data Interpretation

Here we outline the general steps of the data interpretation process. Note, however, that the notion of "steps" can be deceptive. Steps can make a process look simple, linear, and even rigid when in fact they require critical thought and fluidity on the part of the researcher. These steps are meant to be useful in providing a scaffold for the data interpretation process as presented here. This is not *the* way, but *one* way of approaching data interpretation that has been useful to the many preservice teacher-researchers with whom we teach and learn. There are other ways to undertake data interpretation; perhaps you will invent your own process. However you arrive at the end of data interpretation, the goal is still the same: *making meaning of the data*.

The six steps of the data interpretation process are generally as follows (see Figure 6.2):

1. *Revisit, reflect on, and reread data and perform ongoing analysis.* Synthesize across the data by creating mind maps, charts, highlighting data, and/or creating timelines.

2. *Create tentative category headings of interpretation.*

3. *Expand your interpretation.* Add raw data to the interpretation.

4. *Apply interpretative layers.* Add the perspectives of others.

5. *Return to the questions.* Apply questions to your interpretation; look for what is missing.

6. *Draft and expand synthesis statements.* Synthesize and organize what you know.

In the next section, we will outline scaffolds for getting started with the first step of data interpretation. It may be helpful to read this section and then choose the scaffold that best fits your way of learning and knowing. This section is interactive, and assumes that you have organized your data and completed ongoing data analysis. *Note: If you used charts to organize your data as described in Chapter 3, be open to new categories of data interpretation.* It is useful to think outside and around any categories created during ongoing data analysis, even if you return to them later as your work through the interpretative layers.

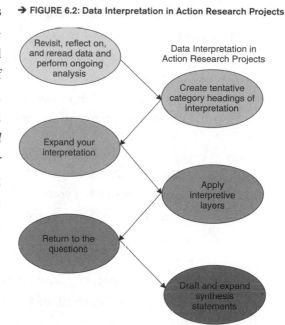

→ FIGURE 6.2: Data Interpretation in Action Research Projects

Data Interpretation in Action Research Projects

Revisit, reflect on, and reread data and perform ongoing analysis

Create tentative category headings of interpretation

Expand your interpretation

Apply interpretive layers

Return to the questions

Draft and expand synthesis statements

Cultural Context 6.2: *Reading Empirical Research*, found at the end of this chapter on p. 178. Curious how the above steps differ from what might be thought of as "traditional" or "empirical research?" If so, travel this side road.

Scaffolds for Data Interpretation

Approach data interpretation with anticipation, a sense of curiosity, and an openness to possibilities that may lie outside of your current paradigm for thinking. Be deliberate about setting aside space and time to do final data interpretation. Don't attempt to do all of your data interpretation in one evening or one sitting. Allow "think breaks" between the times you work on interpretation to make connections and create space for "Aha!" moments. As necessary, seek support and feedback from your critical colleagues.

Revisiting, Reflecting, and Rereading Collected Data and Ongoing Analysis

Getting started on data interpretation begins by reviewing data collected, rereading journal entries and analytic memos, and critically deconstructing tentative conclusions and assumptions found in these documents. Our students report that getting started with data interpretation can be the hardest part of action research. We agree. The initial step in interpreting is to simply *play* with the data, interacting with it in a dynamic, fluid way. This can be uncomfortable. Practice self-reflexivity. Be mindful of preconceived answers or conclusions you may desire.

Take a break and read Self-Study 6.1: *A Cautionary Tale of Data Interpretation: Pamela's Story and the Case for Self-Reflexivity*, found at the end of this chapter on p. 173.

We suggest four options as ways to get started with this first step of final data interpretation. For any option, start with butcher or poster paper, a large whiteboard, or even a graphic thinking tool such as the popular computer program *Inspiration* (www.inspiration.com) or a tablet application like *SimpleMind+* (Xpt Software & Consulting B.V., 2013). While these activities may seem rather out of place in formal research, we have found that such creative approaches to interpretation are very useful.

1. Create a mind map (diagram). Start by writing your critical question in the middle of the workspace. Branch off from your critical question using lines, arrows, and shapes to represent what you have learned about your research project and what questions you still have. Review analytic memos to determine the branches of the mind map: what tentative lessons were you learning? You may want to have a branch for "critical incidents." Include those moments of teaching you just cannot forget (for good or bad!). Another option is to include categories from your literature review and use these as branches of the mind map. Mix and match and add your own as necessary!

2. Create a timeline of your study. If you did this study as a student teacher, start the timeline with your initial entrance into the classroom, even if you were not collecting data at that time. Add just the dates of important "landmarks" during your learning-to-teach and data collection phases. Add to the timeline when you collected data. Add specific incidents connected with data collection, such as "Taught lesson using computer simulations." Add any other specific incidents that occurred during the data collection period. Include even those incidents that may not seem related. Complete the context for your study by adding memorable incidents from your entire student-teaching period. You may want to include emotions as well as actions. After creating the timeline, try highlighting with different colors incidents that seem to be most important. Often these are incidents you reacted to emotionally, e.g. "Lousy day," or "Wow! Today went great!" That said, we often overlook the power of normalcy. *What seems "normal" and why?* This is a good question to ask during final data interpretation.

3. Create a chart with three columns: 1) What I thought I knew about my research topic/question; 2) What I now know about my research topic/question; and 3) What I still wonder about my research topic and question (Figure 6.3). Work through the first column prior to reviewing your data and analytic memos. Then, as you review your data collection, continue to complete the chart. Don't hesitate if there are items that end up in more than one column and feel free to draw dialogue-bubbles outside the otherwise neat column spaces. Leave a lot of blank space on your chart to work with later.

➜ FIGURE 6.3: Forming Initial Categories

What I thought I knew about my research topics/question	What I now know about my research topic/question.	What I still wonder about my research topic/question

4. Work with several different colors of highlighters as you read through your data collection and analytic memos, using different colors to highlight what appear to be related incidents, evaluations—*repeating themes*, made in the data. The trick with using this method is that you don't know when you start rereading data what you will mark or with what color you will mark it. Just begin reading. When you find the first interesting comment in your journal, highlight it with color one. When you come to another memorable incident, consider if it is related to the previous journal remark and then highlight with the same color or another color if it appears to be different. Continue reading in this fashion and enjoy watching the color pattern emerge!

Create Tentative Category Headings of Interpretation

The next step is to synthesize across the data to create tentative categories of interpretation. This is a continuation of reading across the data and synthesizing what you are learning. The categories are tentative and open to change as you work further through the steps of interpretation.

If you used mind maps, read across all of the different "branches" of the mind map. Could some branches be merged? Are there other branches that seem more important than others? Are there branches you would like to rename to better represent what you are thinking? Perhaps other branches no longer seem to stand-alone? Use different colors of highlighters or draw arrows (or do both) to collapse and create new "branches" from your mind map.

If you used a timeline or the three-column chart, use different colors of highlighters to find relating themes in your timeline or chart. For example, you may group all of the "most successful," "not so good," and "most normal" incidents or data together. You may find common themes in your journals and memos. A theme emerges from the data as you consider items that appear related. You may find it useful to revisit your literature review: what categories of knowledge do you identify? How are these categories represented in your chart or timeline?

If you read with highlighters, analyze the color patterns your work has created. Revisit your thinking. What does each color group seem to represent? What are the salient qualities of each of these groups? You may find it useful at this time to now place your thinking into a mind map or chart as described above.

No matter what medium you have used, once you have created tentative categories of interpretation, you are ready to name (or re-name) these categories. Play with the language you use to write tentative headings of interpreted data groups. Write several different headings. What headings best seem to synthesize the data categories best?

Finally, deconstruct the tentative headings and categories of data interpretation you have created. Ask:

• "What appears to be missing from this data? What have I excluded and why?" This may require rereading field notes, journals, memos, and other pieces from your data collection.

- "How do these emerging categories reflect my own beliefs about teaching and learning?" If the categories only affirm what we are thinking as researchers, we may need to look again. Using your literature review and seeking help from your critical colleague are helpful in this pursuit.

- "What are the limits of these categories?" What is it you do not know and cannot know about these categories?

📖 Take a break and consider the criteria for trustworthy teacher action research. How is practicing self-reflexivity, seeking multiple perspectives and making strong connections critical to the above process? How do these first steps document the journey of *becoming* a teacher? How might they lead to meaningful results?

Expanding Your Interpretation

The goal now is to expand the representation you have developed to answer the question, "How do I know this new information?" This is a critical step in the process, one in which you find data to support your intuition and hunches. This step should result in a greatly enhanced mind map, timeline, or chart. Add data to the mind map, timeline, and/or chart that supports what you have learned. There are several options for doing this. Try literally cutting out data from your data collection and placing it on the mind map, timeline, or chart. Another option is to reference data via the date and kind of data so you can find it in your data collection easily. Or, list the data with a descriptive phrase.

Again, *play* with this data. Just because you place the data in one category doesn't mean it has to stay there! Move data around: what new ways of thinking does this create? Draw arrows making connections; invent codes or symbols that help represent your thoughts as they are forming. Be creative. Use student voices in your work. Mark places of conflict, discontinuity, or uncomfortable self-spaces of learning, "Aha!" moments, places of affirmation concerning your research topic, and places that raise further questions about your research topic. Highlight the data and/or incidents that represent the most learning. These often represent further points of conflicts, discontinuity, or uncomfortable self-spaces. You may find that some conclusions and areas are not well supported by data. This may mean that this area either needs further data collection to be trustworthy, may need to be dropped as a focus, or perhaps the category can be collapsed into other categories. Alternatively, you may find that category headings you earlier wrote do not seem to "fit" with the data. Revise category headings to reflect changes in thinking.

Critical to this step is to practice deconstruction, contextualization, and critical self-reflexivity. Ask yourself, "Why these categories?" Are you making interpretations that the data do not truly support but do align with your expectations or biases? Is the data in anyway unique to the context of the school? Be willing to return to the data collection and read across the data as necessary.

Data Interpretation Illustrated: Liri's Journey Through Data Interpretation

Liri's action research project focused on teacher–student writing conferences. Her original intent was to focus on teacher talk, talk that would encourage her fifth grade writers to engage and own their writing and develop their writer identity. Her data collection included: writing lesson plans; weekly journals; audio-recorded teacher–student writing conferences; note-making completed while listening to the audio-recordings; selected transcriptions of conferences that "seemed important" during the data collection period; and, two analytic memos. During her data collection and while completing ongoing analysis, it became clear to Liri that teacher talk was only one piece of the teacher–student writing conference. Her note-making and journals provided evidence of this and she began to analyze more than just talk in her data.

Liri began data interpretation by reading through her data collection, focusing most closely on the conferences she had not only audio-recorded but also transcribed. She made a habit for several days to play the audio of the conferences during her commute to school. Her data interpretation included walks with a friend to talk about what she thought she was learning, as well as some evenings at a coffee shop reading and doodling along side of various pieces of her data collection. After working through about half of her data set, Liri created a mind map on her iPad of categories that she found emerging from her data: "Please, get your stuff together"; "Argh! Behavior!"; "Manipulation"; "Just get something down!" and "Picture Perfect" (see Figure 6.4). Each heading represented her response to different situations she faced as a teacher in the teacher–student writing conference. She continued to read through her data, only now she would color code the data according to these categories. Using this, she was able to return to her mind map and clearly reference data to support each branch of her mind map.

Liri printed a copy of her mind map and began taking notes about each category. She began to reference specific conferences that seemed to represent the heading or category she had created (Figure 6.5). It became obvious that a "picture perfect" conference was one that did not include any of the conditions of the other categories. This caused her to reframe her critical question, "What are the

→ FIGURE 6.4: Liri's Draft 1 Mind Map

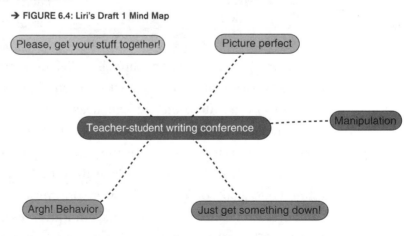

conditions of an effective teacher–student writing conference?" As soon as she wrote this new question, her critical colleague asked her, "Yes, but what do you mean by 'effective'? Is effective only what makes you feel good as a teacher?" This question sent Liri back to her data. She found herself stuck in a binary. In her journal, she wrote, "An effective teacher–student conference makes me feel like a good teacher. All those others make me feel like a failure." She did not want to stay in this place, and decided to work through additional layers to get beyond a good/bad teacher scenario.

→ FIGURE 6.5: Liri's Draft 2 Mind Map

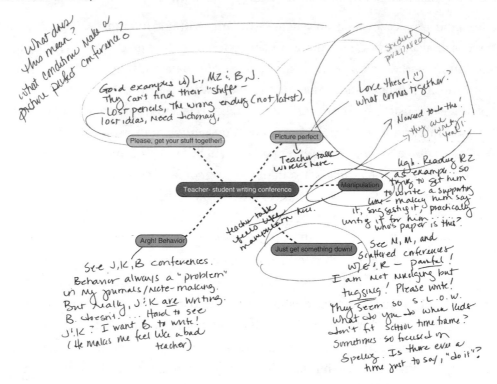

Applying Interpretative Layers

→ FIGURE 6.6: Interpretative Layers

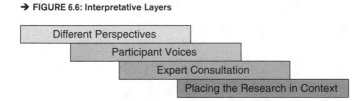

Interpretative layers are the different layers of meaning we apply to our data (see Figure 6.6). Each layer of interpretation allows the teacher-researcher to see the data from another angle. The voice representing each layer affirms, denies, or leaves in question a hunch, belief, or assumption. The layers reflect macro- and micro-ways of seeing, exposing cracks or even whole patterns that may have been overlooked. As you layer your interpretation, add ideas to your map, timeline, or chart.

Imagine altering a photo using digital technology. It's fun play. The subject of the photo stays the same, but the way we see the photo is changed by applying alternative filters, shades of color, and brush strokes. Sometimes these tools alter the original picture in such as way as to bring out details or features that were previously unseen. Layers of interpretation create a similar sense of collected meaning. Layering gives research what is termed "thick description" (Geertz, 1973; Patton, 2002), weaving trustworthiness into the research project. Not all of the layers described may be appropriate for your study; choose those that will bring the most meaning into your work. Even after doing this, the meaning will be partial and incomplete. You may find that rather than arriving at one place, you have arrived at various places of interpretation. You may find more questions than answers or solutions. Here's the question: are you making significant discoveries for yourself in your journey of becoming a teacher?

As you read through the descriptions of each interpretative layer, take note how they promote trustworthy teacher action research.

Interpretative Layer 1: Different Perspective(s)

Seek another perspective on your data by sharing your analytic memos or other synthesis statements with your critical colleague, mentor-teacher, student teaching supervisor, university instructor and/or another specialist in the area. Sometimes, parents of students you are working with can give a critical missing perspective. Not all voices may be necessary; choose those that will reflect an important new light on the study.

Interpretative Layer 2: Participant Voice(s)

In qualitative research, this layer of interpretation is often termed a *member check*. In collecting this layer of meaning, you return to the participants in the study—most likely, your students. Employ any method of interview that works best for your action research situation. A whole-class discussion, focus groups, surveys, or written responses all work well. Do this by using your synthesis statements and asking the participants to respond to them. This may be one of the most important layers of interpretation you can add to your study. In doing a member check, you are asking the people closest to the study, "Do you see what I see in this data?"

Interpretative Layer 3: Expert Consultation

Return to the literature and consider your data interpretation in the light of experts. How does the literature support your emerging theories or synthesis statements? Are there gaps, discontinuities, or disagreements between what you are discovering and what the literature says? Revisit your distant colleagues and theorize about these issues together.

Interpretative Layer 4: Placing the Research in Context

Step away from your research study. Consider your research in the context of your student-teaching/practicum/teacher-education program experience. How do critical incidents that may seem at first to be unrelated influence your data interpretation? How is your data interpretation limited? How have your own developing abilities as a teacher influenced the study? Are there issues, conflicts, and details unique to this class/school/community that may influence the way you interpret the data? How are your own beliefs, assumptions, and views of education shading the way you view the data?

Data Interpretation Illustrated: Liri Works Through Layers of Interpretation

Liri continued with her data interpretation by adding more information to her mind map as she worked through each of the interpretative layers described above. You can see her expanded mind map in Figure 6.7. Liri began to use her mind map more as an outline rather than as an inclusive mind map of all her data and literature references. She selected, for example, key quotes and references representative of the data and included this on the mind map. She kept expanded notes for each branch of the mind map in her journal.

→ **FIGURE 6.7: Liri's Mind Map: Applied Interpretative Layers**

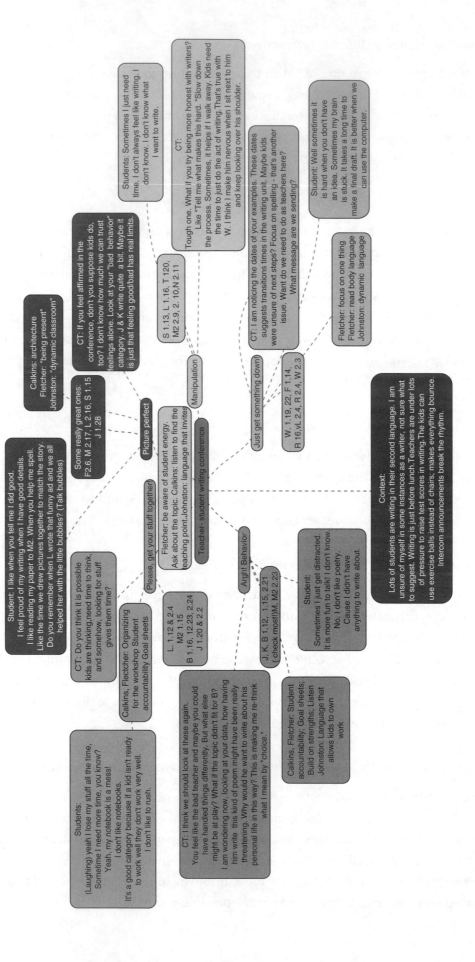

Student: I like when you tell me I did good. I feel proud of my writing when I have good details. I like reading my paper to M2. When you help me spell. Like the time we drew pictures together to match the story. Do you remember when L wrote that funny ad and we all helped her with the little bubbles? (Talk bubbles)

Calkins: architecture
Fletcher: "being present"
Johnston: "dynamic classroom"

CT: If you feel affirmed in the conference, don't you suppose kids do, too? I don't know how much we can trust feelings alone. Look at your "bad behavior" category. J & K write quite a bit. Maybe it is just that feeling good/bad has real limits.

Students: Sometimes I just need time. I don't always feel like writing. I don't know. I don't know what I want to write.

CT: Tough one. What if you try being more honest with writers? Like "Tell me what makes this hard." "Slow down the process. Sometimes, it helps if I walk away. Kids need the time to just do the act of writing. That's true with W. I think I make him nervous when I sit next to him and keep looking over his shoulder.

Student: Well sometimes it is hard when you don't have an idea. Sometimes my brain is stuck. It takes a long time to make a final draft. It is better when we can use the computer.

Some really great ones:
F2.6, M 2.17, L 2.16, S 1.15 J 1.28

S 1.13, L 1.16, T 120, M2 2.9, 2. 10,N 2.11

CT: I am noticing the dates of your examples. These dates suggests transitions times in the writing unit. Maybe kids were unsure of next steps? Focus on spelling - that's another issue. Want do we need to do as teachers here? What message are we sending?

Fletcher: focus on one thing
Fletcher: read body language
Johnston: dynamic language

Picture perfect

Manipulation

Fletcher: be aware of student energy.
Ask about the topic. Calkins: listen to find the teaching point. Johnston: language that invites

Just get something down

Teacher- student writing conference

W. 1.19, 22, F 1.14, R 16, vL 2.4, R 2.4, W 2.3

CT: Do you think it is possible kids are thinking,need time to think, and somehow, looking for stuff gives them time?

Please, get your stuff together!

Arg!t Behavior

Context:
Lots of students are writing in their second language. I am unsure of myself in some instances as a writer, not sure what to suggest. Writing is just before lunch Teachers are under lots of pressure to raise test scores in writing. The kids can use exercise balls instead of chairs; makes everything bounce. Intercom announcements break the rhythm.

Calkins, Flectcher: Organizing for the workshop Student accountability Goal sheets

L. 1,12 & 2.4
M2 1.15
B 1.16, 12.23, 2.24
J 1.20 & 2.2

J, K, B 1.12, 1.15, 2.21 (check most)|M, M2 2.23

Student:
Sometimes I just get distracted. It is more fun to talk! I don't know. No, I don't like poetry. Cause I didn't have anything to write about.

Students:
(Laughing) yeah I lose my stuff all the time. Sometime I need more time, you know? Yeah, my notebook is a mess!
I don't like notebooks.
It's a good category because if a kid isn't ready to work well they don't work very well. I don't like to rush.

CT: I think we should look at these again. You feel like the bad teacher and maybe you could have handled things differently. But what else might be at play? What if the topic didn't fit for B? I am wondering now. looking at your data, how having him write this kind of poem might have been really threatening. Why would he want to write about his personal life in this way? This is making me re-think what I mean by "choice."

Calkins, Fletcher: Student accountability; Goal sheets; Build on strengths; Listen Johnston: Language that allows kids to own work

Liri has sought the perspective of her mentor-teacher and she helped her move beyond the good/bad teacher binary by raising questions. For example, when the mentor-teacher asked Liri, "Do you think it is possible kids are thinking when they appear to be wasting time or unorganized? Maybe they just need time to think, and somehow, looking for stuff gives them time?" This startled Liri; she had not thought of this perspective. Liri considered her own study habits. When she was stuck writing a paper, she often found herself looking around on iTunes for new music or cleaning out a desk drawer . . . all the time thinking about what to write next. This moved Liri to consider how as a teacher, she needed to consider more carefully what Fletcher and Portalupi (2001) refer to as learning from body language. Liri returned to her data and found, as an example, a time when a writer was trying to decide what color of pencil to use. Liri had been impatient with the student. She just wanted the student to "get her stuff and start writing." But now she wrote in her journal, "Is this an example of a writer creating time to think?"

Liri also returned to her student-writers and asked them about writing conferences. She shared her different headings and asked writers about them. This gave her yet another way to think about her data. For example, students often referred to lacking time or feeling rushed. When they described memorable conferences, they were often remembering favorite writing topics and moments of collaboration. It seemed as if good writing conferences not only made Liri feel like a good teacher, they also made students feel like good writers. Having a topic worthwhile to talk about, being able to work with a friend, these were all important to student-writers. Liri begin to wonder how reading the data from her other categories might change if she were to read through this new lens of information.

Returning to her distant colleagues proved a rich experience for Liri. "Now they [her distant colleagues] make sense," she told her advisor. It was during this layer of interpretation that Liri returned to the work of Johnston (2004) and the original focus of her action research, that of teacher talk. Reviewing her data yet again, she realized that using "language of influence" was easiest in those "picture perfect" conferences. What made the difference? Liri, through talk with her mentor-teacher and critical colleague, realized that when she felt she was losing control of a conference, either because she didn't know what to say next or children were "misbehaving," she often began using language of "control." She spent time journaling about this, noting that it was in these very instances, she most needed to use language of "agency and becoming" (Johnston, 2004), like "You don't seem interested in this writing topic. What other possibilities exist for you? What other choices might you make?" She wondered how this kind of language might change her own perspective from "trying to get a student to just write anything" to a more open space of possibility.

Finally, Liri stepped away from her mind map and thought about context of her action research. What about her school context made this data set unique? What *mattered*? Many students were writing in their second language. Maybe this is why they cared so much about spelling, were so unwilling to "just give it a try." The use of exercise balls as an option for traditional chairs seemed great for kids, but for Liri, having bouncing bodies around her was a whole new school experience. How was this influencing her perceptions of student behavior? Writing occurred just before lunch. How might that influence writing conferences? And right before lunch seemed to signal more announcements from the public address system, often interrupting the flow of a conference. This, too, needed to be considered. Furthermore, she wondered about the high expectations of her school to raise students' writing scores. Liri felt this pressure. She wondered how it affected her, as a student-teacher.

Having worked through the layers of interpretation, Liri felt something like exhaustion and found herself worrying she would not be able to "pull it all together." Her mind map had exploded with detail; she had much to think about. How to synthesize across all this newly interpreted data and the many questions it raised?

Drafting Synthesis Statements

Having worked through the layers of interpretation, you are ready to identify what seem to be the major themes—or *categories*—of your study. These themes or categories have been emerging as you have worked through the steps of data interpretation and as you have written headings for each of your categories. Each synthesis statement should be very succinct yet descriptive. Writing synthesis statements is a process; be willing to revise. Each revision represents revised thinking. Study the following revisions of Thomas and Macy's synthesis statements:

- *Rituals and routines are important to creating classroom community.*

- *Not just any ritual or routine is important in creating classroom community. Such rituals and routines need to be meaningful and engaging. They should be aligned with student learning, and often they are done with an adult as a mentor. They are fun for children—in many such rituals and routines, children may not even know how much they are learning! Somehow, they don't become "old" or "used." Taken together, it is best when the rituals and routines of a classroom reflect a coherent belief sytem of the teacher.*

- *Meaningful classroom rituals and routines develop a caring and respectful community of learners when they: 1) are developed around a coherent child-centered belief system; 2) are authentic and engaging as they teach and support classroom learning; and 3) include an adult mentor.*

📖 How do the revised synthesis statements represent revised thinking? What conversations do you imagine occurred between each synthesis statement revision? What appears might be criteria for a good final data interpretation synthesis statement? How are these synthesis statements different than any you may have written during ongoing data analysis?

Data Interpretation Illustrated: Liri and Synthesis Statements

As Liri looped back through her interpretations, she discovered her original data interpretation headings were getting in the way of her revised thinking. After playing with the different contents of each branch of her mind map she merged the data of "Please, get your stuff together" and "Manipulation," coming to see both of these as her own reactions to feeling a loss of control during a teacher–student writing conference. Applying layers of interpretation opened up different ways of reading the data. She played with all of her headings and revised them as follows (the former heading is followed by the revised heading):

- "Please, get your stuff together" and "Manipulation—"There is more to read and notice than the written text"

- "Argh! Behavior"—"Opportunities *to* and Challenges *of* Practicing Agency"

- "Just get something down"—"Honor the hard work of writing"

Drafting synthesis statements took more time than Liri expected. Liri drafted, deleted, and started over (and over) multiple times. Here are her final synthesis statements:

Synthesis Statement 1

When conducting a teacher–student writing conference, I need to learn to read more than the written text of the student. I must also learn to read my own emotions, interest and fears, along with the body language and actions of the student-writer and the context of the classroom and the day.

Synthesis Statement 2

There are times as a teacher, I feel like I am losing control of a writing conference and as a result, I often use "control" language. In fact, this is the time to practice the language of agency, to re-frame the situation and ask the kinds of questions that truly invite students to own their writing and to help students think of other possible behaviors, topics, or even alternatives to writing.

Synthesis Statement 3

Writing is hard and rewarding work. I need to remember to honor the process of writing, which is different for everyone, requiring different amounts of time, conditions, and even materials for each student-writer.

⬛ Study Liri's synthesis statements. How do they convey self-reflexivity and becoming a teacher? What do you think works about these synthesis statements? How would you revise your criteria for synthesis statements based upon Liri's work? Are there recommendations you would give Liri?

🖐 Would you like more practice with synthesis statements? Find "Practice with Synthesis Statements" on the companion website.

Expanding the Synthesis Statements

Once synthesis statements are written, you can expand the statements to organize and outline your final data interpretation. We suggest using the synthesis chart in Table 6.1. Write

→ TABLE 6.1: Synthesis Categories

Synthesis Statements	Key Supporting Literature	Key Supporting Data (including data from layer interpretations)	Additional Theorizing	Continuing Questions

the synthesis statement in the first column. Include the literature that best supports the synthesis statement in the next column. Our students find it useful to include any salient quotations from distant mentors (and if they do so, to include the page number of the quotation!) Now, return to earlier draft interpretation work and select pieces of data that most support the synthesis statement being expanded. This is representative data that illustrate and clarify the ideas behind the synthesis statement.

Pause after completing these first three columns—allow yourself space to think. Visit with your critical colleague and *theorize* (as oppose to declaring or concluding) about your synthesis statement. This is taking the statement a bit further, asking questions like: *What might the consequences, intended or not, of this statement be? What related areas of teaching and learning might this also influence? How is this statement also a question? How is this statement limited?* Doing this kind of theorizing will lead you into the final column: *continuing questions*. What do you still wonder about your action research topic? What areas of the action research topic has your theorizing opened up that you would next like to explore?

Data Interpretation Illustrated: Liri's Synthesis Chart

The first row of Liri's synthesis chart is in Table 6.2. Read through her synthesis chart. Consider:

- How does the chart serve as a useful tool for Liri?

- In what ways does the contents of the chart illustrate: evidence of becoming, self-reflexivity, multiple perspectives, and a strong sense of connection?

- In what ways might Liri's final data interpretation, as illustrated in the synthesis chart, lead to meaningful action?

⌖ Interested in another story of data interpretation? See "Criteria for, Recommendations, and Questions: Children and Adolescent Literature about Disabilities" on the companion website.

→ TABLE 6.2: Liri's Synthesis Statements

Synthesis Statement	Key Supporting Literature	Key Supporting Data *(including data from layering interpretations)*	Additional Theorizing	Continuing Questions
When conducting a teacher–student writing conference, I need to learn to read more than the written text of the student. I must also learn to read my own emotions, interest and fears, along with the body language and actions of the student-writer.	Fletcher, R. & Portalupi, J. (2001). *Writing workshop: The essential guide.* Portsmouth, NH: Heinemann. "Listen . . . We all know the word, but putting it into practice is harder than it sounds" (p. 49) Johnston, P. (2004). *Choice words: How our language affects children's learning.* Portland, ME: Stenhouse Publishers. "Feelings of discomfort or uneasiness can be useful indicators . . . Often we smother these feelings rather than deal with their source . . . " (p. 19) Graves, D. H. (1994). *A fresh look at writing.* Portsmouth, NH: Heinemann. "Our research data show that entire years— or even school careers— can be wasted if we don't let our students teach us" (p. 16)	See journal entries from 1.23, 1.28, and 2.218; Note-making from conferences with B, J, & M2 (highlighted with blue in data collection); See blue highlighted areas of analytic memos; See notes from my conversation with cooperating teacher about my data interpretations. Data Snapshot: Conference with J. I wrote in my memo "this conference was a train wreck." I so want J. to be successful (and I want to be the one that makes her successful!) and she is so hesitant to use English. I found myself feeding her ideas/words, doing most of the talking, not listening carefully, so I missed what she really wanted to write entirely. (Didn't notice this until I listened to the audio!) My sticky note that I wrote right after the conference says, "J. was restless, squirming all over the floor." Learn to read the writer's text: check to read *me*, read the body language.	The ability to "listen" is so underrated. It seems related to the Graves (1994) quote— listening is about letting kids teach me. Listening is a full body activity! I keep reading, and I really do believe (!), that teaching and learning go hand-in-hand as a teacher, but I am finding I am so socialized after years of being a student to think that as a teacher I am the one that has to be the expert talking all the time! If I am talking, I am not listening, not able to read the entire conference situation. When people say, "get to know your students," that sounds good and it is important, but it seems like it is more than just getting to know your students, it is about getting to know your students, their habits, their ways of thinking and how this "fits" with the teachers way of doing things. All of this is involved with learning to "read" and "listen" during a teacher–student conference. My data is limited and biased b/c I have been learning to teach and felt a lot of pressure to perform. Will it be different in my own classroom?	What are the layers of "listening"? How can I explore listening as a full body act even more as a teacher? When I do have my own classroom, how do I learn to check myself from falling back into the expert/talker role?

Other Views of Data Interpretation: Alternative Scaffolds and Variations on These Scaffolds

We have set out a process for final data interpretation. Know that not every step may be useful or necessary for you. Additionally, there is no one "right" way to do data interpretation. We have provided for you a process that works with almost all of our students and for ourselves as researchers. You may find other ways to record your draft thinking, categorizing, theorizing, and grouping. For example, you may want to draw your interpretations or use more word associations. You may find that these scaffolds are not necessarily helpful. Use whatever method you can to make meaning of your data. Just make sure the meaning you make is based upon the data, the expert knowledge of distance colleagues, and other voices from suggested layers of interpretation. Data interpretation is more than interpreting according to your own opinion or experience alone. Data interpretation, remember, ought to move your thinking forward, provoke, and open up new and interesting questions as you are continually in the process of *becoming* a teacher.

One Last Look at Criteria for Trustworthiness

Even after our students complete their data interpretation (sometimes working through the process several times), they are still haunted by a doubting voice that says, "You have no right to say these things; you're not being objective; this only means something to *you*." Beyond simply repeating our previous retorts of such voices found earlier in this chapter, we suggest now that you formally respond to each of the criterion for trustworthy teacher action research, thus equipping you to be ready to give an answer to those who may ask about your work. As always, be honest in your assessments. Note what you have learned along the way, what you would do differently another time, and most importantly, what your take-away is as you continue your journey in *becoming* a teacher.

🗊 Evaluate your interpretations of each criterion in your notebook.

🖑 A downloadable version of this list is available on the companion website.

Criteria of Trustworthiness in Teacher Action Research

- *Criterion 1: Evidence of Becoming.* Trustworthy interpretations illustrate the process of becoming a teacher. Is this transparent in your work? Does your work demonstrate critical thinking, problem solving, and a growing, "living knowledge" of teaching and researching?

- *Criterion 2: Trustworthy interpretations demonstrate self-reflexivity.* Have you practiced self-reflexivity in your work? Can the reader identify how you have changed? Are you transparent in identifying paradigms, biases, and assumptions as well as new theories of teaching and learning?

- *Criterion 3: Trustworthy interpretations seek multiple perspectives.* Does your work reflect the perspectives of participants, mentor-teacher(s), university advisors and supervisors? Is the expert advice of distant colleagues used in your interpretations? Do you have "thick" data to illustrate your themes and recommendations?

- *Criterion 4: Strong sense of connection.* Trustworthy interpretations make strong connections between the cultural contexts of the classroom, school and community; distant colleagues; and your own unique journey of becoming a teacher. Is this sense of connection palpable in your study?

- *Criterion 5: Trustworthy interpretations result in meaningful action.* How does the knowledge and meaning derived from your action research project make you more insightful and wise as a teacher? Do the results demonstrate a future teacher who has the abilities and dispositions to continually study and re-frame practice? How is this study meaningful to students, the school community, or the community at large? How does the work represent praxis?

Outcomes of these core elements of trustworthiness in data interpretation include the following:

- *Acknowledgments of limitations.* Do your interpretations show a clear under-standing of limitations such as the guest status of the researcher in the classroom, researcher biases, and time constraints?

- *Interpretation that is tentative rather than absolute.* Do your interpretations avoid broad generalities, leave issues open, suggest further questions, and admit partial understandings influenced by your own values, belief systems, and biases?

- *Ethical and professional use of data reflecting respect for participants.* Have you only included data gathered from participants in an ethical, authentic way? Do the data accurately reflect participants, the context, and your journey of becoming a teacher? Can it be said that your use of data represents integrity and respect for participants and the school context?

This chapter follows a formal progression for final data interpretation. Review this progression:

1. *Revisit, reflect on, and reread data and perform ongoing analysis.* Synthesize across the data by creating mind maps, charts, highlighting data, and/or creating timelines.

2. *Create tentative category headings of interpretation.*

3. *Expand your interpretation.* Add raw data to the interpretation.

4. *Apply interpretative layers.* Add the perspectives of others.

5. *Return to the questions.* Apply questions to your interpretation; look for what is missing

6. *Draft and expand synthesis statements.* Synthesize and organize what you know.

While this is a formal process of data interpretation, we argue that critically intelligent teachers of influence engage in this process informally as a matter of daily practice, as a way of creating living, organic knowledge on which to base "tomorrow's lesson." In particular, we find this process helpful when living in the classroom raises questions that keep us awake in the night, when a classroom interaction leaves us feeling unsettled. Then, the principles of final data interpretation might be used in this way:

1. A question comes from a classroom moment that keeps us awake in the night, leaves us unsettled.

2. This leads us to critically revisit and reflect on how we "read the data of the moment" at the time of incident or over the time the question has emerged.

3. We play with other ways we might have "read the data of the moment" and seek multiple perspectives on how we might read the "data of the moment."

→ FIGURE 6.8: Cycle of Action Research

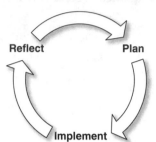

4. Which leads us back to a revised question based upon that incident that keeps us awake at night.

5. So we synthesize our thinking . . . *and*

always already *becoming* teacher as we begin the process of action research one more time, all over again.

Chapter 6: Content Questions

1. How would you describe final data interpretation?
2. What is the role of synthesizing, deconstruction, and contextualization in final data interpretation?
3. How are the criteria of trustworthy teacher action research also actions of teacher action research?

Chapter 6: Process Questions

1. What strategy for getting started on final data interpretation seems to resonate most with you? Why?
2. How will you apply layers of interpretation to your project?
3. What challenges to you anticipate as you begin final data interpretation? What strategies will you use to work through these challenges?

Self-Study 6.1: A Cautionary Tale of Data Interpretation: Pamela's Story and the Case for Self-Reflexivity

Here is a story used here as a cautionary tale illustrating the importance of critical self-reflexivity and data interpretation. This is a true story about a student teacher who we will call Pamela. Pamela was asked by school district officials to investigate a new reading program being field tested in her school. Her data interpretation journey illustrates how paradigm matters—why we need as teacher-researchers to immerse our interpretations in self-reflexivity and multiple perspectives. Pamela excitedly consented to study the school district's new reading program, and we encouraged her to create her action research project around this topic, which she did. It was clear from the beginning that the school district was very enthusiastic about the new reading program, and was hoping Pamela's study would add some weight to their impending decision to implement the program district-wide.

Pamela completed a thorough literature review, seeking out faculty who were expert in literacy programs and who advised her of the powerful and dangerous aspects of the new reading program. She collected a reasonably rich data set, adding participant voices and multiple perspectives. She was clear about the context of her study (English Language Learners) and engaged with the students, parents, and reading program for eight months during her student teaching.

Of the four students Pamela tracked closely through the eight months, three displayed a pattern in which their Lexile reading scores improved somewhat initially, but then declined to previous levels. The students reported in interviews that the program was "boring."

Pamela expressed some concern and puzzlement about these negative results, and provided additional data about each student to attempt to explain her findings. However, she was ultimately unable to provide a trustworthy interpretation, writing the following in her results section:

Out of everything that I have been observing and learning from these students, the most important improvement has been their increased confidence. I know that even for those students that I didn't follow closely their own self-confidence has increased in their ability to read. For me to be able to state that with no question in my mind, I can say, "This program is successful!" (Pamela, Action Research Paper)

Pamela was unable to practice critical self-reflexivity about what her data was saying. She was unable to let go of her preconceived ideas about what the study was "supposed" to show or prove. Letting go of our "private universe" of ideas about our AR question is the hardest part of data interpretation. We refer to this passage by Elliot Eisner (2002):

Our inclination to control and predict is, at a practical level, understandable, but it also exacts a price; we tend to do the things we know how to predict and control. Opening oneself to the uncertain is not a pervasive quality of our current educational environment. I believe that it needs to be among the values we cherish. Uncertainty needs to have its proper place in the kinds of schools we create. (p. 11)

continues ➔

How can you open yourself to uncertainty, to the scrutiny of data? How do you react when someone suggests a different reading of your data? What are your personal paradigms that might limit the way you can read data?

1. What kinds of school and/or community systems, organizations and/or structures exist that may need to be questioned for their influence upon your find data interpretation?
2. In what ways is your action research turning out "just as you thought it would"? (Indeed, it may be that your theorizing was correct! But it is also important to double-check these kinds of conclusions for biases.)

Cultural Context 6.1: The Numbers Tell the Story

There is an old story based upon a vaudeville act that both Palmer (2003) and Kohn (1999) use to illustrate the dilemma of data analysis and interpretation, particularly when the data to be interpreted has to do with numbers. It is worth retelling here:

A man is walking down the street at night. He comes across another man looking rather frantically for something under a streetlight. The first man asks, "What are you searching for?" The second man replies, "I've lost my watch!" The first man volunteers to help the second man look for the watch. They look everywhere but find nothing. Finally, the first man says, "Certainly, your watch is not here. Are you sure this is where you lost it?" The second man replies, "Oh, no, I didn't lose it here. I lost it farther up the street." Exasperated, the first man exclaims, "Then why are we looking for the watch here?" The second man replies, "Because the light is better here."

Indeed, this is always the danger in data analysis and interpretation: We want to look where it is easiest, where there is light, where we aren't forced to look at ourselves. We want to look where the seeing is easy and, we hope, the solutions are easy. This can be true interpreting the informal assessment generated from life in the classroom, as well as when interpreting formal research data.

In Western culture, the light in education often shines brightest on clear, unambiguous data. We seek the bottom line. Numbers are nearly sacred; they are often the final word in a debate. They have the appearance of objectivity and fairness, and therefore wield power and influence. Statistics are used by the dominant culture to sell everything from toothpaste to educational policy. As Kohn (1999) writes,

Any aspect of learning (or life) that resists being reduced to numbers is regarded as vaguely suspicious. By contrast, anything that appears in numerical form seems reassuringly scientific; if the numbers are getting larger over time, we must be making progress. (p. 75)

Smith (1998) retells the story of scientific theory in education. He argues that our fascination with statistical analysis and standardized testing in education comes from our desire for control. "Rigorous control," he notes, "was the key element that education adopted from laboratory theory" (p. 55). Experimental research is often referred to as *scientific inquiry*. Experimental research relies on controlling the conditions, or variables, under which the inquiry is carried out. For experimental research to be valid, all variables must be adequately accounted for.

This means that when experimental research is applied to education, major assumptions must be made about students, parents, culture, class, and communities. Experimental designs "control" or account for such variables by use of a large sample size. The assumption is also made that the person recording the data and then interpreting the numbers can be detached from the setting, the interpretation, and the students. It assumes the researcher is objective and that the researcher's personal paradigm won't interfere with the interpretation process. Obviously, this is a problematic and potentially dangerous aspect of experimental research in education. The assumption of full researcher objectivity is what Harding (1996) calls a "god trick," the belief in a kind of vision of "seeing everything from nowhere" (p. 253).

continues →

The same kind of "god trick" can make us ignore what we really need to see and to feel in order to believe we are controlling our reality by being objective.

Control is a sneaky desire. It lures us by promising safety and stability. It can make us believe that what feels chaotic can be ordered and aligned in neat categories. It makes life—especially life in a classroom with 32 very independent, individual human beings—seem desirable and "do-able." But the desire for control, partnered with the call for objectivity and the sacredness of the "bottom line," is dangerous in that it can paint a picture of classrooms that is sterile and devoid of the dilemmas, conflicts, joys, and rewards of the lived experience of teaching. The end results of numbers printed across the page can seem more like a spectacle of what is left after the dementors from the *Harry Potter* children's book series (see, e.g., Rowling, 1999) have sucked life out of the living. Little wonder that teachers sometimes ignore educational research and standardized tests results and consider them "outside" of their practice as teachers.

Ironically, the field of science best teaches us about how our paradigm for thinking can limit our ability to interpret "scientific rigorous research" from outside our own box of belief (Zukav, 1980). For three centuries, science believed itself to have arrived at a full understanding of classical mechanics, the physics of motion. The understanding of the universe constructed by Galileo and Isaac Newton became so accepted that it was considered common sense. Ironically, the most rigorous experiments of the day held clues about the fallibility of classical Newtonian physics, but the received paradigm was so powerful that most scientists considered the results to me no more than anomalies. Albert Einstein was one of a few scientists to take the "anomalous" results seriously, realizing that the only way forward was to tear down the structure of physics and rebuild it from scratch. In the early 20th century, Einstein, with his radical theories of special and general relativity, altered the way we view space and time itself. What Einstein proposed, at first, appeared to be nonsense. But, as Zukav (1980) notes, "The history of scientific thought, if it teaches us anything at all, teaches us the folly of clutching ideas too closely" (p. 251).

In data analysis and interpretation, there is always a danger that we will find evidence to support that which we *want* to believe, that which appears to be common sense according to our paradigm, and that which makes us feel less discomfort and more safety. Numbers, in our society, tend to do just this.

But the very thing that make numbers dangerous also make numbers useful. If we can understand the limits of objectivity, we can use the principles of objectivity to improve our own practice and educational policy. If we can learn the basics of statistical analysis—putting numbers into proper context—then numbers can be powerful ways of knowing and understanding. To return to the lesson from science: Einstein applied rigorous scientific research *and* imagination to disprove three centuries' worth of physics, just as earlier scientists applied rigorous scientific research and imagination to prove their erroneous theories. To simply say, "Numbers are bad," "Don't ever use an objective test," or "Disregard all statistical analysis" would be to miss another way of looking. This is why multiple viewpoints are critical to teacher-action data analysis and interpretation.

In this section, we want to provide a framework for deconstructing numbers in education within a North American cultural context. Entire books are written about this topic, so you will need to look further

continues →

for an extensive review of statistical analysis in education (see Coladarci, Cobb, Minium, & Clarke, 2004; Gorard, 2001). The goal here, however, is to keep the tension at play between what is dangerous and what is useful, and how teachers can better understand and use the data produced by statistical methodologies. To begin this discussion, here are some broad questions to ask whenever you meet statistical analysis in education. When considering objective tests, standardized tests, or statistical analysis in educational research, ask:

- Are the questions themselves meaningful? What framework for thinking decides which questions are meaningful? Do the questions reflect the context for learning and teaching? Here is a general rule: *Know the context and critical questions of the research before quoting the results.*

- How are key concepts or interventions being defined? Read these definitions carefully; do not assume there is universal agreement on what, for example, "fluency in reading" means.

- What other context brings meaning to the numbers? Numbers alone, just like stories alone, always isolate knowledge. While we admit that our knowledge is always partial, we return to the principle of trustworthiness: *The more viewpoints entertained, the more trustworthy the data becomes.*

- Why was this particular methodology chosen? Why was an objective test chosen? Is this the best way to assess the knowledge the researchers were looking for? Why a standardized test? Why statistical analysis? Were these assessments chosen for efficiency or because they are the best way to respond to the questions posed?

- Were the methodologies employed valid and reliable? Results printed as numbers don't make the results meaningful in and of themselves. How has the researcher accounted for variables? What variables are noted? Are there others that appear missing (and, by implication, ignored)?

- What are the limits of knowledge produced by the results? Are those limits acknowledged? Read for what is missing. Read for assumptions. Think about context: What additional information is needed to make the numbers more meaningful and/or the picture more complete? Sometimes we make leaps of faith in data interpretation, from what is actually there to what we *want* to be there. Do such leaps of faith exist?

There is one more broad principle that we want to apply in our deconstruction and lessons on numbers. This lesson reportedly comes from Albert Einstein's office wall. It is worth posting on every teacher-researcher's wall: *Not everything that counts can be counted and not everything that can be counted counts.*

Cultural Context 6.2: Reading Empirical Research

One of the hardest parts of understanding empirical, scientific research is the technical language used. While many empirical studies are very powerful and worthwhile for study by educators, their usefulness is sometimes cloaked in a morass of terminology, statistical tables, and graphs. Worse, it is often difficult to distinguish bad **empirical research** from good because both use the same mathematical language and employ words like *significant* in precise ways that require careful reading and deconstruction.

Finally, the objective nature of empirical research is such that it tends to minimize and mask the biases and intentions of the researchers. However, these biases and intentions exist in empirical studies, and in our opinion, play an important role in all phases of empirical research, from inception to design to interpretation of results. Empirical studies all too often leave to the reader the critical task of determining researcher biases and intentions and the role they may have played.

To begin to experience these useful and dangerous elements of empirical scientific educational research, imagine the following dialogue:

Q: *What do you mean by empirical research?*

A: By empirical research we mean research that relies exclusively on direct, and observable evidence, or data, as the basis for conclusions and interpretations. Technically, this definition could encompass almost all of what we would reasonably call research. After all, most research relies to some degree on data. In practice, though, empirical research attempts to reduce or eliminate subjectivity by relying as exclusively as possible on objective and (ideally) quantifiable evidence or measurements, rather than on the opinions, biases, or intentions of the researcher.

Q: *How is empirical research different from experimental research?*

A: Experimental research, as a subset of empirical research, does two things. First, it attempts to establish cause-and-effect relationships among variables. It does this by carefully designing an experimental test whose results permits the researcher to reasonably claim the existence of a cause-and-effect relationship. Second, it limits its data to strictly quantifiable measurements, so as to permit a rigorous, unambiguous, and mathematical analysis of results.

Q: *Can you give me an example?*

A: Sure. Suppose you wanted to know whether a certain form of instruction, such as using math manipulatives, results in an increase in the ability to solve math problems. You could design an experiment to test whether there is a cause-and-effect-relationship between using math manipulatives (proposed cause) and problem solving ability (desired effect).

Q: *So I would start using math manipulatives in my classroom and measure its effects on problem solving ability through testing students before and after instruction?*

A: Yes, but that is only part of the story. Suppose overall problem-solving ability among your students went up after you started using manipulatives. Are there any other possible reasons they might have improved in problem solving?

continues →

Q: *I suppose so. What if my science unit on inventions somehow helped them do better on their math? Or maybe the gains were caused instead by the worksheet-driven part of the math curriculum. How could I be sure that it was the manipulatives that caused the gains in learning?*

A: This is where having an experimental design becomes important. In order to establish the cause-and-effect link between manipulatives and problem solving, you need both a treatment group and a control group. Think of how we test a new drug: the treatment group receives the drug, and the control group gets a placebo. The results obtained in the treatment group are compared to those in the control group. If the treatment group results differ from the control group, then we can be more sure it was due to the treatment.

Q: *Can you talk about this using our example?*

A: Sure. Your class—the group being taught with math manipulatives—is the treatment group. The control group would get taught math without manipulatives. But it's a little more complicated that that; there are all the other variables to consider: age, gender, and mixture of ability levels, especially in math. The control group would need to be very similar to your class in these ways. Also, the control group would need to be taught in the same way as your class in all the other subjects except math, where no manipulatives would be used until the experiment was finished. In this way, the treatment—math manipulatives—is isolated as the only factor that could plausibly have caused differences between the groups in learning.

Q: *Hmm. But how would I get a control group? It seems like it would be hard to find a class of kids just like mine, taught just the same as mine, by a teacher similar to myself.*

A: It's even a bit worse than that. Strictly speaking, experimental research requires random assignment of subjects to treatments. Ideally, this would mean randomly assigning students (subjects) to treatment and control classrooms or groups within a single classroom. Often this is infeasible, so researchers use other means such as seeking out and matching groups that already exist; in other words, you would literally find a classroom like yours in a different school and use it as a control group! Other *quasi-experimental* designs (termed such because they don't use random assignment) seek to measure student improvement over time, so that differences in initial ability between treatment and control groups don't matter as much. Unfortunately, the construction of control groups is an area in which researcher bias can play a crucial role is biasing the outcome of an educational experiment. One point to remember is that no experiment, at least in educational research, is perfect. The point in experimental research is to create a situation in which *statistically significant* differences between the treatment and the control groups can be reasonably attributed to the treatment.

Q: *Statistical significance—I hear this term a lot. What does it mean?*

A: Let's suppose that in our example your class's average score on problem solving after using manipulatives for several weeks is somewhat higher than of the control group. Assuming you are comfortable with the validity of the control group, would you then feel comfortable reporting to the school board that manipulatives worked better than nonmanipulative-based teaching?

Q: *Not necessarily. I think I see what you mean. If the scores were drastically different I would be pretty*

continues →

sure the treatment worked. But for a small difference I wouldn't be so sure. Maybe if we both retook the test again the results would be reversed. Maybe the other class just had a bad day. On the other hand, if practically all of my students did better than practically all of the control students, even if by a lesser amount, then I would be pretty sure there was a difference. But if the difference was small, it may not be worth reporting. I'm guessing that statistical analysis comes into play here.

A: Correct. Using statistical tests, we can do two things. First, statistics such as mean and median summarize numerically the difference between the treatment and control groups. Second, and most important, statistics are used to analyze the two groups of scores so as to determine whether they are actually different due to the treatment, or different simply due to uncontrollable, "random" effects. If the difference is deemed as random, then the two groups actually have the same "true" score. The mathematical procedure used to make this determination is called an **ANOVA**—*analysis of variance*. The formulas used in an ANOVA discern from the distribution of the scores in both groups to determine how sure we are they are statistically different. The score (called a *p-score*) is reported as a number between 0 and 1. A *p*-score of 0 means there is no chance that the difference between scores is due to chance; we can be 100% sure it was the treatment. A *p*-score of 1 means that we are utterly unsure of how to explain the difference. Most of the time the *p*-score is somewhere in the middle.

Q: *How sure is sure enough?*

A: Traditionally, educational researchers use $p < .05$ as the cutoff for confidence in a result. This translates to 95% confidence. When we achieve 95% confidence, we use the term "statistically significant" to describe the result.

Q: *Is significance hard to achieve?*

A: It can be, especially for effects (differences) that are small or even medium. Unless the treatment makes a very sizable difference, the result of an experiment involving two classrooms of 30 students each is unlikely to be statistically significant.

Q: *So how do we create significant results?*

A: The most common way is to increase the sample size. The underlying mathematics of the ANOVA is such that the greater the sample size (referred to as *n*), the greater the experiment's power to identify smaller differences as statistically significant. If the experiment includes 10,000 students, even a very small effect may be deemed significant while a much larger effect among 50 students may be deemed not significant. So in experimental research, the greater the *n* the better. There are other ways to increase an experiment's power, such as using different statistical procedures to attempt to control other variables not taken into account in forming the control group, or creating so-called composite variables that more closely target the desired effect. Sometimes the statistical tests used to achieve significance are quite complex and create a dilemma for the reader in interpreting the procedures properly. You must bear in mind that the researcher's goal is to achieve significance, even for potentially very small effects, so sometimes very complex measures are taken to squeeze every last ounce of power out of an experiment.

continues →

Q: *That doesn't seem quite right. Let's say you manage to achieve significance for a small effect. Shouldn't a small but statistically significant difference mean less than a potentially large but statistically insignificant difference?*

A: Absolutely. When reading studies, one must look not only at the statistical significance, but practical significance as well. Experimental research studies sometimes focus exclusively on statistical significance, leaving issues of practical significance to the reader. In these cases it's up to you to decide whether the results of research have practical significance or usefulness in your context. That's why you have to become literate in all forms of research likely to affect your teaching practice.

Now that that you have the basic tools to read empirical research, continue reading the next section to see how it works.

Reading, Interpreting, and Deconstructing Quantitative Research

In this section we will guide your through reading, interpreting, and deconstructing a sample article (Gningue, 2003) representing "typical" quantitative research done by a teacher-researcher. Of course, no research is truly "typical"; there are literally hundreds of possible experimental designs. The proper interpretation of many designs requires specialized knowledge in statistics and therefore lies outside the scope of this book. Every study has its own strengths and weaknesses. The intent of this exercise is to develop a critical stance toward all forms of research, including those that involve quantitative analysis.

We present and annotate selected sections of text, as well as the ANOVA analysis. With each selection, you will be prompted to return to some of the questions suggested earlier in this section.

Reading the Abstract

Most research articles include an abstract, a self-contained summary of the purpose, methods, and findings of a research project. Consider the abstract of our sample article (Gningue, 2003, p. 207):

This article describes two professional development experiences for middle and high school mathematics teachers: one long term, the other, short term. The training of the long term group took place over an entire semester, in a 15-week, 45-hour graduate course, at an urban institution in New York City, that accented the use of computing technologies, especially the "TI83 Plus" graphing calculator and the "Geometers Sketchpad," to enhance the teaching of mathematics in secondary schools. The training of the short-term group took place in a series of three workshops totaling 7 hours, with teachers from the institution's Professional Development School, using essentially the same kind of technology tools. Attitude changes about the use of technology, obtained through a 16-item pre- and post-survey given to both groups, are presented. Comments from teachers' written reports and reflections about their beliefs in the effectiveness of using technology in the mathematics classroom are included as well. Professional development in computing technologies can be effective in changing teacher' attitudes and beliefs if implemented through a long-term, sustained, and coherent form of training that provides teachers with opportunities for active learning in the use of relevant technology tools in general.

continues →

📖 Answer the following questions in your notebook or journal and make additional comments:

- What is the researcher's critical question? Is this a "workable" critical question? (Refer back to Chapter 2 if necessary.)
- What intervention is being studied? In other words, what is being tried?
- What is the context of the study? In what ways has the researcher been successful and unsuccessful at employing the "control group" concept? How large are the groups being studied? What affect will this have on the results of the research?
- What is the main source of numerical data for this research?
- What other data will be used to bring additional meaning to the numbers?

Reading the Methods

→ TABLE 6.3: Research Participant Descriptions and Context (Gningie, 2003, pp. 211–212)

"Long-Term" Participants	"Short-Term" Participants
. . . (n = 12) included four female and eighth female teachers . . . who were students in the Master's of Mathematics Education program . . . The investigator chose this course for the study because it was redesigned to meet the request of students in the Master's program for more implementation of technology. Participation was voluntary. They were informed that lack of participation would have no influence on course grade.	. . . (n = 11) included six female and five male teachers. . . . none of these teachers had used technology to teach mathematics concepts. The technology training of the PDS [Professional Development School] teachers took place because one of the year's main PDS goals was to increase mathematics teachers awareness of technology-based curricula . . . the [decision was made] to use the only two citywide Professional Development Days available that year, to conduct three workshops to train them on how to use computing technologies to enhance the curriculum . . . not much computing technology was available at the PDS site.

Consider now details about the study teachers and context, given in Table 6.3. This study uses a *repeated measures* design. This means that the survey was used in a pre-test/post-test format with two groups, one receiving the treatment of interest (long-term professional development) and one receiving (in this case) an alternative treatment (short-term professional development).

📖 Answer the following question in your notebook or journal and make additional comments:

- In what ways are these groups well matched, meaning that comparisons between them will be valid? In what ways are they not well matched?

Reading the Numbers

We now show and explain two examples of ANOVA tables from the sample study (Gningue, 2003, pp. 215–216), one analyzing item 1 of the attitude survey, showing a significant difference between pre- and post-test scores for the "course" group, and another analyzing item 2, showing no significant pre- and post-test differences (see Table 6.4).

continues →

→ **TABLE 6.4: ANOVA Tables (Gningue, 2003, pp. 215–216)**

Item 1. Calculators should "only" be used to check work. (0 = strongly disagree, 4 = strongly agree)

Group[1]	Test[2]	Rank[3] 0 1 2 3 4	Mean[4]	SD[5]	MD[6]	t[7]	p[8]
Course ($n = 12$)	Pre	1 3 2 4 2	2.25	1.29			
	Post	6 5 0 1 0	0.67	.89	1.58	3.50	.027*
PDS ($n = 11$)	Pre	3 3 2 3 0	1.45	1.21			
	Post	1 8 0 1 1	1.36	1.12	0.1	.166	.871

Item 2. A graphing calculator can be used as a tool to solve problems that I could not solve before. (0 = strongly disagree, 4 = strongly agree)

Group	Test	Rank 0 1 2 3 4	Mean	SD	MD	t	p
Course ($n =12$)	Pre	2 2 2 4 2	2.17	1.40			
	Post	0 3 0 6 3	2.75	1.14	−0.58	−1.17	.267
PDS ($n =11$)	Pre	1 0 3 4 3	2.73	1.19			
	Post	1 1 2 3 4	2.73	1.35	0	0	1.00

* $p < .05$. This indicates for the reader which comparisons indicate statistically significant differences at the 95% confidence threshold.

1 Group: Denotes the two experimental groups, "Course" (received long-term training) and "PDS" (received short-term training).

2 Test: The analysis compares pre- and post-test scores.

3 Rank: Raw data from the Likert scale-type instrument. Numbers indicate how many participants ranked the item at each level.

4 Mean: Average ranking among group members.

5 SD: "Standard deviation" (SD) is a measurement of the variability in the data. SD indicates for the reader how much the rankings tended to vary between participants. The higher SD, the greater the variability, or "spread" in the data. In interpreting data, the SD must be viewed alongside the possible range of data. If the SD is small (large) compared to the range, this means that the spread of data within groups is small (large). The pretest SD was 1.29 compared to a mean of 5, meaning that there was substantial variability between the participants in how they responded (note that there was no consensus in the rankings for this item). The post-test SD was .89. There was somewhat greater consensus between participants on the post-test.

6 MD: Mean Difference: This is the average difference between pre- and post-test results for the participants in each group. For the "course" group, the difference was 1.58, for the "PDS" group the difference was 0.1.

7 t: t-score: The t-score is a statistic that gives a measurement of the statistical difference between the pre- and post-test for each group. t is based on the pre-and post-test means, SD, and n, the number of participants. The higher the t-value the greater the statistical difference between the pre- and post-test scores.

8 p: p-score: t-scores are converted to p-scores, a measure of the probability that the pre- and post-test scores are in fact different statistically. In this case, the "course" group comparison yielded a p-score of .027, meaning that we can be 97.3% certain statistically ($1 - p$ converted to a percentage) that difference in the pre- and post-test scores are different for reasons other than chance. This exceeds the generally accepted threshold of 95% confidence, so the difference in scores is deemed "significant." On the other hand, the "PDS" group comparison yielded a p-score of .871, indicating a confidence of only 13%, far below the threshold. We must conclude that the difference in scores for the PDS group is likely due to chance.

📓 Answer the following questions in your notebook or journal and make additional comments:

* On Item 2, it appears that there was a noticeable "mean difference" (MD) between pre- and post-test results for the "course" group, but the difference was not judged "statistically significant." How do you interpret this?

* Suppose the researcher wished to further study item 2. How could she redesign the study in order to increase the chances of finding a significant difference between pre- and post-test scores?

continues →

Reading and Deconstructing the Results

In total, the above study found that a "favorable shift" in the course group only occurred statistically for two items, 1 and 14 (Gningue, 2003, p. 219). Four other items (2, 3, 4, and 15) showed positive changes in the means that were not judged statistically significant.

Read the author's interpretation of the data (Gningue, 2003, pp. 218–219). To what main factor does the author attribute the difference between the "course group" and "PDS" group:

[Course Group:] What may explain the course's positive outcomes may be the length and extent to which concepts were studied. It took teachers 15 consecutive weeks to learn, practice, reflect, and be tested on the different activities involving the "TI83 Plus" graphing calculator and Geometers Sketchpad.

[PDS Group:] [T]he training seemed to have no effects on its participants views about the use of technology. . . . Such results were not surprising since the length and the extent to which the concepts presented to PDS teachers were very short, and their experiences with technology limited because of time constraints.

Summarize the author's interpretation of the results.

Deconstruction means to suggest possible alternatives to the author's interpretations of the study. Before looking at additional data from the study, take a moment to brainstorm possible alternatives to the author's interpretations as noted above.

The study's author includes some additional data in the form of participant comments and reflections. Consider these comments made by two of the workshop (control group) participants in regards to learning how to use the calculators in their classroom (Gningue, 2003, p. 221):

This is fine information, but I wonder why we are spending time on stuff we don't have, and I can't see when we'll have this stuff. We need to focus on attainable goals and situations. I suggest we get trained on how to do things with little or no technology, because that's where we are. (John, PDS teacher)

Good crash course, but the material relevant to 6th grade curriculum was not reviewed (Christine, PDS teacher).

The author interprets these comments by noting,

Indeed, the workshops did not provide teachers with time to develop a plan for using suggested materials and methods in their classrooms. A long, sustained, and more coherent form of training would have provided more opportunities for active learning, and could lead more PDS teachers to report more favorably about their use of technology. (p. 221)

Answer the following questions in your notebook or journal and make additional comments:

- Based on the above participant data, what alternative interpretations could you suggest?
- What are the strengths of this study? What are the weaknesses?
- How does the reader's *stance* (personal interests, beliefs, biases, and paradigm) affect the reading of this study? How could different readers draw very different conclusions about the study, and how would these different conclusions be grounded in different paradigms?

CHAPTER 7
TELLING THE STORY OF YOUR ACTION RESEARCH

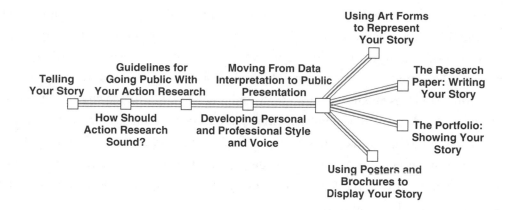

Chapter 7 asks, "How do you go public with your action research project? How do you develop both personal and professional voice? How can you represent the journey of your research ethically and authentically?" Sharing and celebrating what you have learned with others during the action research journey is an act of joy and humility. Bring your own ideas, voice and style to this chapter: what are other possibilities for presenting your research? Imagine well!

Telling Your Story

No journey carries one far unless, as it extends into the world around us, it goes an equal distance into the world within. —Lillian Smith (1954), *The Journey*

You now have a story to tell.

You've learned something important about teaching and learning. You have constructed meaning that makes the act of educating students more just, compassionate, and meaningful. You have (we hope) done a thorough job of analysis and interpretation, creating rich meaning from your raw data, just as the artisan twirls raw wool and dye into multicolored strands of yarn.

How will you share your story? How will you weave the many-colored yarn of your data interpretation into a tapestry that tells others of the mood, the patterns, the interconnections, and the "warp and woof" of your journey? Having reflected inwardly on the data, how will you extend the meaning outward, toward your colleagues in education?

"Going public" is an essential part of action research for three reasons. First, the process of going public is the process of articulating the actual learning that has happened, bringing together in one coherent whole both the journey and the destination. Second, sharing energizes professional educators—we love exchanging and brainstorming ideas, learning from each other as we read and experience (though vicariously) each other's travels. Third, sharing is celebration—there is great joy and satisfaction in sharing meaningful discoveries.

How you go public and share your research project will most likely be prescribed to some degree by the requirements of your teacher-education program. You may be required to write a formal paper, present a portfolio, create a poster or brochure for public display, or show other compiled evidence of your work. You may have the flexibility to use alternative means to go public, such as artistic representations or even performance. In this chapter we outline several of these possibilities. Use whatever specific information applies to your project and requirements.

If you are like many of our students, you may be leery of the process of putting your journey to words. Academic papers and projects you have done in the past may have seemed like dry, academic exercises lacking in personality and creativity. Action research, even written as formal academic work, must be anything but dry and impersonal. It is critical, no matter what the presentation mode you use, that your work reflect a blend of personal and professional tone and style, and that it is interesting, engaging, and yes, even captivating to the reader. This process takes some time and effort; we can give you general guidelines for developing your personal/professional style and voice.

In this section, the side roads of cultural context and self-analysis merge with the main road of action research. This is symbolic in that at this stage of your action research journey all "roads" merge as you complete the project and travel on to your next place as a professional educator. It is practical since any public presentation is a combination of the cultural context of academics and your personal style and expression.

Finally, throughout this section, there are specific suggestions, outlines, checkboxes, and other guides for going public. Don't let the seemingly straightforward guides limit your imagination. Eisner (2002) writes, "Imagination is no mere ornament; nor is art. Together they can liberate us from our indurated habits" (p. 10). As you go public with your action research story, let the process of creating be influenced by both imagination and art. What you have learned in the action research process that has opened up possibilities you might otherwise not have imagined about schooling? How have *you* changed? What emotions have you felt during the course of doing action research? How will you represent these? Don't consider data interpretation "done" as you begin to design your presentation; stay open to surprises even as you arrange, organize, and represent your work in its "final" stage. Your research may come together on a deeper level even while in the final stages of work. After all, as the poet William Stafford writes, "You can't tell when strange things with meaning might happen" (1993).

How Should Action Research Sound? The Cultural Context of Academic Work

When you hear the word *academic*, what do you think of? Just for fun, and harkening back to an early activity in this book, brainstorm a list of adjectives you might associate with *academic*.

Read through your list of words: Do you see yourself? Our students tend to think of both starched white collars and slumped-over disorderly tweeds mumbling in dim light when they consider the idea of an academic. It is time to face the fact that as one who has deliberately designed, implemented, and interpreted an action research project, *you* are an academic! You may need to revise your images if they don't fit you.

TELLING THE STORY OF YOUR ACTION RESEARCH

There are a number of myths surrounding the act of being academic. One is that such work is rarely practical. This myth contrasts with your action research project. While it is surrounded by the voices of experts, is grounded practically in the classroom, it is *research in action,* concerning practical dilemmas and questions. Another myth is that academic work is rarely personal. Your action research project, again by contrast, represents personal meaning making and places *you* at the center of the work.

A final misconception may be that academic work all "sounds the same," and is "devoid of voice." Listen to the voice and style in each of the following selections from well-known researchers, taken from opening paragraphs of published works:

The problem of this essay is that I need to do some fieldwork but don't know where to go. For quite some time now I have been stalled in ethnography—stopped, stuck, dead in the water. And since I am convinced that the technology called the essay can take me places I have been unable to imagine, I have decided to attempt a nomadic journey, to, in fact, travel in the thinking that writing produces in search of the field. (St. Pierre, 1997, p. 365)

In 1969, I was a junior at the University of Wisconsin and a member of Students for a Democratic Society (SDS), an organization formed to protest the war in Vietnam. Many of my activities as a member of SDS revolved around recruitment—talking to other students and getting them to come to rallies and be active in the demonstrations against the war. . . . After a simple recounting of some facts about napalm, brutality, and lives lost, the recruit was often on board. However, one group of students seemed to respond differently to my sales pitch; they were the art students. Their response was often that their politics were taken up in the art studio, not on the streets. I did not understand or accept this response. My response was one of anger at what I regarded as their conservatism and lack of activism. (Gitlin, 2005, p. 15)

People have gotten killed
And I really don't want anyone to suffer or die
But despite my sorrow and guilt I can't help but think
"First World blood is so much more expensive than Third World
blood."

My legs are trembling and so are my hands grasping the paper with the scribbled poems. I am very conscious of the fact that my jeans and shirt are not appropriate apparel for the evening. I surreptitiously try to display my *Allah* medallion more prominently, but my fingers refuse to cooperate. (Chaudhry, 2000, pp. 96–97)

These pieces were all published in either prominent educational research journals or collections of research works. The authors use *personal* (and thus their *political*) engaging voices, enticing the reader into the work to follow. "Academic" presentations can be personal, convincing, and inspirational, a living celebration of learning.

That said, the cultural context of higher education, the "academy," often does privilege certain kinds of research and presentation style more than others. Strictly rationalized patterns of thought sometimes carry more weight in academe. Modernist roots of thought mesh well with our "increasingly technicized cognitive culture" (Eisner, 2002, p. 8). Not surprisingly, statistical analysis and an objective, stereotypically scientific voice in presentation are privileged in much educational research, especially in the United States (see Cultural Context 6.1: *The Numbers Tell the Story*).

For example, many of us were taught to use the third-person voice in academic writing, avoiding the personal pronoun *I*. Consider the following opening passage, which uses a more traditional academic voice:

> Over the past 20 years, our understanding of reading acquisition and reading disabilities (RD) has increased dramatically. This understanding has been informed by the ongoing consolidation of a substantial scientific knowledge base in beginning reading, consisting of converging, multidisciplinary research evidence (Adams, 1990; National Reading Panel, 2000; National Research Council, 1998). One of the most salient and compelling conclusions to emerge from this knowledge base is the vital and cumulative consequences of establishing or failing to establish beginning reading skills in the early grades (Cunningham & Stanovich, 1998; Stanovich, 1986). (Coyne, Kame'enui, Simmons, & Harn, 2004, p. 90)

As readers and listeners, we expect to hear or read certain kinds of styles in certain kinds of contexts. When attending a lecture series on world affairs, for example, one most likely does not expect to hear a presentation that is slapstick in nature or uses a great deal of slang; if attending a variety show highlighting local talent, however, one might expect just about anything! Cultural norms determine what is "acceptable" and "appropriate" in a given situation. Negotiating research methodology, voice and style within the academic culture is an ongoing evolution. We provide some guidelines; you will need to do some work to find what is appropriate in your own setting.

Guidelines for Going Public With Your Action Research

As a preservice teacher presenting action research, expect to negotiate the tension between being professional and personal; you may think that somehow the two cannot go together. Preservice teachers should consider some general guidelines when presenting action research. For instance, it is appropriate to share:

- personal struggles of becoming a teacher during the action research project (how much is shared depends on how these struggles influence the actual process and results);
- conflicts that influence the action research process and results;
- moments of chaos and joy, and "mistakes," as they relate to the action research process and results.

It is not appropriate to share:

- personal stories that may be harmful to other people by exposing issues, moments, or questions they have not given you permission to share;
- negative incidents that reflect anger you have not yet worked through;
- judgments based upon your own value system and not data.

The merging of the professional and the personal has to do with *how* you share them. For example, here are two different ways a preservice teacher might write about her relationship with her mentor-teacher as it relates to her action research project:

I did not agree with my mentor-teacher, who apparently did not think it was important to take the extra time to do the preparation for the *Jeopardy* review game for the students in her fifth period class. Her class didn't do nearly as well on the final exam as my class, and I attribute this to my mentor-teacher's lack of commitment in preparing the review game.

The *Jeopardy* review game was successful; students did do well on the final exam and it appears this was a positive factor in these results. It did take me a great deal of time to prepare the game. My mentor-teacher and I discussed this: was it worth the gains in student learning to fall behind in other areas of my own work? How does a teacher find balance in making such decisions?

The second example not only uses different wording, but implies a different approach to this common preservice teacher dilemma. The first example reflects an attitude of judging, the second an attitude of questioning. Note that the second paragraph does not mention that students in her mentor-teacher's class did not do as well on the exam. Why? The action research project was not being conducted in the other classroom. There could be a number of other reasons that students in that class period did not do as well on the exam, besides the absence of the *Jeopardy* review game. However, the writer does mention the important question about use of time. This discussion is critical to the action research project and to future teaching plans the preservice teacher might design. Attention to this kind of detail makes the presentation of your work not only both professional and personal, it also make it ethical.

Additional Guidelines

Other general kinds of guidelines for academic work that the cultural context of the academy requires are as follows:

- Research writing should be very clear in identifying *who, what, where, when, how,* and *why*. None of this should be left open to readers' interpretations.

- Credit should be given where credit is due. In other words, cite sources when directly quoting or referring to someone else's ideas.

- Be explicit about limitations. This is particularly important to preservice action research projects where the limitations include critical variables like the amount of time spent collecting data and the amount of data.

- Maintain confidentiality. Use pseudonyms for all names.

- Be tentative in pronouncing grand narratives or making sweeping conclusive statements. For preservice teachers and their action research projects, this means using language like, "The data suggest . . .," "The data appear to . . .," "This is also supported in the literature, as well as in . . .," or "In my experience in this classroom. . . ."

Any action research presenter should also be mindful of the following:

- Purpose: What is the heart and soul of what you want to share? Spend your time and energies here.

- Audience: For whom are you presenting? How much do they know about the context of your study and of your student teaching experience? Present your work for the appropriate audience.

- Limitations: What time, physical and/or other cultural boundaries exist that will determine how you present your action research project? (For example, how much time do you have for a presentation? Are electrical plug-ins available for use of technology?)

Developing Personal and Professional Style and Voice

Style

Style in writing is not something glib—oh, yeah, she has style. It means becoming more and more present, settling deeper and deeper inside the layers of ourselves and then speaking, knowing what we write echoes all of us; all of who we are is backing our writing. —Natalie Goldberg (1990), *Wild Mind: Living the Writer's Life*

In the epigraph above, Goldberg is speaking of writing style, but she might well be describing the process of creating art, a presentation board, or the choice of font for a title page. *Style* as we use it here is about who you are and who you have become as a teacher. Style is how you represent the "layers" of yourself as a teacher in going public with your action research.

Most of our "style" comes from the context in which we live our lives; a theme that is present throughout this text in the "Cultural Context" side roads. Most of us wish our style as teachers to be "professional." Our vision of "professional" behavior, attire, and presentation is based upon the intersections of class, gender, ethnicity, and other cultural values, all embedded in the place where we learn these "professional" traits. In the context of going public with your action research project, you need to think about how professionalism is defined by your university culture. While there are some general kinds of norms that the academy (in a general sense) tends to privilege, every university, school within the university, and teacher-education program has its own rendition of professional. Reading the culturally privileged norms—the often unspoken codes—can be important in any professional educational setting. Once you know them you can decide whether to conform, how much to conform, or whether to choose your own way.

For example, you may propose to present your action research project as an interpretative dance. You believe this is "acceptable" since the syllabus indicates you may use "alternative forms of representation." However, as you proceed with your plans, you are asked to "complement" your dance with more and more traditional pieces of writing. In such an instance, you may be experiencing a "cultural code" that does not accept "dance" as "professional" or "appropriate" for university work.

Many styles may be considered *professional*. Being professional does not imply a "cookie cutter" look, set of actions, or language. There is room for individuality. If necessary, negotiate and nudge the systems of "tradition" to find your own way.

So, what do you consider your "personal style"? If your teacher-education instructor asks you to look "professional" for an event, how does that translate into behavior for you? What are the professional expectations for dress at the school where you student teach? How does the culture of the community where the school is situated influence this? Use Figure 7.1 to map out what the terms professional and personal mean to you.

→ FIGURE 7.1: Venn Diagram: Personal and Professional

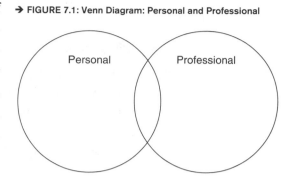

Voice

Being professional is more than looks alone. Seen more deeply, professional identity is about *voice*. What *voice* should you use when going public with your personal action research journey? *Voice* is a term we use in writing, but again, it can apply to all kinds of presentation. Everyone, Fletcher (1993) tells us, has an inner voice: "The writer may not know exactly what the inner voice represents (Unconscious? Superego? Spirit?) but the writer does know one thing: the inner voice is spokesperson for the inner life" (p. 68). What is the "inner life" of your experience telling you about your action research journey? Let your inner voice interpret the discoveries you have made in your journey. What specific moments come to mind, what student faces appear in your memory? What dialogue from the classroom do you hear? These lived moments in the classroom, the collected data that represents a story—*your* story. Going public with your story requires personal style and voice, overlaid with a professional framework, giving your presentation richness and reality of the reflective of life in the classroom.

Assuming you've been through the data interpretation phase and are contemplating going public with your action research at this time, pause for a moment and reflect on your "findings" or "results."

List these and then brainstorm words, colors, metaphors that best represent these results. How can you both personally and professionally represent these ideas in the voice projected in your final presentation? How will this look, sound, and be interpreted by others?

Some Guiding Thoughts on Going Public

Strive to be genuine and sincere in presenting your action research project. It is enough that you have journeyed through this process of learning to teach. Do not try to represent more or less than your own personal story of becoming a teacher. Seek to honor the students and the other professionals who have assisted you along the way. Circle back and answer these questions: "Why teaching?" "What kind of teaching?" "Who have I become?" And enjoy this final phase: it represents a great deal of effort and learning on your part. Celebrate this by designing a meaningful final presentation for both you and your colleagues.

Moving From Data Interpretation to Public Presentation

Listen to the past, future, and present right where you are. Listen with your whole body, not only with your ears, but with your hands, your face, and the back of your neck.—Natalie Goldberg (1990), *Wild Mind: Living the Writer's Life*

Listening is critical in getting started in the actual process of planning your action research presentation. In front of you, you have clusters, charts, categories, a timeline, and/or scribbles from your data interpretation. Now what? Listen. Follow Goldberg's advice by allowing your hands to scribble (and your head to follow), your feet to dance the rhythm of your story, by remembering moments of learning so rich that the hair on the back of your neck stands up. Listen to that data and the interpretation you have done. Return to the activity in the above section and use some of these memories as starting points.

Additionally, use the data interpretation tools to make the transition from interpretation to presentation. The act of organizing your thoughts on data interpretation for a presentation allows you to better articulate what you have learned.

Examples

Laurel used a series of clusters in completing data interpretation. As a result, she had three clusters centering on study skills she had introduced and used in the chemistry classroom: perspectives (students, her mentor-teacher, and her own) of the usefulness of each of these study skills, what the actual data said that supported or contradicted these perspectives, and a final cluster with unanswered questions. Laurel decided to organize her story according to each study skill she had tried during her action research. She created a new cluster by putting "study skills" in the center; she then made subcircles of "wall graffiti," "warm-up questions," "concept test cards," "chalkboard strategy," and "review games" (the study skills she implemented). Around this she organized the lessons learned; the perspectives from students, her mentor-teacher, and herself; and the literature she wanted to highlight. In another cluster, she organized her questions into categories and chose the ones she most wanted to discuss. Laurel posted these clusters around her computer and began to write the first draft of her "results."

Ian used his final synthesis statements from each category to organize his presentation. He put these in the order he wanted to use in his paper; he selected the ones he had the most data on and the most conviction about to focus on in his presentation. Using an unstructured outline format, he included under each selected synthesis statement the data and details to support the statement. From this outline, he began to put together his oral presentation.

Both of these examples highlight the first step in moving from data interpretation to presentation: organizing the interpretations into a format from which you can begin to actually put together your presentation. Use the pre-presentation planner in Figure 7.2 to organize your thoughts in a more linear way. Write concise statements for each heading; force yourself to be brief and to the point. If you already have this chart or something like it, feel free to skip this exercise.

→ FIGURE 7.2: Pre-Writing Chart

The main points I want to make in my presentation	Connecting points from the data	Connecting points from the literature	Question I still have from this area

This chart is downloadable from the companion website.

Now you are ready to actually begin writing the story of your research, organizing a portfolio, preparing for a research symposium, or creating alternative forms of representation. Skim through the following sections for an overview of the options. If you know which format you are going to use to go public, focus on the guidelines presented in the appropriate section.

The Research Paper: Writing Your Story

Writing the story of your action research can be a profound experience. This doesn't mean that it may not be difficult, but it can be another step of transformation as you organize the lessons learned, articulate the experiences, and finally share with others your new insights. Writer Anne Lamott (1994) describes this as "becoming conscious": "When you're conscious and writing from a place of insight and simplicity and real caring about the truth, you have the ability to throw the lights on for your reader" (p. 225). The process of writing your action research journey is an opportunity to "throw the lights on" and celebrate in sharing.

We recommend organizing your paper using nine major sections. These sections represent those commonly found in research papers. We've used these headings to introduce you to the tradition of research writing, but we have "tweaked" them to better represent preservice action research as presented in this text. The nine headings are:

- Abstract

- Introduction

- What I've Learned from Distant Colleagues (also referred to as the *literature review* or the *theoretical framework*)

- Clarifying My Action Research Project

- The Road Map of My Action Research Project

- The Story of My Action Research Project

- Further Reflection and Questions About My Action Research Journey

- References

- Appendixes

Of course, there are many other acceptable headings for organizing a research paper. Your program or course may require something different, or may skip some of the above headings altogether. We only offer the following template as a suggestion. Each of these headings is further described below.

An annotated and downloadable template, and examples of completed action research projects, are available on the companion website.

In addition to these nine headings, you will need to construct within each section your own *signposts* (Rankin, 2001) to further direct your readers. Signposts include the following:

- *Subheadings.* These are especially useful in long sections of writing. Group these sections into smaller organizational units so your reader can follow along. For example, you might include subheadings that represent themes you found in your literature review. (Note: Many of our students report being taught to avoid using subheadings in formal writing. We require it as common practice in educational research texts.) Be consistent in your use of terminology and/or structure with sub-headings throughout your paper—check with your professor for possible required stylistic preferences.

- *Transitional paragraphs.* These provide a road map to your readers, giving them direction about where the piece is going to go next. For example, in a transitional paragraph, you might state the purpose for the entire section and then introduce subheadings that will follow, and include a summary statement for the section.

- *Connecting or linking terms.* Words such as *however, in addition,* and *furthermore* help link together ideas for the reader.

The Abstract

The abstract consists of a single, concise paragraph describing the purpose, procedure, and results of your study. Use no more than 200 words. Don't write the abstract until you are nearly finished writing the larger research paper. Then draft the abstract as a summary, and redraft it until it reads as clearly and concisely as possible.

The Introduction

The goal of the introduction is to combine information about the setting and the story behind the action research project into a smooth narrative that gets the reader engaged in the work's context; the critical question is also introduced here. This section is usually about three to five pages long. The reader should have a good idea what the paper is about before finishing the first page. In the introduction, be cognizant of the following:

- *Context.* It is important to communicate to the reader a clear picture of the overall context of your action research project. The way you write the beginning of your paper lays the foundation (weak or strong) for the credibility and trustworthiness of your results and conclusions.

- *Storytelling.* Instead of telling about your setting, illustrate it for the reader using stories and anecdotes taken from your notes, reflections, and data. Introduce major players in your analysis and results.

- *Active and layered description.* Use multiple data sources to illustrate the setting and story behind the research. It must be clear to the reader that you are thoroughly immersed and engaged in your setting, and are therefore qualified to make credible analyses and interpretations. By referring to some data here you signal to the reader prior to the rest of the paper what type of research this is and how data was generally collected.

- *Your story.* It is also important to communicate to the reader a clear picture of yourself as the student teacher-researcher and how your own biases, experiences, and assumptions not only influence the study but also provided the fodder for your critical question. This may be woven into your illustration of context by including your own thoughts and memories. If there are key quotes that tell your story in another's words, consider including these quotes in this section. Make it clear how you arrived at your critical question.

- *Your critical question.* Bring your narrative to a climax in which you lay out your critical question in detail. Explain briefly what your action(s) consisted of. Tell briefly what your conclusions look like—don't try to keep the reader in suspense.

How to Write Good Introductory Paragraphs

Opening paragraphs can be the most difficult to write. For some reason, the blank page of the computer monitor blinks ominously as we begin. Try using (and expanding on) a quote, telling a personal story, or even writing an invitation. Here are a few examples from our students.

Example 1

On the first day of school at a large suburban high school, a freshman English teacher welcomed 130 new ninth grade students as they nervously made the transition from middle school to the big new world of high school—from childhood to semi-adulthood. With their eyes glazed they heard about the stringent requirements and responsibilities that were ahead, and I was surprised by a promise she made to them. Mrs. D. told the students that if they turned in every single assignment throughout the year, she would give them a passing grade—no matter how poorly they did on said assignments or tests. Surely this guarantee was far too generous, I thought. It's a "Get Out of Jail Free" card for students who don't meet standards!

Example 2

All study of human thought must begin by positing an individual who is attempting to make sense out of the world. —Howard Gardner (2004), *Frames of Mind*

The car shuttered and lurched as she edged onto the highway just as the sun began to peak in its crown from behind the westward range, illuminating the sky to the east and the yellow lines ahead. A new day awaited, a day that marked the start of a teaching journey. She took a deep breath, accelerated . . . popped the car into fifth gear and paused momentarily to reflect on the golden events of the past, and the uncertain events that loomed close in the near future. Over, around, up and down mountainous and forest trails she'd trekked, identifying creatures great and small, green and otherwise with young, avid learners clamoring at her heels. After three years of experience teaching in the outdoors, she felt prepared for what lay ahead on this journey, but wondered exactly what she could expect from this new environment.

Example 3

Welcome to the Avi Coffee Shop. Come in, find your friends, pick up something interesting to read, and be ready when the maître'd stops by to bring you a snack. However, it will not be coffee and croissants. More likely it will be hot cocoa and a granola bar, or apple juice and popcorn. You are not at Starbucks, you are in Mrs. Browning's fourth grade class. Friends, interesting literature, snacks, and great conversation are what Avi Coffee Shop is about; come on in and join in the conversation!

What I've Learned From Distant Colleagues

The goal of this section is to introduce the reader to the major issues and/or themes learned from distant colleagues in the literature surrounding your critical question. By broadening your readers' understanding of the major issue surrounding your research, you further solidify the credibility and trustworthiness of your work. This section is generally about three to five pages long.

We find that it is best to organize this section in one of two ways: either group the literature you are reviewing by themes or review the literature to provide an overview of the history leading up to the framework for your action research project. For example, one of our students organized her literature review according to these themes: (1) literature on the effectiveness of reading aloud; (2) strategies for increasing reading fluency and comprehension; and (3) meaningful reading fluency and comprehension assessment strategies. Another student organized her literature review as a historical overview of assessment in mathematics. Her review looked at the evolution of mathematical assessments to the present emphasis on problem solving.

Choose a format that will allow your readers to make the connection between your literature review and the action research study by establishing the theoretical foundation of the action, curriculum review, self-study, or ethnography you later describe in your action research paper. (Note: This section will contain the majority of your citations, although we suggest bringing in the voices of distant colleagues throughout your paper.)

Clarifying My Action Research Project

This is a concise one-page section focusing your reader on the essential elements of your action research project. Assume a more professional style and tone to precisely answer:

- *who* is involved in the project;

- *what* the critical question is and what was implemented or analyzed;

- *where* the project took place (description of setting);

- *when* the data collection occurred (dates of implementation and/or data collection, length of study);

- *how* data collection was completed (these are brief statements—the next section gives this information in more detail);

- *why* you conducted the study;

- the limitations of the study.

This subsection may seem redundant given that you have already revealed your critical question and action(s) earlier. The intent here is to clearly focus your reader and to use a technical, professional tone that clearly defines the study before the reader begins the story of your research.

The Road Map of My Action Research Project

The goal of this section is to inform your reader about:

- the interventions, analysis, or strategies you implemented;

- the data collection strategies and sources you used;

- the contents of the data sets you collected;

- the methods you used to analyze, interpret, and deconstruct the data;

- changes you made in your research design.

This section should be three to five pages long. Continue the professional tone of the "Clarifying My Action Research Project" section. This "Road Map" section is a technical piece of the paper in which the reader gets an inside view of your research process. The idea here is that someone else could do the same research in their classroom by following your detailed descriptions of methodology.

The Story of My Action Research Project

The goal of this section is to illustrate what you have learned as related to your critical question. Use your data to tell the story of your research and support your conclusions and emerging theories. This section is the heart and soul of your action research paper. This is where you tell *your* story. The section is rich in voice, style, and data. Remember this classic bit of writing advice: as you write, *show, don't tell.* Interweave important data into your narrative. Include tables, charts, and quotes from interviews and your observations and reflections. Use your data to illustrate your ideas, and to provide the readers the freedom to draw their own conclusions as well. Explain how you interpret your data. Support your interpretations with examples. Use multiple data sources to support major assertions or ideas. Include multiple voices and perspectives. Be sure to include other voices, such as those of critical colleagues, students, and distant colleagues (literature review). *Deconstruct your work*, providing counter examples and alternative interpretations.

Two examples of writing are given below; one *tells* the story; the other *shows* the story. The voice in the first example is flat and somewhat detached; the second example includes a lively voice and style and makes the most of narrative structure. The examples are based upon an action research project to develop the artists' abilities of grade three students.

Example 1: Telling the Story

One student found it very difficult to give up the idea that "good" art is art that is a realistic depiction of what is observed. This student struggled in her art efforts; she often destroyed her work. During the self-portrait drawing assignment, however, she appeared to have a change of attitude. Although she accidentally created a hole in her picture from rubbing too hard, she found a way to incorporate the hole into her final self-portrait. I was very pleased, and encouraged her work and her ability to do this.

Example 2: Showing the Story

Rosie, the class perfectionist, was crushed: she had rubbed too hard and ripped a hole in her self-portrait. When asked for another paper, I reminded her of our class motto, "There are no mistakes—only opportunities." A little later, she came back with a finished portrait. Rosie had taken that hole, that "mistake," and purposefully ripped it a bit more, turning it into a halo! The ripped edges gave the portrait a unique and beautiful texture. "You know what?" she said, "That hole is my favorite part of the picture." In that moment, Rosie discovered her artist self.

Further Reflection and Questions About My Action Research Journey

In this section, you bring themes together and begin the process of concluding your paper. Consider the following questions as writing prompts for this final reflection of your action research journey:

- What are some of the most important lessons you will take into your teaching career?

- What will you do differently next time?

- What additional questions did this research project pose for you?

- What was your action research journey like? How has this journey transformed your image of teacher, teaching, students, schools, learning? How have your paradigms been altered, confirmed, and/or challenged?

- What have you learned about action research? How has your definition of action research changed? How do you see yourself using this process in the future?

How to Write a Memorable Conclusion

Conclusions are tough: how do you end a good date, or say good-bye after a long visit? More than likely, you will write your concluding paragraph several times before you are satisfied. An effective way to write the concluding paragraph is to use a quote, either from someone famous, your students, other participants, or from your own researcher's notebook. Another possibility is to end with a short story, a vignette, from your data that illustrates the central focus of the study. Sometimes, a combination works well.

In the example below, the student teacher had conducted an action research project about homework. In his classroom, students either did not turn in homework, or they turned in poor-quality homework. He attempted two different kinds of homework strategies to improve both quality and completion rates. However, he found that a reward system that gave students "free time" points for turning in homework regardless of quality trumped all his other homework strategies. This is how he concluded his piece:

To conclude my research I decided to ask the entire class one question. "Would you rather earn homework points by turning in an assignment that you know you could do better on or sacrifice the homework points but get the best score in the class on a big assignment?" Seventy-six percent of the class said they would choose the homework points. Only six of the 25 students polled would take the top score. Students are getting mixed messages. They're motivated to get the homework points even though we want them to produce their best work. They're motivated by the wrong thing; completing assignments no matter what the quality is. Absolutely, they still struggle to complete their work, but they do understand that completing work is what is valued regardless of the quality. More than anything else, I've learned that students are smart. They learn early on in the school year what is important, and most students strive to achieve that. As a teacher, I need to be aware of this and careful not to send a message to my students that I don't want them to receive. Students will provide us with the information we need to create the types of classrooms we want if we look for it. I credit the students for teaching me the lessons that I will take from this action research project, one of which is summarized by this quote: "good values have to be grown from the inside out" (Kohn, 1994). How to do this is my next action research project.

This conclusion returns to the heart of the action research study. It summarizes the main lesson the student teacher-researcher learned. And it encourages the reader to ask, "What kind of mixed messages do I send my students?" This makes for a memorable final curtain call!

References

Consult carefully with American Psychological Association style guidelines, or whatever other citation methods are required in your program, to ensure that references are written correctly, as they are another important element of trustworthiness. Having proper references is important in ensuring that credit is given where credit is due. Plagiarism is not only legally and ethically wrong but cheapens the quality of your journey. Attend to references carefully.

Appendices

A writer places in the appendixes additional information that supports or illustrates points in the paper. Items in the appendixes allow the reader to go deeper or gain a clearer view of what is being said in the main text. Appendixes are important, but they are not a "dumping ground." For example, not all data goes in the appendixes; however, a log of data sets may be appropriate. Not all student work would be placed in the appendices, but a sample that clarifies an assignment would be appropriate.

Possible inclusions in the appendixes might be:

- a log of data sets or specific items from a data set;

- assessments;

- surveys, questionnaires, and interview questions;

- letters sent to parents (including those used in obtaining informed consent from your students);

- lesson plans;

- artifacts.

Note that anything placed in the appendices must be referenced in the text of the paper. Check the appropriate citation guidelines on how to do this.

A Final Word on Writing

Take this final word of advice from author Ray Bradbury (1994) on writing: "If you are writing without zest, without gusto, without love, without fun, you are only half a writer. . . . For the first thing a writer should be is—excited. He should be a thing of fevers and enthusiasm" (p. 4).

This is most likely one of the last projects for your teacher-education program. Have fun! Be yourself! Enjoy! Become a teacher with both zest and gusto and let it show in writing your action research project.

The Portfolio: Showing Your Story

A portfolio is another demonstration of your action research journey. While portfolios share some organizational principles with formal papers, portfolios are much more visual and inter-active, allowing the audience a closer, less-processed look at your research work. A collection of artifacts organized into a three-ring binder notebook or in electronic format allows readers to travel with you through the stages of learning. Your portfolio should demonstrate your abil-ity to be reflective in using assessment data to better facilitate learning for students, and to answer questions you have about your teaching practice.

We recommend organizing your portfolio into the following categories:

- Introduction
- The Road Map of My Action Research Project
- Discovery Documentation
- What I have Learned from My Action Research Project
- Further Reflection and Continuing Questions About My Action Research Journey
- Annotated Bibliography.

The Introduction

This section functions as a narrative that provides an overview of the action research project. Write the introduction to your portfolio much as you would if writing the more traditional research paper. As part of the portfolio introduction, answer the questions *who, what, where, when, how,* and *why* (see the section "Clarifying My Action Research Project" above). The rest of the portfolio fills in the details of the overview presented in the introduction.

The Road Map of My Action Research Project

In this section, include a brief overview (one or two paragraphs) of how you collected data. Follow this with a chart or other visual image showing how the data was collected; an anno-tated timeline may be a good option. The visual image should demonstrate and support the trustworthiness of the data. Include a data collection log that lists the data sets you collected.

Discovery Documentation

Communicate the essential themes of your action research journey in this section. You may include charts, graphs and/or tables of data collected, pictures relating to the action research project, samples of student work, lesson plans, and reflections from your researcher's notebook. The secret to an effective "Discovery" section is organizing documentation in a meaningful way with appropriate narrative so that a reader can clearly understand the story you are telling. We think you will find it most effective to organize this section in chronological order, beginning with your first data set and moving through your student-teaching experience. (If you used a timeline for data interpretation, this is a good tool to return to in organizing this section.) Select the documentation that best illustrates the primary discoveries you have made. You do not need to include *everything*; it is better to select for quality representation.

As an example, suppose you decide to illustrate the importance of assigning equally important roles to students during cooperative learning. To do this in your portfolio, you could choose one lesson you taught without clearly defined meaningful roles, and another where these roles were clearly defined. This subsection would begin with a brief narrative introduction; the introduction provides the reader a road map for reading the documentation that follows: the purpose of this subsection, a brief description of the two lessons, and a list of the artifacts to follow. The artifacts would include the two cooperative learning lessons (with the roles specified), pictures of students working on the two projects, sample student work, and, finally, selections from your researcher's notebook from each of the two lessons. Each artifact should be clearly labeled. If you have written analytic memos, include them in this section as well.

Sometimes student teachers need to demonstrate through a portfolio how they have met or are moving toward specific standards. If this is true, you may want to consider organizing this section around each standard, or specifically making the connection between the standard(s) and the content of each display in the introductions.

The depth of this section depends on the amount of data you have collected (in a short study, you may display the entire data set), the parameters determined by your teacher-education program, and the physical boundaries of a three-ring binder notebook. A variety of documentation will enrich this section, but all documentation should support the primary discoveries of your action research project.

What I Have Learned From My Action Research Project

This section summarizes the major themes, recommendations or highlights of your project. You may want to organize this section by synthesis statements. For each synthesis statement, include salient data and voices of distant colleagues that support the statement.

Further Reflection and Continuing Questions About My Action Research Journey

This section of your portfolio is a written narrative raises questions you still have about your action research project. These may be areas for continued research. They may represent wonderings, "I wonder what might have happened if I would have realized earlier the power of music to motivate my students." This is also a place for final reflection on the process of action research and your plans for continued implementation of action research as a practicing teacher. Use the instructions from the above section, "Further Reflection and Questions about My Action Research Journey," for additional guidance in completing this section.

The Annotated Bibliography

An annotated bibliography includes the citation of each source followed by a brief summary (one concise paragraph) of the source (the annotation). The annotated bibliography should demonstrate your ability to find appropriate sources to support teaching and learning as demonstrated in your action research project. The connection between the citation and the action research project should be evident in each annotation. Consider organizing this section by themes or categories that represent your research design and synthesis statements to better demonstrate the connection between the literature you have used and your project.

A sample entry could look like this:

Calkins, L. Ehrenworth, M., & Lehman, C. (2012). *Pathways to the common core: Accelerating achievement*. Portsmouth, NH: Heinemann.

The authors provide an overview of the English Language Arts Common Core State Standards in a useful and practical way. I found the book useful in increasing my understanding of what the CCSS really say and what this means to me as a teacher. Most useful to my study is the section on developing performance assessments. I used these guidelines to plan for data collection.

Formatting the Portfolio

Organization is of utmost importance in a portfolio; items must be arranged in such a way that a reader can travel easily through your journey. Include a table of contents, title pages, and brief narratives as guides. Consider aesthetics as well. The use of color, borders, and different fonts can add to the overall professional and personal presentation. Aesthetic devices ought to complement, not overpower, the content. More is not usually better in this category. Be inventive, invite humor, allow your personality to shine through the documentation and illustrate the teacher you have become.

The Web-Based Portfolio

We like the idea of web-based portfolios. They allow for more inventiveness by allowing the use of digital photography and movies, as well as using hypertext navigation to ease the readers journey through your work. You may have access to a portfolio-making tool as part of your teacher-education program or you may use various tools available online, such as Google-Docs (www.google.com). Check with your educational technology instructor or other tech-savvy colleague for ideas.

Using Art Forms to Represent Your Story

"A Guide to Artform-Based Presentations" is available on the companion website.

Why would anyone want to make their action research presentation into an art project? Consider the following story. Christy completed her student teaching in an elementary classroom with a very diverse group of learners. Particularly troubling to her was how to bring some of the students who had difficult learning disabilities and emotional challenges into the class-room community. Her project was empathetic, compassionate, and deliberate in attempting to create an inviting, safe, and responsive classroom for all her students. Christy collected rich and interesting data but when it came time to interpret this data and organize it, Christy was stuck. None of the tools we suggested seemed to help. In working with Christy, we real-ized that she often used art to express herself in other assignments and projects. Her action research journal was full of symbolic drawings. So, Christy drew her interpretations, first as sketches, and then, as her final project.

Dewey (1954) has written, "The function of art has always been to break through the crust of conventionalized and routine consciousness. . . . Artists have always been the real purveyors of news, for it is not the outward happening in itself which is new, but the kindling by it of emotion, perception and appreciation" (pp. 183–184). There are many ways to repre-sent, as art the story of your action research: painting, sculpture, music, interpretative dance, fiction, storytelling, digital photography, and digital video, just to name a few. Performance narratives often include poetry and dramatic representations of specific experiences or data. Artistic forms of representation can provide rich and expressive ways to tell your story, to capture that part of the experience that does not conform to words alone. The process of cre-ating art can be particularly meaningful to both the artist and the audience as relationships between experiences, emotions, and literature are explored. In developing such representa-tions, the guidelines at the beginning of this chapter should still be followed. How they appear in your presentation is a matter of your interpretation. Since art representations are still rela-tively new to academic culture, check with your professor for additional guidelines.

"An Example of Using Art to Think and Present Research" is available on the com-panion website.

Using Posters and Brochures to Display Your Story

A poster presentation template is downloadable from the companion website.
Research symposiums or other pubic settings are often the culminating venue for sharing action research projects. One format commonly used at such events is a "poster session." Poster board presentations are common at professional conferences. Creating a poster may be a good skill/art to develop as you move forward professionally.

The professional requirements of most poster presentations boards include:

- your name;
- the title of your research project;
- the name of your university and date of publication;
- the critical question(s);
- the research design and select data;
- final reflection and continuing questions.

Be attentive to spelling, punctuation, and mechanical errors. Include essential elements only; too many words make the board "busy." Artifacts or pictures of artifacts may be included. Remember, if you are displaying pictures of students, you should have permission to do so.

It's a good idea to provide your poster audience a short handout to go along with your poster. We recommend a trifold brochure for this purpose, a summary of your action research project. Trifold formatted brochures are printed front to back; templates are available on most word processing programs. The professional requirements of most brochures include:

- your name;

- the title of your research project;

- the name of your university and date of publication;

- the critical question(s);

- the research design and select data;

- final reflections and continuing questions;

- a bibliography of key sources;

- your contact information.

As for posters, be attentive to spelling, punctuation, and mechanical errors. Include essential elements only; allow for enough unprinted space to make the brochure easy to read.

These are the professional requirements for a presentation board and brochure; but personal style should reflect who you have become as a teacher. Combine color, texture, symbols, and artifacts to represent your story and yourself as a teacher. Keep in mind how this intersects with the professional in making your presentation aesthetically appealing while representing you and your story.

Celebrating and Sharing: Find Joy and Humility Through Action Research

We may find joy in celebrating each others' strengths, but there is also unleashing of joy when we join together in our humility. —Rachel Kessler (2000), *The Soul of Education: Helping Students Find Connection, Compassion, and Character at School*

Going public with your action research project is a time for celebration. As you share with your colleagues, there is strength in realizing how much you have learned, grown, become. There is also recognition of how much more there is to still discover. There is *joy* in both.

Chapter 7: Content and Process Questions

1. How do you define voice, style and professionalism in academic presentations? How does this reflect your paradigm?

2. Anne Lamott (1994) is quoted in this chapter, "When you're conscious and writing from a place of insight and simplicity and real caring about the truth, you have the ability to throw the lights on for your reader" (p. 225). What are the critical insights from your study? What "lights" do you want to throw on for your reader?

3. What parts of your action research journey are most difficult for you to share? Why? What parts are easiest to share? Why? Work through your responses with a critical colleague.

CHAPTER 8
LIVING ACTION RESEARCH AS A PROFESSIONAL EDUCATOR

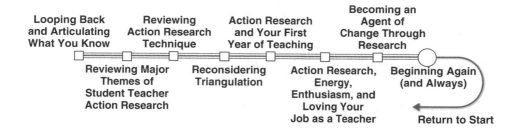

Coming to the end of the action research project, to the end of a teacher education program, and *you are ready to begin again*. Maybe that's the best part about teaching: there is always another day, another new start. How will you use what you have learned from the action research process to be a more intelligent teacher of change? How will you use strategies and ways of thinking learned during the action research process to "be the change" you would like to see in education? Read this chapter with an eye to your own future—and the future of the children and adolescents you will teach, local communities where you will live, and the global community where we all engage.

Looping Back and Articulating What You Know

Becoming a teacher . . . means more than acquiring technical knowledge and expertise. It means becoming a teacher morally, through one's commitment to the children one teaches and to the wider social purposes for which that teaching is done . . . . It means becoming a teacher emotionally . . . through caring for and engaging passionately with others . . . . Becoming a teacher also means becoming a teacher politically by having to negotiate and adjust to the continuing constraints of schooling . . . .

— *Andy Hargreaves and Noreen Jacka (1995), "Induction or Seduction?*
Postmodern Patterns of Preparing to Teach"

Reread the epigraph above. How has your experience with action research prepared you to be a teacher along moral, emotional, and political dimensions? Who have you become as a teacher, and where might your continued self-evolution and reinvention take you? How do you see the art and science of action research as a scaffold that might support who you become as a professional educator? Respond to these questions in your notebook or journal; if possible, discuss them with your colleagues. Respond in writing, drawing, or by clustering your thoughts.

Action research can serve as a bridge between the world of student teaching and that of your new career as a professional educator. The skills, attitudes, and spirit of inquiry inherent in action research can be useful in meeting the challenges of your first year of teaching. Teacher-action researcher as a part of your professional identity can act as an ongoing scaffold as you become a teacher who is morally, emotionally, and politically astute. As you near completion of your teacher-education program (or at least the end of your action research project), take time in this final section to loop back through some of the primary themes of this text as you contemplate growing yourself as a professional educator.

Reviewing Major Themes of Student Teacher Action Research

The role of your personal paradigm in influencing who you are as a teacher is a central theme of the present volume.

📖 Begin by reflecting on what you have learned about your own paradigm, how your paradigm has changed, and how it might continue to transform you as an educator. Completing the following phrases through writing/drawing your own synthesis statements.

- My paradigm for thinking about education has changed in these ways:

- I can identify the following key influences on my paradigm for thinking about teaching:

- The above translate into the teacher I have become as illustrated by:

- These are areas within my paradigm through which I want to continue to question, grow, and explore:

Another major theme of this text is the role of cultural context in teaching. Who you are and how you are positioned (according to gender, race, ethnicity and other defining categories) work alongside your values and beliefs (paradigms) to influence all of your perceptions and practices as a teacher. What have you learned about *context* during the action research process?

📖 Complete the following phrases through writing, drawing, or clustering:

- When I first began reading about cultural context (community and school values, socioeconomics, gender, religion, ethnicity, and other defining categories) in this book I thought:

- I understand how context influenced by action research project and teaching in these ways:

- When I accept a teaching position, this is what I want to remember about cultural context:

Reviewing Action Research Technique

Throughout the action research process, you have learned the art and science of observing students, interviewing or listening to students and other participants in the educational setting, and collecting artifacts or assessments to inform your teaching. Continued growth in these skills can strengthen the bridge between being a beginning teacher and being a teacher of influence.

📖 Consider what you have learned and how you want to enhance these skills by responding to the following prompts. Use specific stories and/or examples when possible.

Observation

Complete the following statements:

- This is what I have learned about making observations in the classroom (include some tools that have become favorites):

- My observations can be useful and dangerous in these ways:

- I find I am most willing to overlook:

- The quick judgments I am most likely to make include scenarios like:

Interviews

📖 Consider what you have learned about interviewing, listening, and seeking students' voices and other perspectives in completing the following statements. Use specific stories and/or examples when possible.

- This is what I have learned about interviewing students and other participants in education (include tools that have become favorites):

- When interviewing students, I find I am most interested in the following:

- I find it most difficult to listen to_____because:

- Based upon my responses, this is what is useful and dangerous about they way I interview (listen to, seek other perspective from) others:

Artifacts: Collecting and Interpreting Assessment Documentation

📖 Consider what you have learned and how you want to grow your abilities to collect and assess artifacts by responding to the following prompts. Use specific stories and/or examples when possible:

- What I have learned about collecting student artifacts as assessment:

- What I have learned about the limits of assessments:

- I consider the following critical points in designing, collecting, and interpreting student artifacts as assessment (and this is what makes them trustworthy):

- In the future, I plan to grow my abilities in this area by:

Reconsidering Triangulation

Throughout this text, we have discussed triangulation as a means of building a trustworthy set of data. Triangulation, or actively seeking multiple perspectives and voices, can be a powerful tool in many teaching scenarios. For example, understanding a student who is constantly a behavior challenge in the classroom requires triangulation, or data gathering from many sources, such as parents and other teachers. When you hear a "rumor" about a district's decision regarding pension plans, you may want to "triangulate" what you hear by looking at several perspectives before you believe it entirely. When you perceive a lesson or unit to be a "disaster," triangulating the data may provide useful insight. When you hear, "Research says . . ." keep triangulation in mind. Triangulation is the larger concept behind critical thinking: it is the act of suspending judgment while seeking multiple perspectives, voices, solutions, and possibilities. What have you learned about triangulation that you want to take with you into your first teaching position?

Respond to the following prompts using specific examples and/or stories:

- This is what I have learned about triangulation and its usefulness in the teaching/learning process:

- This is what I have learned about triangulation and making classroom decision:

- This is what I have learned about triangulation and assessing classroom climate:

Recall Hargreaves and Jacka (1995), who state that one must become a teacher *morally*, *emotionally*, and *politically*. We add to this list that a teacher must become a teacher *intellectually*. Loop back through your responses above: who do you want to continue to become *morally*, *emotionally*, *politically*, and *intellectually*?

Action Research and Your First Year of Teaching

Who do they think they are, talking back to their teacher with such disrespect? When I was 8 years old, I would have never dreamed of speaking to an adult that way. Did I go to college for this?
    —*Patricia Anguiano (2001), "A First Year Teacher's Plan to Reduce Misbehavior in the Classroom."*

The skills of observing, listening, and collecting artifacts coupled with a paradigm informed by action research can position a first year teacher to successfully face a multitude of challenges. If you are anticipating your first teaching position, consider the weeks just prior to your first day in the classroom, as well as those initial first two weeks of teaching. How might you use the skills of action research as presented in this text?

We see the following possibilities; compare and contrast them a list of your own making. Once you have your first teaching position, return to Chapter 2: *Listening to Your Setting*. Find out as much as you can about the context of your new position—and if you believe you are very familiar with this setting, it may be wise to test those assumptions—by using the activities described in Chapter 6. Use this information to plan systems of organization, structures, and relevant lessons for the first two weeks of school.

- During the first two weeks of school, use surveys to gather data about students' attitudes, learning styles, homework habits, interests, and strengths; complete essential academic assessment to establish the diversity of learning levels.

- Be deliberate in planning for systems of management and structure based upon what you discover about your students and their community, as well as your own comfort levels and needs in this area. Be deliberate in teaching these systems. Finally, be deliberate in setting up ways to gather data concerning the effectiveness of these systems.

- Although you may be exhausted after those first days, take time to write in your notebook or journal, sketch, cluster, or otherwise freewrite about your days; record both your own behavior and that of your students. Start a list of questions and resist answers or solutions that are too easy.

- After the first two weeks, plan some time and space to analyze, synthesize, and deconstruct your data; let this data guide your next steps as a teacher.

- Consult critical colleagues, both local and distant, to find encouragement and ideas.

This is a short list. As we have said before, a list can be dangerous, reducing what is complex and messy to overly simplistic answers and actions. Our list is an illustration of how to position yourself as a new teacher-researcher with a certain way of thinking, a particular teaching stance. If your days are hectic, you may say, "I don't have time for a frequency count chart!" But consider the alternative, which is trying one solution after another as if attempting to aim at a target while blindfolded. It may be worth it to adopt a more intentional approach suggested by action research.

The first year of teaching is about classroom management issues, rethinking big concepts like *control* and *authority*, and reframing what you believe about yourself and your students. Seeking multiple perspectives and the voices of critical colleagues, considering context, and developing the techniques of action research as a way of thinking and practicing can provide a road map allowing you to stay—for a long time, and satisfied—in education.

Thinking About the First Year

Scenario 1

Fletcher's ninth grade language arts class threatens to drive him just a little crazy; it isn't that students are mean or even really disrespectful, but they are "everywhere at once," talking, laughing, and enjoying what seems like everything but the content, which is suppose to Shakespeare. Fletcher isn't sure how he is going to get the class through four major plays during the semester. After one particularly frustrating day, Fletcher writes in his journal about what he *does* know: (1) students think Shakespeare is boring; (2) they reportedly "don't get it"; (3) most of the students are reading just at grade level or slightly below; (4) over two-thirds of the students have never seen a play; (5) students' behavior seems to decline just after directions have been given, when they are to read individually, and 10 minutes before class ends.

Without coming to conclusions or providing possible solutions to this scenario, consider how action research techniques might be used to gather additional data and create an informed plan of action:

- What techniques of action research are already being used in the scenario?

- How might interview techniques be used to provide additional data on the dilemma?

- How might observations be useful?

- What artifacts might be deliberately collected and analyzed?

- What additional perspectives or voices might be helpful in analyzing the situation?

- What assumptions may need to be deconstructed?

Scenario 2

Dorrey never knew 22 first graders could be so "out of control." They never seem to stop moving or talking. Misbehavior significantly increases during math. The school's math curriculum incorporates multiple tactile and kinesthetic techniques, and Dorrey is amazed at what a first grader can do with a handful of colorful cubes. She asks a colleague to come and observe during a 30-minute math session. Here are some of the results of the observations:

- Six different kinds of manipulatives were used during the 30-minute class period.

- There were eight total transitions.

- Children consistently began playing with manipulatives prior to listening to all of the instructions given by the teacher.

- The lesson introduction did not appear to connect to the use of the manipulatives.

- Children at two table groups appeared to be "bartering" with the manipulatives; children at a third table were constructing interesting designs.

- The four English Language Learners [those for whom English is a second language] did not follow any of the directions.

- Dorrey mostly stayed at the front of the class and shouted over the children to various table groups.

Without coming to conclusions or providing possible solutions to this scenario, consider how action research techniques might be used to gather additional data and make an informed plan of action:

- What techniques of action research are already being used in the scenario?

- How might interview techniques be used to provide additional data on the dilemma?

- How might observations be useful?

- What artifacts might deliberately analyzed?

- What additional perspectives or voices might be helpful in analyzing the situation?

- What assumptions may need to be deconstructed?

Your first year of teaching may very well include scenarios like these. Becoming a teacher who thinks and acts using action research principles early in your career can help you maintain the energy and enthusiasm necessary to happily remain in the teaching field. Be realistic about your goals: you won't likely do a formal action research project, but you can begin to think in this way now and grow your professional future.

Action Research, Energy, Enthusiasm, and Loving Your Job as a Teacher

Gandhi said, "We must be the change we wish to see in the world." I want to see students feeling excited about learning. I want to see students being engaged in school because it is relevant not only in content but also in technique. I want to see teachers who are skillful at employing varied techniques to appeal to the multiple intelligences of learners, using technology as a tool that allows for the pursuit of curiosity and encourages individual strengths to shine forth. This research has taken me giant steps toward becoming the change I want to see in the world of teaching.

—Carley, a student teacher-researcher

Carley wrote the above reflection at the end of her action research project and her student-teaching practicum, one week prior to graduation from her teacher-education program. Like most of us in education, Carley is beginning her career idealistically. She is equipped with many skills, and is *ready* and *willing* to make a difference in the world through her role and contributions as a teacher. Her action research project has taught her ways to become the teacher she desires to be.

Even as Carley and her colleagues in the program contemplated graduation, they sensed that it would take determination to maintain their dream of being a teacher of influence. Consider their comments exiting their teacher-education program:

- It is important to remember how this feels, this at-the-beginning feeling, and keep a part of it with us as we move through our careers.

- The challenge is to keep learning, [to] continuously reflect, [and to] maintain a circle of peers to consult and confide in when the going gets tough.

- Could it be that our biggest challenge as teachers is to remain as we are, and not become too obsessed with the details of our daily routine that could cause us to take the path of least resistance?

We agree that the biggest challenge may be getting bogged down in routine, mandates, testing requirements, losing that "at-the-beginning" feeling, or finding oneself too tired to contemplate even the idea of reflection. In fact, there is a fair amount of research that suggests this is exactly what happens to many teachers. "Burnout leads to teacher dropout. This condition has been referred to as 'battle fatigue'" (Hansen & Wentworth, 2002).

What is your plan for combating "battle fatigue"? How did you see mentor-teachers coping with burnout and cynicism? What can you do to grow your idealism with experience and become a teacher who makes a difference? How can you keep and grow idealism?

We have found that action research can be effective in staving off dreary routine or finding oneself trapped as a teacher in a role, place, or job that no longer has passion or interest. Implementing action research as way of living practice, as a way of thinking and being in the classroom empowers teachers to:

- stay focused on students;

- keep a vision and enact choice;

- have a plan, or an approach to questions, conflicts, and dilemmas;

- continue to learn in areas of interest and passion;

- use data to make persuasive and powerful arguments on behalf of students;

- experience rewards through solutions and accomplishments;

- collaborate with like-minded colleagues to effect change.

Cochran-Smith and Lytle (1993) have found that in school communities supporting teacher research, "teachers may be willing to confront their own histories, hear the dissonance within their own profession, and begin to construct working alliances with colleagues, students, parents, and communities" (p. 84). Stories of action research in school support this finding (Babkie & Provost, 2004; Hansen & Wentworth, 2002; Joyce, Mueller, Hrycauk, & Hrycauk, 2005; Lane, Lacefield-Parachini, & Isken, 2003; Luna et al., 2004; Meyers & Rust, 2003; Mohr et al., 2004; Raisch, 2005; Sax & Fisher, 2001; Senese, 2002, 2005). In this sampling of studies, teachers as researchers challenge their own assumptions about teaching while changing their practices; they effect change on school curriculum, programs, and polices and though collaboration find renewed energy and vision. Ultimately, action research "establishes the teacher as the ultimate arbiter over what is to count as useful knowledge" (Elliot, 1994, p. 137), and having that kind of control over what counts and gets counted as knowledge can be just one more way of keeping idealism and passion alive.

An Illustration of What Living Action Research Can Be: Rachel's Story

We interviewed Rachel in her classroom on a sunny afternoon late in the school year. Rachel is a bilingual fifth year teacher in a large school district. Approximately 85% of the children attending the elementary school where she teaches come from backgrounds of poverty. An additional 75% of the students in her fourth grade class are English language learners, representing a continuum of language acquisition. Most of these children speak Spanish and have moved to the area from Mexico. Rachel's classroom is filled with drawings and artwork, all done by students; this is their shared and collaborative learning space.

You do not have to spend much time with Rachel to know that she is passionate about teaching, her students, and public education. Listen just a little longer and you come to understand that she is committed to democratic principles of education centered around facilitating education for all children so they might participate well in the larger society. For Rachel, action research is "what teaching is all about." She does action research both formally and informally as part of her teaching practice.

As a fifth year teacher, Rachel remembers her first year of teaching as "really hard. It was a hard class and I didn't have a lot of support from colleagues. I wasn't ready to take a lot of risks that year. I worked on classroom management. We did a few good things that year. It took a lot just to do what the other teachers were doing. But by the next year, I was ready to take on some projects. I felt like I could risk more." And by the next year, she found like-minded colleagues both within and outside of her school community, including connecting with organizations like Rethinking Schools. Rachel continues to gain inspiration and encouragement from these colleagues and she teaches with passion for what is socially just and good.

Her first formal action research project took place the year before our interview. Because the children in Rachel's classroom come from backgrounds of poverty, their homes are not filled with books or other reading material. Yet very close to where many of them live is a beautiful public library. Rachel begin to wonder what would happen if she introduced her students to this open, public source and space of seemingly unlimited resources. How could access to a public library enrich her students' lives? Would this enthusiasm for print generate more ownership and use of their classroom library? If such rich literacy was available to her students and their families, might this be a benefit far beyond fourth grade?

Rachel decided to introduce the children to the public library in an intentional way. They visited the library, talked with the librarian, and each child received their very first library card—a kind of membership into the greater society's literacy club! Children learned how libraries are organized, and, critically (as Rachel discovered), they set about the task of organizing their own classroom library according to categories that were meaningful to them. They were proud of both the public space they came to know and the personal space within their classroom; classroom visitors were quick to be given a tour of the classroom library. Rachel documented her project with surveys and recorded how children and their families increased their use of the public library. In the end, children not only had access to the library as a resource, but knew how to use this resource, and *did* use it; they "owned" a skill for life.

During the school year of our interview, Rachel experienced another challenge. In fourth grade, students at the elementary school were to cover the science topics of electricity, life cycles, and water. Rachel created another action research project, a thematic unit about the nearby Columbia River combining these three science topics. In facilitating this unit Rachel wanted to make sure the children learned to be critical thinkers, entertained multiple ideas, read "facts" in context, and made informed decisions. She also realized that many of her students "didn't have a sense of place." Rachel hoped the unit would help students identify with their new home and come to "own" some of the controversial issues surrounding salmon and hydroelectric dams.

Because Rachel loves questions and is willing to engage in multiple perspectives, it followed that the unit began with children generating their own questions. From this beginning, children visited a dam and heard of the many benefits of hydroelectric power, but from a Native American speaker they also learned of the loss of culture and a way of life. They analyzed geology and land forms and considered the impact of dams on the environment, and finally, after so many facts and perspectives, they debated whether or not dams should continue to be utilized or breeched. Rachel is willing to tackle controversial subjects with global and local complexities because she believes deeply in the fourth graders' abilities to think, learn, and participate. Controversial subjects, after all, require critical thinking skills.

During the unit, Rachel used techniques of action research informally by observing, interviewing, and collecting student work to access how students used critical thinking in reading, discussing, drawing, and writing about issues related to the dams. Rachel's documentation demonstrated that children are learning what is required by state standards (the required curriculum), fulfilling the requirements of the school and district. The unit also fulfills Rachel's learning goal: students are learning to be critical thinkers so they can better participate in a democracy as future active and engaged citizens.

Rachel continues to take risks on behalf of students. It isn't easy at her school, as "[t]here are a lot of pressures" since the children at the school often test below "acceptable" levels on standardized exams. There is a lot of emphasis on scores and basic skills, so visits to public libraries and science inquiry units must integrate reading, writing, and math as much as possible.

That's why Rachel didn't know if her garden project would ever happen. Yet she couldn't help but contemplate a little plot of soil within the schoolyard. "Can we do a garden?" she wondered, particularly given the pressures to raise the school's test scores. "What would happen if kids were growing things? Would they understand how things are tied together? Make connections?" Would they begin to connect salmon, red worm, plant, and human cycles together? It was one of those dreams Rachel didn't want to give up, so despite the fact that she doesn't know much about gardening, she began to collaborate with the children in her classroom. Together, they came up with questions, ideas, a list of "expert resources," and together, they are growing a garden.

For Rachel, action research is "taking risks and learning with the kids." It is about deepening an understanding of the world through seeking multiple perspectives and experiences. Action research gives her a vehicle to make her teaching dreams happen. It is about valuing controversy as a way of learning through conflict and thus gaining insight into ways of living and thinking outside of one's one paradigm. She practices this way of thinking for herself; she invites her fourth graders to join in the learning.

Not long ago, a friend sent Rachel a postcard with an old picture of the Berlin Wall being torn down. She shared the card and some of the history with her students. One of the fourth graders raised his hand and said, "That's like the wall between Mexico and the United States." Rachel thought about that comparison; it informed her again about the history of the children in her classroom. It made her wonder more about the variety of experiences of the students in her class and their individual stories of coming to live in this area. She took an opportunity during a summer break to travel to that border, to see the wall that divides, the eyes peering through and perhaps dreaming, or scheming of a way to cross over to the other side. She visited with deportees who have risked and will continue to risk everything to come to the United States. With her group, Rachel visited by day factories that provide employment and by night shanty towns of deep urban poverty where the workers can barely afford to live on their wages. Rachel is still processing this "ultimate" action research project, this inquiry into the place of her students' stories. Maybe she should undertake an inquiry unit into walls, something about the borders that divide us, real and otherwise, she thought. How would such a unit empower students?

In reflecting upon her five years of teaching, Rachel told us in our interview, "The first year I was so challenged, just how to get teaching in order and all of the management issues; it is easy to get boxed down by political pressures, testing, there is just a lot that is really challenging. But this is what keeps me going, these kinds of projects. They are things that I deeply care about, for real; it is not like I have to pretend to the kids that I am excited about learning with them. These topics are real, relevant, and important."

We hear in Rachel's words how action research allows a teacher to take a vision and transform that vision into a reality. In this way Rachel reminds us of why we teach, of why we believe deeply in education, and how we can stay energized in education through action research. Action research, for Rachel, is a way of living practice as "inquiry as stance" (Cochran-Smith & Lytle, 1999, p. 296). It is not something extra, but a way of being in the classroom in pursuit of democratic ways of teaching and learning. Purpel (1999) writes, "The major question that we need ask educators is not 'What is your philosophy of education?' but 'What is your philosophy of life and what are its ramifications for education?'" (p. 77). Learning to "live the questions" as a philosophy for life is to become a teacher-researcher of influence in education.

Becoming an Agent of Change Through Action Research

I began to think about the many ways, both great and small, in which we teachers advocate for the children in our care. Advocacy is about decision making and then moving forward to press a point home. On a daily, hourly basis, within the classroom context, we make choices that impact the lives of children and families, move forward with action plans, and thus transform the school itself from educator/service provider to change agent. In my own teaching, I have always understood that beneath the lessons, the observations, the daily attention to detail (are the sponges damp?) lies the principle that education is fundamentally about change of the human condition.

—Martha Torrence (2002), "Teaching as Advocacy"

We become agents of change as teachers when we transform ourselves from "service providers" to teachers with an agenda and corresponding action plan. Shor (1992) defines such agency as "learning and acting for the democratic transformation of self and society" (p. 190); Aronowitz and Giroux (1985) define it as becoming a "transformative intellectual" (p. 45). Two of our students have noted that being a change agent means "having the courage (and the willingness to take the time and energy) to begin making small changes within my circle of influence," and "focusing on each student as the individual, finding out what they need, and meeting them there."

When we listen to Rachel's story, we hear the story of her evolution as a teacher: the first year was about classroom management, the second year about reaching out, and beginning to take risks and make connections with like-minded colleagues. Rachel's first formal action research project was one *she* undertook and organized, but now Rachel's action research projects are collaborative efforts *with* students. One of our student teachers noted, "Every day I feel my focus shifting away from 'How am I doing as a teacher?' to how much [my students are] learning. . . . Are they 'getting it'? How do they feel today? What have I learned about my students today?" This shift in primary focus from self to students, and from students to local and global communities, is paramount to expanding one's sphere of influence and recognizing the role a teacher can have in transforming self, students, and society. But how does a teacher new to professional education get there? How can action research be the bridge to this kind of being a teacher?

→ FIGURE 8.1: Characteristics of Transformation

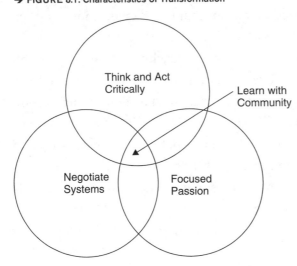

In studying the action research projects of preservice teachers in our program and their continuous evolution as professional educators, we identify four critical and overlapping characteristics/skills that appear to propel them toward action, agency, and transformation: learning with community, the abilities to negotiate and think and act critically, and focused passion. These are outlined in Figure 8.1.

Learning With Community

A crucial element of action research is having critical colleagues who can give perspective as a teacher seeks multiple solutions in practice and act to effect change in school communities. This continues to be true for professional educators. Having critical colleagues, a community with which to learn, keeps one energized in teaching by raising relevant and authentic questions, bringing possibilities to the conversation, and ultimately shaping vision. Such colleagues (both local and distant) can bring meaning to your career. Who this community is matters. McLaughlin (1993) has concluded:

The character of the professional community that exists in a school or a department—collegial or isolating, risk taking or rigidly invested in best practices, problem solving or problem shirking—plays a major role in how teachers see their work and their students and is why some teachers opt out, figuratively or literally, while many teachers persist and thrive even in exceeding challenging teaching contexts. (p. 98)

There are many voices or discourses that inform our identity as teachers (Britzman, 1993; Marsh, 2002; Phillips, 2002). Who you choose to engage with and who you choose to listen to may affect who you become as a teacher more than anything else. Early on, seek colleagues of influence who are positive, who offer encouragement, and who willingly engage with questions, ideas, and seeking alternatives. These future critical colleagues (both local and distant) will influence how you negotiate, think critically, and even shape your passions and emotions (Zembylas, 2003). So teacher, beware! Choose your company mindfully.

Thinking and Acting Critically

To think and act critically is to live and practice action research on a daily basis by using observation, interviews (critical listening), and artifacts (assessment) to analyze, synthesize, and deconstruct the multiple voices and situations of the classroom and greater community. To think and act critically in this way is to seek to expand paradigms and spheres of influences through critical and transformative action plans. Students from our programs who understood and practiced this concept and skills as preservice teachers have gone on to be agents of change as professional educators. They have introduced innovative and successful programs, practices and technologies; they have challenged systems of power on behalf of students.

Negotiating Systems

As a student teacher conducting action research as a guest in another's classroom, you have most likely needed to negotiate, to learn to work within the system. There is an art and science to negotiation that we identify with former students who become outstanding teachers. These teachers learn to negotiate by understanding concepts like those of *sacred, cover,* and *secret stories* (see Chapter 1, *Inside Track: Secret, Cover, and Sacred Stories*). Such teachers learn to discern power dynamics at schools, among staff and administrators, and among students. Wise negotiators honor differences; they view conflict as an opportunity. By thinking and acting critically, they are able to negotiate for change.

Focusing Passion

Passion is a powerful motivator for change. In our own experience, we have found that preservice teachers who are passionate about learning, specific content, or particular issues are passionate about others and education, and determined to work for a more just society in order to find vision as professional educators. Passion/vision doesn't always equate with action, but when such teachers combine this with thinking and acting critically, skills of negotiation, and learning with community, they become agents of change in their school communities. In fact, they find vision within these other spheres, not just within themselves.

The result is action, agency, and transformation. This is a process, a journey, one in which we never arrive. This is living action research as practice.

Forming a Vision, Creating a Plan

A vision can give us meaning; a plan can keep us from feeling trapped. Both can keep us energized and joyful as teachers. Brainstorm responses to the following prompts. Then, complete the diagram shown in Figure 8.2 using the responses. Keep the diagram and refer to it over the next several years as you teach. Just as in action research, be willing to change the plan as needed, yet doing this kind of vision planning now can provide a scaffold for you as you move toward your career in education.

→ **FIGURE 8.2: Plan of Action**

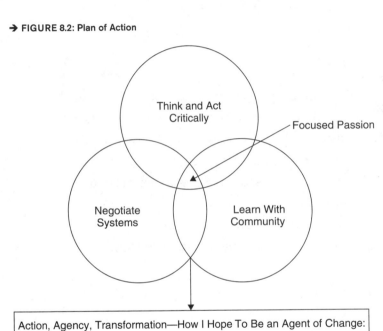

Action, Agency, Transformation—How I Hope To Be an Agent of Change:

Learning With Community

What characteristics are important to you in colleagues? What is your "ideal" teaching community? What kinds of questions do you want to ask during an interview? What distant colleagues can you continue to seek?

Thinking and Acting Critically

Review your responses earlier in this chapter. Make an assessment of your abilities to think and act critically (to observe, interview, collect artifacts; to analyze, synthesize, deconstruct). Where would you like to specifically focus on the next stages of being a teacher?

Negotiating Systems

Think back over your student-teaching experience. Consider situations where you did well and not so well at negotiating systems. What can you learn from this? Deconstruct your own behaviors during times of conflict. How do you approach conflict? How *could* you? What have you learned from your own experience and from the experiences of others about systems of power at school sites? What are your emerging theories for working with and around such systems?

Focusing Passion

Brainstorm a list of the activities, ideas, content, and situations from student-teaching and your teacher-education program that give you energy. Likewise, make a list of activities, ideas, content, and situations from student teaching and your teacher-education program that drain your energy.

When you talk about teaching, what issues, questions, ideas motivate you to increase the rate of your talk, the intensity with which you articulate your words, or actually raise your heart beat a bit?

Using these notes, complete Figure 8.2, giving yourself a vision of who you would like to continue to become as a teacher. Save your completed diagram; tuck it away in a place where you can find it again. Create notebook or journal entries from it, partake in dialogue with your colleagues about your plans, and continue to grow your vision of a teacher-researcher of influence.

Finding Critical Colleagues

There are many publications and organizations providing support to new teachers; through these, search out distant colleagues from whom you might find inspiration, hope, and good teaching ideas. It is difficult to make suggestions, but at the end of this chapter you will find a reference list of a few of our favorite publications, ones that we think may be helpful in creating a scaffold for your invention and reinvention of the teacher-researcher identity.

Beginning Again (and Always)

It is good to have an end to journey towards, but it is the journey that matters, in the end.
—*Ursula K. Le Guin (1969), The Left Hand of Darkness*

We still love late August—that's the month in our community when school is beginning (again). We find ourselves drawn to aisles of department stores, checking out the latest in crayons and markers, playing with technogadgets, and anticipating that rush of the first day of school, the crush of students, schedules, and the promise of what might be. That's the beauty of school, though, at any grade level—one always gets another beginning as a teacher, a kind of guaranteed "do-over," another chance to *become*. It is not about arrival as a teacher; it is about the continuous looping of life, never back to the same place, but always another place, even though it may seem familiar. French philosopher Michel Foucault (Foucault, Martin, Gutman & Hutton, 1988) reminds us, "The main interest in life and work is to become someone else that you were not in the beginning. If you knew when you began a book what you would say at the end, do you think that you would have the courage to write it?" (p. 9). Foucault continues, "The game is worthwhile insofar as we don't know what will be the end" (p. 9).

At the beginning of this text, we wrote, "If this book could be more—if this book could touch, smell, argue, exclaim, sigh, even dance—then it might be more representational of action research as we have come to know it." What we hope is that you have come to know action research in this way as well—and, even more, as a way to continue to evolve and reinvent yourself as a teacher of influence.

Total "Modern" statements (2, 4, 5, 8, 9, 11, 14, 16, 18) you agreed with:

_____

Total "Postmodern" statements: (1, 3, 6, 7, 10, 12, 13, 15, 17, 19) you agreed with:

_____

What your scores could mean:

- If your totals are different by more than 3, it means you have a propensity for one paradigm over the other.

- If your totals on both are less than 4, you may be somewhat non-committal. You may find that your views swing one way or the other as you become a teacher.

- If you scored more than 7 in either modernism or postmodernism, you appear to have a very strong propensity for that paradigm.

- If you scored more than 6 in both paradigms, you may be confused!

Appendix B
Data Set/Teacher Images

Pictured Teacher's Gender

Male	Female
7	25

Pictured Teacher's Ethnicity

White	African-American	Native American	Asian-American	Latino	Other Ethnicity
28	4	0	0	0	0

Other Observations

Teacher Centered in Picture	Teacher Not Centered in Picture	Non-Traditional Educational Setting	Students Teaching Students
31	1	0	0

APPENDIX C
DATA SET/TEACHER GIFTS

Item for Sale	Primary Colors	Symbol	Slogan
Teacher album	Red, blue, yellow	Apple Pencil ABC	
Coffee mug	Red	Apple	World's best teacher
T-shirt	Red	Test tube exploding	Trust me, I'm a science teacher
Tote bags	Red, green yellow	Apples Chalkboards	
T-shirt	Red		Don't make me use my teacher voice
Coffee mug	Red, yellow, green, blue		Inspire, teach, guide, praise, influence
Button	Red	Apple Pencil	A teacher gives, a teacher shares, but most of all a teacher is a friend
Teacher gift bucket	Pink, green	Teacher with book, smile, cartoon	We love you, Mrs. ___"
Craft ideas: snowmen	Pink		
Acrylic tumbler	Red	Apple	Plant the seeds for tomorrow
Chocolate bar	Green	Rule, globe, apple	Teachers make learning sweet
Coffee mug	Red, green, yellow	Apple, ruler	Personalized with name
Teacher memo sheets	red	Apple	Personalized with name
Metal sign	Green, red	Heart	I (heart) Mrs. (personalized)
Christmas ornament	red	Apples, composition notebook, green worm, books	Worlds' greatest teacher
Canvas tote	Red, black	Red school house, apple, chalkboard, alphabet	
ABC wooden desk organizer	Red, yellow, black	Books, pencils, ruler, globe, alphabet	
Water bottle	Yellow, red	Apple	World's greatest teacher

APPENDIX D
DISSECTING AND RE-FORMULATING YOUR CRITICAL QUESTION

For each of the critical questions below, use the directions from Chapter 2, "Dissecting and Re-formulating Your Critical Question" to practice the art of revising and drafting a workable critical question.

There is a downloadable version of these questions on the companion website.

Action Research Questions
What effect does storyboarding as a pre-writing activity have on elementary student writing quality and attitudes?
Will the use of graphic organizers increase students' retention of historical facts?
Does the use of math journals increase middle school comprehension of math concepts?
Is it possible to differentiate through cooperative learning labs in the science classroom?
How can I effectively use collaborative learning to increase confidence in English Language Learners?
Will the use of technology (iPod, *Garage Band*, and digital video-recordings) increase student participation and project completion in my freshman English class?
How does personal connection to a foreign language help students to use the language outside of the classroom for further learning?
How do students' funds of knowledge appear as I listen and observe their conversations and interactions in the classroom environment?
How can competition be used well to encourage students in weight lifting?

APPENDIX E
DATA COLLECTION TOOLS EXPLORED

More downloadable data collection templates are available on the companion website. The following data collection tools are detailed in this Appendix:

E1:   Note-Taking/Note-Making

E2:   Anecdotal Notes

E3:   Logs, checklists, and rating scales

E4:   Mapping

E5:   Shadowing

E6:   Surveys, Questionnaires, and Attitude Response Scales

E7:   Formal, Informal, and Focus Group Interviews

E8:   Sociograms

E9:   Multiple Intelligences Approaches to Interviews

E10: Working With Artifacts

Appendix E1
Note-Taking/Note-Making

Overview

- Note-taking/note-making is an ethnographic approach to observation.

- When doing note-taking/note-making, the observer writes what she/he sees and hears, attempting to record without judgment.

- Note-making is completed after the observation; note-making is the space where the observer raises questions, records hunches, and analysis.

Variations and Uses

- Note-taking/note-making may be done by a mentor-teacher or other supervisor. A lesson may also be video-taped and then observed using note-taking/note-making.

- There are many variations depending on the desired outcome. For example, time increments may be added to the observation form. Sometimes, only specific items are observed, for example, only questions might be recorded. One way we have used this strategy is to divide the observation into two categories: "What the teacher does" and "What the students do." Consider the purpose of the observation and then decide the specifics.

- Note-taking/note-making can be used for a variety of purposes. It can be used to observe a whole class lesson, with small groups, or only for specific teaching events. Used over time, note-taking/note-making can show progress and reflect or identify process.

- Note-taking/note-making becomes easier and more efficient with practice! Experiment with the method even in non-school settings –this will increase your effectiveness with the strategy.

Example

Carrie completed the note-taking/note-making in Table E1.1 while watching a video-recording of herself teaching a science lesson in a middle school classroom:

→ TABLE E1.1: Note-taking/Note-Making of Video Observation, Self

Observations	Note-Making
1. Daily science—students working on it. Some talking. 3 minutes for DS	Giving too much time for daily science.
2. Gabe enters room. Takes off jacket and organizes ear phones.	Gabe tardy from Phil Johnson's advisory group.

(Continued)

3. Asking questions during daily science. Using lots of words like appropriate, classify.	Yes I talk a great deal. Feel tension in getting control. Adjust daily science to get kids more involved?
4. Noise from outside in the hall during daily science. Sixth graders.	Distracting—Keep door closed.
5. David makes a comment for tundra.	David's comments tend to go on and on, but the class has been quite respectful of what he has to say. He is a wealth of information, that's for sure.
6. Jamie makes comment.	I have a difficult time listening to one kid talk and not losing the rest of them.
7. Jonathan asks to sharpen pencil.	Temporary cease fire.
8. I clarify potential and kinetic energy to review from yesterday.	This talk went fairly well. Kids seemed to get it at the time, but know that there are many who are still confused.
9. I ask questions. Breanna has hand up. I don't call on her. She sets her head down on the table.	Favoring hand-raisers. Begin calling on those that don't have hand up to more equitably distribute attention to all kids.
10. David answers question.	Called on David again. Struggle with this because he raises his hand a lot and I call on him a great deal because I want everyone to feel included. I don't want to not call on him because he always knows the answers.
11. Breanna raises hand again. I allow people to call out to get through the lesson.	Ignoring people with hands-raised. Allowing loud folks to answer questions, dictate flow of class.
12. I circulate around the room. Gabe yells out "dangerous" energy. I ignore it.	First detectable "smart" remark by Gabe goes ignored.
13. I am using lots of words to explain energy conversion. Students yelling out in class.	My actions say that I don't care if you yell out in class. What cannot be seen by my outward appearance is the growing frustration within. I'm getting harried and frustrated at myself for my resistance in addressing it. Truly, it was no longer the child's problem, but my own.

Appendix E2
Anecdotal Notes

Overview

- A way of collecting critical moments and recording them in the midst of a busy classroom.

- Anecdotal notes are an effective way to collect data concerning specific students, small groups of students, or for use in a self-study as a quick reflection device.

- When taking anecdotal notes write down quick descriptions or quotes and then come back to them later for interpretation. Complete the analysis and interpretation in the margins and then in your researcher's notebook more formally.

Variations and Uses

- Some teacher-researchers have found that sticky notes and a clipboard are a good way to record anecdotal notes. The notes can then be easily organized at a later date.

- Another variation is to set up a chart with space for notes. For example, if there are five science lab groups in the classroom, organize a chart with two columns and five rows. Use the chart and a clipboard to collect the notes. There are a number of possible ways to set up such anecdotal charts—again, consider the purpose and devise and revise the kind of chart that works best in your teaching situation.

- Anecdotal notes are best done deliberately. Collect the notes over time to show progress and process. As with all data collection strategies, you will improve with practice.

In the example below, Kelly designed a chart with all of her students' names. She recorded anecdotal assessment notes about the math lesson. Note how she also recorded the context for the observation by describing the lesson.

➔ FIGURE E1.1: Example One—Anecdotal Notes

Date: *January 14*
Time: *9:45*
Event: *Computer lab simulation – 9th grade.*

Group 2 having problems: can't decide who gets to actual key in the information on computer. R. insist it is his turn. M. says R. always gets to do this. I asked for a peer mediator to step in and left the group….

Group 3, doing well. They've already got data entered. I can hear group 2 still bickering.

Groups 1 & 5 appear to be on-task. J. is wondering – what group is he suppose to be in?

Back to group 2: R & M have resolved the matter for now. Group may be behind in assignment.

Example: Kelly's Notes

2/11

Counting by 2s Grid to Penguin Pairs Chart

The worksheet included two charts. The first was a 100s chart with only the even numbers. In the first rows the even numbers were present as dotted lines that the students were to trace over. Further down the chart fewer and fewer numbers were provided and students were to continue writing in only the even numbers. The second chart consisted of two columns; the first listed numbers 1–20. Students were to complete the second column by entering the number of penguins in 1 pair, 2 pair, 3 pair, etc. On the day before this worksheet was assigned, students had created a chart with a growing pattern of penguin pairs. The chart ended after row 8.

Observations From Work Time

Seemed to have difficulty understanding that chart showed results of skip counting: EB, RW, LW; DM—did at beginning but seemingly struggled with concept until arrived at meaning.

→ TABLE E2.1: Example Two—Anecdotal Notes

Counting by 2s and Penguin Pairs worksheet

AM	Finished	Seemed to have good CU, skipped 16 on PP chart (# of penguins), asked st. to review—pointing at specific error; self-corrected and changed that & following incorrect answers.
AL	Did not finish	Small-motor fatigue evident; after 40, I alternated rows to write numbers; st. provided information; still only got to 70; did not get to pairs/penguin chart
AG	Did not finish	Ended at 84, did not do PP chart
AS	Finished	One of first finished, CU apparently strong as we reviewed together
AB	Did not finish	Ended at 88, did not do PP chart
CC	Finished	CU strong
DF	Finished	Evident difficulty with understanding at beginning, understanding seemed to emerge as work progressed; need 1:1 to check for understanding
DM	Finished	Solidified meaning as worked; complained of getting stuck at 16 on PP chart (student-created penguin chart went as far as 8 pairs), but worked through it to complete chart
DN	Finished	CU, evidence of self-correction
EB	Did not finish	Ended at 38, but traced only, did not fill in missing even numbers; did not do PP chart
EW	Finished	CU strong, finished quickly and completely accurate
JF	Did not finish	All of skip counting, did not do PP chart
LW	Did not finish	Traced all numbers, did not fill in all missing evens; did write in some odds; did not do PP chart
MC	Did not finish	Ended at 80, did not do PP
MK	Finished	CU, accurate
NW	Did not finish	All of skip counting, did not do PP chart
RW	Did not finish	Stopped at 76, did not do PP chart
TJ	Finished	Seemed to have CU, lots of reversals on PP chart
TT	Did not finish	All of skip counting, did not do PP chart

Overview: Logs

- A log is a running record of events. A log may be a detailed list of events throughout an entire period or day. It may be a list of class activities only or it could include interactions with students, routine classroom procedures (taking attendance, lunch count, etc.). Phone conversations, responding to email, conferences, and/or other daily events are recorded.

- The simplest way to organize a log is by recording the date and time at the top of any page and then noting the events through the specific time period data is being gathered. Keep the log in your researcher's notebook.

- Logs are useful in accessing time and placing other data in context.

Overview: Checklists

- A checklist is a structured form of observation. It is perhaps the most efficient way for a busy classroom student teacher-researcher to collect observational data. The checklist focuses the teacher-researcher to record specific kinds of behaviors, occurrences, or responses.

- The simplest kinds of checklists record "yes/no" in response to specific kinds of statements or questions or use slash marks to record the number of times a behavior or occurrences happens. Checklists can be more sophisticated and may use a combination of ways to record the data.

- Checklists are most useful when they are recording meaningful and focused data. You may need to use a checklists several times, analyze the data, and then revise the checklist to make it more useful.

- Checklists are best used multiple times, over time. Used in this way, they document progress and/or patterns of behavior.

Variations and Uses

- Checklists can be completed by the teacher-researcher, a mentor-teacher, a supervisor, or students.

- The more items on the checklist, the more the checklist will demand of the observer; choose the items carefully.

- Analyze the results of the checklist the same day the observations are made.

- A variation of a checklist uses a rating scale (see Tables E3.1 and E3.2).

→ TABLE E3.1: Example Checklist

6th Grade Literature Circle Observation Checklist Date: October 15						
Student	Prepared	Listened	Used Book Examples	Made Personal Connections	Asked Questions	Eye Contact
A	Y	Y	///	///	////	Y
B	Y	Y	/	/		Y
C	N	Y		/	//	Y

→ TABLE E3.2: Combination Checklist

Sharing Circle

Date: 11/12   Time: 12:00–12:15

Name	Shared	Time	Distraction	Comment
A	/	5 sec.		Liked Sammy the Snake activity
B			///	
C	/	1 min.		Talked about Mrs. W's class book
D			/	
E	/	3 sec.		Enjoyed reading and pattern activity
F	/	5 sec.		Shared routine activity-favorite
G	/	3 sec		

* Show and Tell today, students were able to pick one thing they enjoyed about today and would like to share with the rest of the class.

Overview/Rating Scale

A rating scale is a variation of a checklist. It is also used as an observational tool but adds a value according to a continuum rather than just recording "yes/no" or the specific times an event occurs.

Variations and Uses

- Checklists with rating scales can be used by the teacher-researcher or any other outside observer. Students may also use this tool.

- Checklists need to be developmentally appropriate for the age, grade, and language level if used by students.

- Like any observation tool, the checklist should be analyzed just after being used and revised if necessary to collect meaningful and focused data.

- Rating scales may be designed as categories:

How often did the student participate in the cooperative group lab?
Never Seldom Occasionally Frequently Always

- Rating scales may be designed using a number system:

Student participates in the cooperative group lab.
1 = Rarely..........................5 = Active participant

- Rating scales can also be designed to use pictorial representations; this is particularly useful when young children are doing their own observations.

- Anecdotal rating scales can be useful for a teacher monitoring small group work. See Table E3.3 as an example.

→ TABLE E3.3: Anecdotal Rating Scale

1st Grade: Story Re-telling Child's Name _____			Date _____
Literacy Target	**Demonstrates Difficulty**	**Adequately Performs Task**	**Demonstrates Excellent Comprehension**
Accurately re-tells story (plot)			
Describes characters			
Describes setting			
Makes personal connections to text			

APPENDIX E4
MAPPING

Overview

- Mapping is a general term applied to any observational strategy where behavior or movement is recorded and later analyzed. For example, a teacher-researcher may draw a diagram of the classroom and map the movement of students or he/she may note table or lab groups and chart the on-task behavior of students.

- Mapping may be difficult for a teacher-researcher to do, depending upon how involved he/she must be in the lesson.

- Mapping is a useful way to gather specific kinds of behavioral data.

Variations and Uses

Mapping can be used in combination with anecdotal notes. This can be an efficient and useful way for involved teacher-researchers to collect data. The teacher-researcher maps a diagram of their classroom with a seating chart. Anecdotal notes are kept for individual students or groups of students on the chart.

In the example in Figure E4.1 the student teacher-researcher provided her university supervisor with a seating chart to record on- and off-task behaviors during a small group math lesson. The observer checked students' behavior every five minutes. Besides on- and off-task behavior, the observer noted when students left their table groups, along with other anecdotal data. When compared with other

→ **FIGURE E4.1: Mapping**

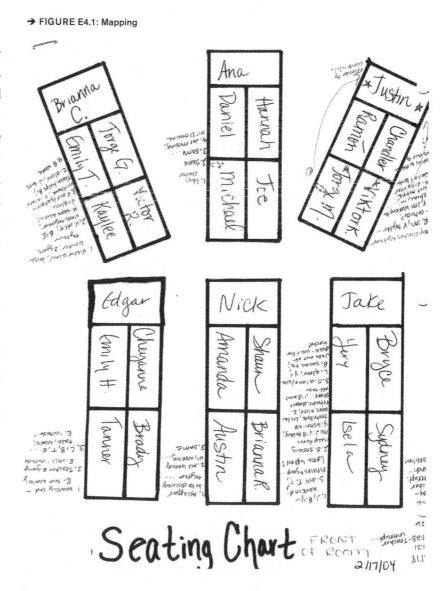

such observations, the student teacher-researcher was able to see certain patterns of behavior emerge. For example, most students who were confident in their math abilities assisted other students who struggled. However, when the higher-ability students did not feel confident in the math tasks, they tended to leave their small groups and ask the teacher. They did not ask the other students in their group, nor did they help these students on these occasions.

Appendix E5
Shadowing

Overview

- A shadow study is primarily used to gather data on a single student. A teacher-researcher may shadow a student throughout an entire school day or for any given class period or content instruction.

- Although there are many variations, shadow studies typically use a form of note-taking/note-making: time increments are noted, the student's behaviors and particular expressions or responses recorded and environmental considerations written as well. Later, note-making is completed; the teacher-researcher theorizes and raises questions about the behaviors.

- Shadows can also be recorded using a log system.

Variations and Uses

- Shadowing is a good way to learn about students whose experiences may be different than your own or students who are given various "labels," such as "learning disabled," or "attention deficient disorder." Teacher-researchers often make assumptions about such students. Gathering data through a shadow study often reveals insights that are otherwise overlooked.

- Shadowing is also a good way to learn about specific groups of students, particularly those you are going to student teach. It allows a teacher-researcher to become more aware of "life in school."

Example

Anne wanted to teach middle school but didn't feel like her own middle school experience in a private school with an environmental emphasis was "typical" of the middle school where she was going to student teach. Anne spent considerable time the first two weeks of her placement doing a shadow study of five students. She followed them throughout the school day to gain insight into a "normal" day of a 12-year-old at her placement school.

APPENDIX E6
SURVEYS, QUESTIONNAIRES, AND ATTITUDE RESPONSE SCALES

Overview

- Surveys, questionnaires, and attitude response scales are used to collect data primarily about how students' perceptions, feelings, or attitudes about skills, concepts, or other classroom issues. These data collection strategies can be effectively and efficiently used by classroom teachers when there isn't time or opportunity to visit with each individual student.

- When writing surveys, questionnaires, and attitude response scales, it is particularly important to craft good questions that will generate the kind of data you wish to collect. This may take some practice, so plan to revise whatever survey you craft, based upon your analysis of the data generated.

- Often times, teacher-researchers write more than one question to gain insight into the same issue. They re-state the question, sometimes in a positive way and then in a more negative way, to ensure consistency in the response.

- Surveys, questionnaires, and attitude response scales are often used as a pre- and post-assessment in a unit, or used over time to demonstrate progress and/or process. The teacher-researcher analyzes this data for patterns and for changes in attitudes or perceptions.

- Surveys, questionnaires, and attitude response scales should be tallied. Patterns and aberrations are noted.

- If there are students who speak other languages rather than that of the dominant culture, it is important that the surveys, questionnaires, and attitude response scales are provided in their language.

Variations and Uses

- Surveys, questionnaires and attitude response scales often use descriptive phrases:

I enjoy reading on my own:

Strongly Agree   Agree   Disagree   Strongly Disagree

- Surveys, questionnaires and attitude response scales sometimes use Likert scales:

Reading a good book is a great way to spend the evening:

NOT! ----- ----- ----- ----- ----- ----- ----- ----- ----- ----- ----- YES!

- Surveys, questionnaires and attitude scales may use pictorial representations; these are especially good for younger children (see example below).

- Surveys may employ user-friendly language:

The discussion today concerning globalization:

Didn't interest me

Raised important questions for me

Made me angry

Made me feel hopeful

- Surveys, questionnaires and attitude response scales may use number representation:

For the following questions, please use this rating scale to respond:

1   Strongly Disagree

2   Disagree

3   Agree

4   Strongly Agree

5   Undecided

_____ *Music is an important part of my life.*

_____ *I listen to many kinds of music.*

_____ *I like to study with music in the background.*

→ FIGURE E6.1: Student Evaluation Example

Student Evaluation

Name_____

1. I like to share in class	☺	😐	☹
2. I feel comfortable in our class to share	☺	😐	☹
3. I feel that other students listen when I share	☺	😐	☹
4. I like working with others	☺	😐	☹

Appendix E7
Formal, Informal, and Focus Group Interviews

Overview

- The interview group is the most direct form of inquiry. In the formal, informal, and focus groups interviews, the teacher-researcher asks the participants for their insights and feedback. The critical piece of an interview, like a survey, questionnaire, or attitude response scale, are the questions asked. Spend time constructing the questions; make sure they are focused and will provide the kind of data that will be most helpful to you.

- The skills of the interviewer are the skills of many great teachers we know: interviewers listen intently, they observe for non-verbal messages, and they know how to follow-up on cues from the interviewee. Effective interviewers and teachers are genuinely interested in hearing what others have to say; asking the questions is not just a requirement or routine. Finally, effective interviewers and teachers recognize they have assumptions about how students (parents and others) will respond so they work to listen around those assumptions.

Variations and Uses

- The *formal interview*, as it suggests, involves a pre-set group of questions. The teacher-researcher asked these questions one-on-one and uses the same group of questions for all students. Responses are recorded via notes or audio-recording. Formal interviews often provide more in-depth data. For example, Sheena's action research project centered on describing how community forms among high school drama students. She conducted formal interviews with each member of the cast. This was an effective choice since the one-on-one setting gave students space to talk more completely about their place in the drama "family."

- During an *informal interview*, the teacher-researcher begins more of a conversation with the student by asking a question and then allowing the interview to follow the responses of the student or other participant. Student teacher-researchers new to informal interviews must still be deliberate in conducting these interviews. It is useful to have pre-formed questions to guide the conversation as needed. The informal interview may use mapping, an anecdotal note format, or even a chart with students' names on one side and a note column on the other side to record student responses. As a form of classroom assessment, informal interviews can be very valuable since a teacher-researcher may walk around the classroom, stop at various desks, and inquiry of students in a natural way such as, "What math problem solving strategy did you use today? How did you use this strategy? Can you explain this to me?"

- *Focus group interviews* are another effective way for a teacher-researcher to inquire of students during the busy classroom day. A focus group is really a small group discussion centered on a particular topic. Responses are recorded via notes or audio-tape. Typically, a cross-section of the student population is most useful, although attention should be given to group dynamics; some small groups of students are more comfortable conversing together than others. The teacher-researcher may have a prescribed set of questions to ask the focus groups or he/she may ask a single leading question and then allow the dialogue to flow. We have seen student teacher-researchers use focus groups in many ways: Michael's fifth grade focus group met during lunch often during the math-based, service-learning project. This is where Michael learned how students were processing not only the math concepts, but also sorted through group dynamics. Cindy's focus group included the small group leaders from the student social studies' teams. By checking in with the leaders, she gained insight about how the class was developing community, along with their conceptual development of concepts.

- When an interview is audio-taped, it is often useful to make a transcription of the interview. Transcriptions take time, but the benefit is being able to read through the words spoken, highlight patterns, raise questions in the margins, and better analyze the interview. Not all interviews warrant this kind of analysis; however, additional insights may be gained through this strategy.

APPENDIX E8
SOCIOGRAMS

Overview

Sociograms are another type of formal interview useful to chart relationships within a classroom. Hubbard and Power (2003) follow these steps in implementing sociograms:

1. Develop questions to ask each student, such as "If you could invite anyone in this class to your birthday party, who would you ask? Rank you choices 1, 2, 3." Or "Who is good at math problem solving in this class?" Or "To whom would you share a secret in this class?" Or, "With whom would you like to be in a cooperative learning group?"

2. Interview young children individually; older children may complete a response sheet.

3. Have students respond quickly—you are after an initial response.

4. Complete a tally sheet of responses. Assign a point value to each response: first choice receives 3 points, second choice receives 2 points, third choices receive 1 point.

5. Now chart the point values for each student and patterns of relationships and power will emerge.

6. Hubbard and Power (2003) identify students by terms like "cliques" (those groups of students who choose each other), "stars" (students who are chosen most often), and "isolates" (students who are not selected by other students)." (Other categories may also emerge.) They also offer this very wise and ethical advice, "You must use some caution in doing sociograms for a class. This is one data source that should not be open to students. *You also need to disguise the names of students in all of your sociogram figures and charts*" (Hubbard & Power, 2003, p. 76).

Example

Christy was a student teacher-researcher whose action research projects focused on developing community among children seemingly separated by language and gender. The sociogram was an effective tool both used at the beginning and end of her research to aide in accessing community among their students.

   Here is an example of Christy's first sociogram. She also charted the data according to boys and Spanish/English speaking students so she could better analyze the group dynamics according to gender and language. This early analysis identified potential leaders as well as "isolates" that Christy targeted during community-building activities.

Action Research-Sociogram

Interview questions asked:

1. If you could pick any student from class to come over to play at your house, who would you choose?

2. If you could pick any student from class to come over to your house to spend the night, but student 1 was sick, who would you choose?

3. If you could pick any student from class to go to the zoo, but student 1 and 2 were sick, who would you choose?

→ FIGURE E8.1: Girls' Sociogram

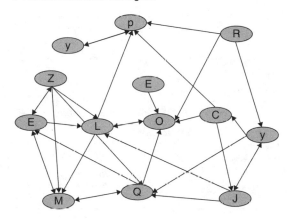

APPENDIX E9
MULTIPLE INTELLIGENCES APPROACHES TO INTERVIEWS

Overview

Interview strategies are dependent upon students' (or other participants) ability to verbally respond to questions. However, we have learned from Howard Gardner's (2004a, 2004b) research that the ability to verbally respond is just one way of expressing attitudes, perceptions, and problem solving. A multiple intelligences approach to interview allows students or other participants to respond to questions in multiple ways:

➔ TABLE E9.3: Multiple Intelligences Approaches to 3 Interviews

Verbal-Linguistic	Logical-Mathematical	Kinesthetic	Visual-Spatial	Musical	Interpersonal	Intrapersonal
Storytelling	Venn diagrams	Role play	Flow charts	Music as analogy	Global perspectives	Metacognition
Word webs	Analogies	Dance	Clustering	Poetry	Collaborative responses	Journal responses
Letter writing	Forming questions as a response	Creative drama	Guided imagery	Rap	Class meetings	Reflective drawings
	Graphs/charts	Play	Visual arts			

These are just some of the possibilities. We recommend *Teaching and learning through multiple intelligences* (Campbell, Campbell, & Dickinson, 2004) as an additional resource for considering multiple ways students might respond to interview questions.

Having students of all ages draw a response as an interview can often be insightful (Figure E9.1). Cindy asked her fifth grade students to draw a picture of an ideal community. After drawing, she asked the students to write a paragraph about the community. Note the variety of abilities and how the drawings support the interview responses and make possible some responses where language is not adequate. If translation is possible, allow students to respond in the language they are most comfortable using.

Marta designed a Head, Hand, and Heart Student Self-Evaluation (Figure E9.2) for use throughout her action research project. Children became more proficient in using the tool as the project covered several months. They could draw,

➔ FIGURE E9.1: Student Drawings as Interview

write words, or sentences in response to a question Marta gave them; she also gave students the opportunity to act out their responses in small groups.

➔ FIGURE E9.2: Head, Hand, and Heart Student Self-Evaluation

Name: Date: Activity:	**Hands:** What I did.
Head: What I thought about what I did.	**Heart:** How I felt about what I did.

Overview

- The term "artifact" conjures up images of items set in special light and under protective glass in museums. In fact, artifacts for teacher-researchers are similar. Artifacts are any documents, projects, arts, or other such items that the teacher-researchers sets aside to study more carefully. Artifacts tell a different story than an interview or an observation; artifacts tend to speak for themselves as evidence.

- Artifacts can be any kind of student-produced work: portfolios, exams, daily work, art work, projects, video-taped or audio-taped productions, and student records and/or rewards.

- Artifacts can be produced by the teacher-researcher: lesson plans, notes, articles, dialogue logs, and/or phone messages.

➔ FIGURE E10.1: Example of Artifact Collection

Four friendly number flowers and two leaves. How many petals and lobes? How many stems?"

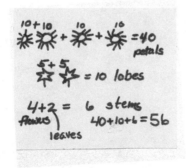

To the left is the sticky note on which I showed my problem solving solution that I discussed with the student who created the problem above.

- School documents can be artifacts, like policy manuals; community newspapers may serve as important artifacts.

- Artifacts can confirm or disaffirm patterns in the data. Learn to analyze artifacts well. Record your analysis in your researcher's notebook.

Variations and Uses

- Digital cameras are a friendly teacher-researcher's tool. Use such cameras to record all kinds of student work and/or other documentation. This is a simple way to collect such documentation and allows the teacher-researcher to return work to students in a timely manner. You may use media software such as iPhoto to organize and annotate your digital images.

- Digital video-recordings and audio-recordings can be used to collect different kinds of artifacts. For example, an audio-recorder in the midst of a small student group can be useful in a number of ways! Video will also allow you to remember the context for your study when you are analyzing the data later. You may even use advanced media software such as Apple's iMovie or Garage Band to organize and annotate your digital artifacts. Be creative.

- Be deliberate in considering what kinds of artifacts will best support your action research project best.

Example of Artifact Collection

Kelly scanned into her computer a copy of not only this first grade student's attempt at problem solving, but also her instructional intervention.

Appendix F
General-Purpose Research Design Template

A general-purpose research design template is included in this appendix:

⊙ This action research design template is downloadable from the companion website. Additional genre-specific templates are also located there.

General Purpose Action Research Design Template
(May be adapted for specific genres of action research)

1. Action Research Project Overview
1.1 Critical Question for my action research project:
1.2 The Context of My Study: Setting, Participants, and Researcher:

Brief description of community
Brief description of school (include the relationship of the school to the community; how the school reflects the community)
Brief description of the physical classroom
Brief description of myself as the action researcher, including community/school connections, comfort level to the setting and the participants
How this information matters to the action research project

1.3 The Context of the Study: The Story Behind the Action Research Project

Describe how the critical question and research project was conceptualized and has evolved
The intervention to be tried; the curriculum to be analyzed; the phenomenon of the ethnography to be studied; or the dilemma or hunch behind the self-study
My interest as an action researcher in this area
My beliefs, values and how my sense of what "good teaching" is are represented in this project
How my position as a student teacher influences this project
How this information matters to this study

2.0 Insights from Distant Colleagues (Literature Review)

List synthesized literature that frames the action research project here.

3.0 Methodology: How the Problem, Dilemma, and/or Issue Will Be Addressed
3.1 Methodology: Data Compilation

Describe the kind of data to be collected (observation, interviews, documents and artifacts)
Describe the purpose for collecting this data (what I hope to learn from the data)
Describe how the data work as triangulation and how each data type will complement each other to create a data set

3.2 Methodology: Context Data

Describe additional context documentation that will be collected to provide context for the data sets

Describe how the researcher's journal will be kept, organized, and when entries will be made

3.2 Methodology: Research Data Compilation

Where will data be kept? (Files, crates, electronically, etc.)

How will data be organized?

Where will journal entries be kept?

How will classroom observations and notes be taken and stored?

How will this data be kept safe and confidential?

3.3 Methodology: Calendar for the Action Research Project

Include a calendar for the project here. Include dates for specific data collection and related classroom activities

Include dates for formal ongoing analysis

3.4 Methodology: Plans for ongoing data analysis and final data interpretation

Analysis

Deconstruction

Synthesis

Contextualization

3.5 Methodology: Trustworthiness

How and where I will practice self-reflexivity

How I will seek multiple perspectives; Whose perspective I will seek; When I will do this

How I will connect back to the literature, the context of the study

How my project will provide evidence of my becoming a teacher

3.6 Methodology: Ethical Considerations of Action Research and Gaining Permissions

What permissions I am pursuing and why

How I will obtain these permissions

How I will keep my data confidential (both during the research and in making the research public)

4.0 Meaningful Results and Going Public

What actions I expect/hope to be the result of my action research project

How I will share my action research

APPENDIX G
GAINING PERMISSIONS/LETTER TEMPLATE

Date

Dear Parent and/or Guardian:

Introduce who you are and your role in the classroom:
I would like to introduce myself. I am Ms. Nancy Marshall and I will be student teaching this term in Mr. Albert's fourth grade classroom. I am delighted to have this opportunity to learn with Mr. Albert and your child.

State the objective of the project:
During my student teaching, I will be studying my own practice of becoming a teacher through an action research project. Specifically, I want to learn more about ways to make homework meaningful.

Strategies that will be implemented:
I plan to implement a number of strategies to enrich the homework experience.

Data to be collected:
During this project, I will monitor homework assignments, survey students about homework, and observe class projects involving homework to better understand this issue. This data will be collected during the normal course of class routine and work.

Timeline for the project:
I will be collecting data for this project between December 1 and March 5.

How the project will be made public:
I will present this project to the faculty and my peers at my university in April.

How confidentiality will be maintained:
Pseudonyms will be used throughout the report I write for the community, school, and all students.

Risks to students:
Data generated by students will be part of the teaching-learning process and will help me to be a better teacher and to provide a better education to your child. There is no risk in participation.

Response needed:
Please sign the permission slip below, indicating whether I may or may not use the data generated during the normal school day from your child's work.

Optional: Video-recording/Photos:

I would like to make video-recordings during this project and take digital photos. These will be used to create a class CD at the end of the project. You will receive a copy of this. I would also like to use this during my presentation. Please indicate if I have permission to use photos and video-clips of your child in my report.

Provide contact information:

Sincerely,

Ms. Nancy Marshall

Email address & school phone number

Mentor-teacher's email address & phone number

Provide a slip to be signed and returned by the student:

Please sign and have your child return this slip. Thank you!

☑ Yes. You may use data generated by my child to be used in your research project.

☑ No. Please do not use data generated by my child in your research project.

☑ Yes. You may use video-tape clips and/or digital photos of my child in your research presentation.

☑ No. Please do not use video-clips and/or digital photos of my child in your research presentation.

Signature of Parent and/or Guardian   Date

Grade Level: Grade Five

Critical Question: *Can small group instruction facilitate a more cohesive classroom otherwise divided by language and gender?*

Context

The context for the study is a rural community, once largely agricultural but fast becoming anchored by industry and urban commuters. Prior to this action research project, the student teacher had struggled with students who refused to work with one another because of gender or language. About 48% of the students are Latina/o and 52% are female. The student teacher decided to use small group learning as her intervention, hoping this would be a way to build community even as students were learning content.

This particular data set was generated during a Colonial America small group project. The data were collected throughout a period of one week.

Data set includes:

1. Observation of small group work

2. Artifact: student journal entries

3. Group leader interviews

4. Artifact: students' writing and drawing the definition of "community"

Instructions

Read through the four data subsets and answer the questions under the heading "Considering the Data."

Data Subset 1: Observation of Small Group Work and Action Researcher's Notes

The class was divided into instructional small groups. I requested the English Language Learning (ELL) specialist to make general observations, but to specifically focus on interactions between ELL and non-ELL students, between male and female student, note positive/negative means of communication, and difficulties in the groups. The observations were made during Day 1 of the teaching unit. Students were deciding upon their roles. Each group was to decide how to further divide into partners. I designed the groups based upon information gathered previously from a sociogram (see Appendix E8).

I chose team leaders based upon their identification as "stars" in the sociogram. This includes: S 26 (female, English first speaker), S 1 (female, bilingual), and S 20 (male, bilingual). One student, S 21 (male, Spanish speaker) is an "isolate" based upon the sociogram results. S 28 (male, Spanish first speaker) and 29 (male, Spanish first speaker) are marginally isolated based upon the sociogram results.

→ TABLE H.1: Observation 1 Results

Group #1	Group #2	Group #3
S 26 went to Raul to include him in group	S 1 asks group "who wants. . . ."	4 of the group members are not participating
S 26 asks for clarification	S 1 asks for clarification	Southern group not working together
Most members actively participating	S 2 sitting behind group	S 28 kicks bottom of S 29's foot; 29 retaliates
Quickly assigned tasks and S 26 recorded	S 21 not involved	S 20 "Tell me what you want to do next"
All students on-tasks	Group attempting to compromise	Group shouts out responses
	Trying to find a role for S 8 (who is absent). S 2 doesn't want to work with S 21 (male); requesting to wait until S 8 comes back to school.	S 20, S 28 & S 29 laugh and carry on (not sure of conversation); certainly off-task.

Considering the Data

- What might you conclude (if anything) from this observation?

- Do you think this observational data is meaningful to the research? Why and why not? Is there a different way the observer might collect data that would be more beneficial?

- What additional data would be helpful?

Data Subset 2: Artifact—Student Journal Entries

All students responded to the journal prompt: *When you were working in your colonial region group, what was difficult and what was easy or good? Did you work well with your partner? What would have helped you work better with your partner or other people in your group?* I have recorded five responses here typical of the entire class:

S 22 (male, E, group 1): "Me and my partner couldn't find the right book and when we did we couldn't find the right page. We knew some stuff already. We talked a lot. If we wouldn't have been together it would have been better."

S 19 (male, S, group 2): "I feel good with my group and with my partner. The good thing is that my partner is working good with me. Yes I am working good with my partner. The hard thing is that he didn't want to work with *me* and now he is working good. The easy thing is that now he is working good and give me a lot of information."

S 23 (male, E, group 3): "I didn't like working with my partner. He isn't nice. He cursed to me all the time in Spanish."

S 9 (female, E, group 3): "The easy part was typing it out. The hard part was finding all the pages and getting the answers we want. Yes, I worked well with my partner. But we both wanted to type."

S 12 (female, E, group 3): "It was too hard to find the stuff. It was easy for me to work with most of my group and it was good we worked together and we finally got it done. It would have helped if my partner would do more and my group would get along."

Considering the Data

- The student journal entries were gathered near the end of the project. Read through this data, highlighting repeating patterns or themes that correspond with the teacher-researcher's questions. (E = English first speaker; S = Spanish first speaker; B = bilingual).

- Compare this data to the observational data. Do you see any connections?

- What additional data would be useful, if any?

- What questions do you have for the researcher?

Data Subset 3: Group Leader Interviews

At the end of the week, I interviewed each of the team leaders with the following questions:

1. What problems did you notice in your group?
2. What difficulties did you face as you tried to divide the group into partners?
3. How did you feel about being given the responsibility/role of team leader?

S 26 (Group 1 leader):

1. One of the problems was S 22 and S 18 kept losing their questions, which was really frustrating. Also it was frustrating because everybody always wanted me to do their work because I was the leader.
2. It was difficult to get people paired up because everyone couldn't be with who they wanted to be with. Like some people didn't want to work with kids who only speak Spanish.
3. I was happy.

S 1 (Group 2 leader):

1. S 2 was gone all the time. Then S 21 stopped working. [They were partners.]
2. It was too hard to do the partners.
3. I just told them what to do.

S 20 (Group 3 leader)

1. We had a hard time finding answers. S 23 and S 28 were not willing to work together and were arguing over answers.
2. Some kids weren't willing to work together. It was okay.

Considering the Data:

- What insights do you gain from these journal entries and the interviews with group leaders? Does this connect with the observational data? Does this data help answer the critical question?
- How and what kind of literature might support this data set?
- What additional data might be helpful?

Data Subset 4: Collection of Artifacts on Students' Definition of "Community"

Class Brainstorming: What are the characteristics of your ideal community?

- Fun
- Helping
- Sharing/working together
- Place with house and river
- A ranch with horses
- Big group of people
- Family
- Love

- Giving joy
- Religion/faith
- Friends
- Money
- Jobs for everyone
- Friendly neighbors
- Kids can play together
- Clean house

Student Artwork Depicting an Ideal Community:

Instruction given to students: "Draw a picture of your ideal community and write a few sentences describing the characteristics of your ideal community." Here are sample data:

→ FIGURE H.1: Sample Data

"Why live out of tha city in ebrabary
Has a Job in We chear food to go get
food we Hafto go to tha city to get
foof we Haft many mony to bay food.
Family is important to my."

We live out of the city and everybody
has a job and we share food. To get
food we have to go to the city. We
have a lot of money to buy food.
Family is important to me.

In my ideal community it is important
to have family and friends around and
to have fun. There is one school and a
bunch of churches. No one gets left
behind.

In my picture I show children playing
and having fun; a church/churches
where people can believe whatever they
want. There is no slavery in this town.
Everybody in the town is helpful and
likes each other's company. Lots of
money and jobs for everybody. The
town is near the mountains and rivers.
The schools have nice and loving
teachers!

Esta es mi comunidad en ensta comunidad
esiste la amistad la alegria nos apoyamos
unos a los otros tambien podemos salir ala
calle ir al mar sin nigun peligro. Tambien en
mi cominidad posemos divertirnos con la
arena cuando estamos de vacasiones o
tambien nos divertimos en la escuela.

*This is my community. In my community
there is friendship and happiness. Everybody
helps each other and we can go out in the
street without danger. Also in my community
we can have fun playing at the beach in the
sand when we're vacationing or we have fun
at school.*

Considering the Data

- What do children value in "community"? What barriers do children identify to "community"?

- How might this data inform the teacher-researcher? What would you do with this data if you were the teacher-researcher?

Final Considerations

This is the critical question for this action research project:

Can small group instruction facilitate a more cohesive classroom otherwise divided by language and gender?

- Taken together, how do the data help the teacher-researcher to "answer" this question?

- What additional data would be helpful?

- What questions would you like to ask the teacher-researcher?

- How might insights from the literature, or distant colleagues, inform the study at this point?

- How would a journal entry from the teacher-researcher support this data collection?

- Do you have suggestion regarding the critical question, research design and/or instructional interventions you might make to this teacher-researcher?

- What do you learn from this practice data set that you want to remember as you conduct your own teacher action research?

APPENDIX I
ANALYTIC MEMOS

Chapter 5 describes effective analytic memos as including:

- The use of raw data as a basis for the analysis.

- The expertise of distant colleagues.

- Multiple perspectives represented by different voices (e.g. students, mentor-teachers, supervisors, critical colleagues).

- The pursuit of significant questions.

- A resistance to conclusions; an openness to discovery.

- A strong sense of connection between all of these elements.

Read through each of the memos in this appendix. How do each of these memos represent these elements? What is missing? Practice responding to one of the memos as if you were a critical colleague.

One of the analytic memo examples includes a response by a critical colleague. Chapter 5 describes a quality critical colleague response as one that:

- raises significant questions, especially by asking "Why?"

- attempts to provide insight the teacher-researcher may not see.

- supports the teacher-researcher in developing and revising themes from the data.

- suggests alternative interpretation or may reference distant colleagues whose ideas may impact the analysis.

- makes suggestions about data collection methods and future data collection.

How does or doesn't the response represent these elements?

We also suggest that you review the Cultural Context sections in Chapter 4. How do each of the teacher-researchers incorporate cultural context in their memos? How might they better address this?

Finally, read through the memos and analyzing them for trustworthiness: what suggestions would you make to the action researchers?

→ FIGURE I.1: Example One: Analytic Memo (no critical colleague comments)

DATE: November 23
TO: Donna
RE: Data Set One.
        Hillside Middle School
        7th Grade
From: Julie

I administered a learning style inventory to my seventh grade math students. Almost half of my students scored the highest in the kinesthetic modality. Even more convincing, eighty-six percent of the students scored either their highest or second highest score in the kinesthetic modality. With these results, I am more convinced how necessary it is to provide opportunities for students to learn though kinesthetic activities and presentations.

When I looked at my topic that I was to teach for my curriculum unit, the greatest challenge to me was, "How am I going to make this information meaningful?" My students have learned this material before with no or little retention. I wanted to really effect change in their learning and thinking. Since my critical question is, "Will teaching math concepts to my seventh grade students with tactile presentations/activities have a positive effect on their learning?" I decided that through the inclusions of these types of activities, I could facilitate my students' learning in a meaningful way.

The observations that I made during the different activities did tell me that the students were engaged. At times, there were a few students off-task, but with more direction, these students usually got back on task. My cooperating teacher remarked how engaged the students were during the *Visual Math* lesson. As part of my action research, I gave a survey two weeks after I completed my teaching unit to have students evaluate what activities helped facilitate learning for them. I was a little surprised by the results. One third of my students indicated that they did not feel that the *Visual Math* lesson teaching factors, prime and composite numbers had helped them learn the math concept. Reflecting on why this may be true for them when it seemed to directly contradict the observations and the related work demonstrating their understanding, I think one reason may be the uncomfortable feeling one has when they are in that disequilibrium stage of moving from *not* understanding to a stage of understanding. This lesson required students to construct for themselves an understanding about a prime and composite numbers. The students had to build configurations out of tiles. A few of the students felt uneasy with this task, as they had not worked with this type of manipulative before. All of my students understood when we were finished with the lesson why the number one is not prime. Their work clearly demonstrates this. I feel this is a tremendous accomplishment. I did not just tell them this concept. They experienced it, and the evidence suggest, they learned it.

The other activity that received the most negative feedback was the computer assignment. During this activity, students were to manipulate an *Excel* program and derive for themselves (with a buddy) divisibility rules. Students felt that this was a hard assignment. One student (female) felt the activity made her feel badly, because she "did not get it right and everyone makes me feel bad." The assignment was difficult, because students were required to think about division instead of being given a list of rules as in the book.

The observations of this activity tell me that students were engaged. The artifacts such as the quiz and the 3-D poster show me that student concept achievement was high. I feel that having physically manipulated the numbers, the students have an experience to hang their knowledge on and will retain this information better than if they had just memorized the facts out of the book.

One of the questions I asked on the survey that I gave was "Did I lecture enough?" Most of the students that I have in this class have not been very successful with the "lecture and then do homework" approach to learning mathematics. However there are a couple of students in this class that have been successful learning through this method. One of these students, even though she did well on tests and quizzes and turned in a wonderful 3-D project, felt that I did not lecture enough. One of my questions I have is about the quality of her learning. Did she learn better conceptually through the activities we did than she would have it I had only lectured and she had completed work out of the text? Is her conceptual understanding higher than it would be if she were to simply hear a lecture and then *do* the math? My hunch is that anytime you are constructing the information for yourself rather than having a person just tell you the information, your conceptual understanding will be higher.

The activities that I planned at times were painful for my students as the activities caused them to stretch themselves and construct knowledge for themselves. The students at times were quick to give up and needed frequent modeling of how to think critically for themselves and to keep at the task at hand. I think with more practice, my students would get better and better at thinking for themselves. It feels like they have been conditioned to sit and listen and wait for the bell of clarification to go off in their heads as the teacher lectures. With these students they have become too accustomed for the bell *not* go off and they have accepted just not getting a concept. Instead, they need practice at grappling with a concept and manipulating it until they can personally make the concept meaningful. I thought students would jump at the chance to use manipulatives, especially the computer. However, the complexity of what was asked made the manipulatives seem less like playing and more like hard learning. I hope to continue this type of teaching with activities for conceptual learning. This type of teaching provides a satisfaction so different than just standing at the front and lecturing with the overhead.

→ FIGURE I.2: Example Two: Analytic Memo (no critical colleague comments)

Date: February 3
To: Donna
RE: Data Sets Two and Three
        Greenway High School
        Accelerated Chemistry
From: Catlyn

It is now January and the quest continues to improve my students' study skills as well as to increase their learning and comprehension of the material being covered in the second trimester of accelerated chemistry. Based on the information gleaned from my first data analysis, this has required me to evaluate my strategies and data collection plan.

Evaluation of the first data set told me that some of the methods I was employing were working. As a result, I decided to continue with the following: warm-up questions, weekly quizzes, problem sets/chapter homework problems, and the use of review days prior to chapter tests.

The start of a new chapter became an ideal time to introduce new study skills activities to my students. The first came as a result of my desire to see if my students are truly understanding the material I am presenting to them as they are taking notes and absorbing new content. In my college chemistry course I found that my professor used an interesting method of doing just this and tucked it away thinking that I would someday put it to use in my own classroom. She used what were deemed "Concept Test Cards" to check for understanding as she proceeded through a lecture. Each student picked up a card as they entered the classroom, and as the lesson progressed one or more concept test questions were asked. Students responded by using their card and holding up a letter corresponding to one of the multiple choice answers to the question. Because each of the letters was a different color, the professor could almost immediately determine whether or not a majority of the students were grasping the concept. She would generally call on one or more students to share their answer, along with an explanation. If more than half of the class answered incorrectly, the opportunity was taken to clarify and re-teach the concept.

During my last two data sets I have been using this same method to check in with my students and have found it to be quite effective in providing quick and immediate feedback. Every time a concept test question is offered, each students' answer has been recorded by myself or my CT. I have found that approximately 85% of the time my students have answered correctly, indicating that they have some sort of understanding of the concept immediately after it is presented to them. In many cases, all but one or two students provide correct answers and when called upon can give a reason for choosing the answer that they did. While this has been valuable feedback, I questioned the validity of this data in showing long term retention of concepts. Because students have their notes in front of them and answered these questions no more than ten minutes after learning about a concept, it should be relatively easy to recall the information being asked for because it is fresh in their minds. Other than a test or quiz, how can I measure whether the concepts are really "sticking"? I also found it interesting that such a large majority of students could answer nearly every single question correctly. Are the questions I am writing too easy? Are students simply cheating and looking to see what their classmates are answering before showing their own answer? Is my teaching so excellent that every kid gets it every time? I would say that the former are much more of a possibility than the latter. With these questions in mind, I polled the students on the effectiveness of the concept test questions at the end of my second data set. I found that 18 of my 25 students ranked this method as being effective to very effective (indicated by a score of 3, 4, or 5). As a result, I continued to use this method in my third data set, this time with a 99% occurrence of correct answers. Perhaps I should also consider including mathematical type problems along with the true/false and multiple choice questions I have been making use of.

Because of my skepticism in the depth of the review potential of the concept test questions, I found myself using warm-up questions more readily at the start of nearly every class period. Typically a warm-up question requires some sort of calculation and reviews something the students' learned during the previous day. These are much more involved than concept test questions and the students are called upon to share their answers and problem solving process. At the end of each chapter, these warm-ups are turned in and counted as a homework assignment. Although no formal observation has been carried out as students work on these problems at the start of class, I have seen that students tend to work diligently to complete their warm-up, often returning to their notes or asking for assistance from another student if they do not understand how to proceed. When polled, students also ranked warm-ups to be an effective study skill activity as 20 of the 25 students said they found warm-ups to be effective to highly effective.

I have found that this trimester has proceeded more rapidly than the previous—the students are progressing at the rate of one chapter every week or week and a half. As a result, it has been more difficult to assign a large number of assignments, but rather more efficient to make use of a review worksheet in order to give closure to each chapter. This is generally given to the students two days prior to their chapter test and they are provided with a limited amount of in class worktime in which they are permitted to work with their peers and ask questions of the teacher. Of the review opportunities provided, I have found this to be one that the students rank highly. Over 90% of the class feels that this is one of the best review tools because it gives them the opportunity to practice everything that they have learned over the course of the chapter, especially if the chapter is heavy on calculations. Although I too find this to be a useful tool, I have found that the students and I agree that it could be more effective if they could check their work to determine whether or not they are doing the problems correctly. This creates a dilemma in the fact that the students turn this review worksheet in to be graded on the day of their test. Would it still be worthwhile if this review worksheet were offered as an optional assignment? If this were the case, would they still choose to complete it and really use it as a study tool? Perhaps this is something that I should ask the students. In addition to the above activities that I now consider to be study skills "staples", I felt the need to provide other quick activities throughout the duration of data sets two and three. In an attempt to better get to know my students as well as to ask them to identify areas in their personal and academic lives that could use improvement, I asked them to set goals at the start of the New Year which they will hopefully revisit at some point near the end of the trimester. I found it interesting that a majority identified the need to prepare sooner than the night before for tests, as well as to ask for help from the teacher when they encounter concepts that they do not understand. I will be interested to see how many feel that they have reached these goals come the end of the trimester.

With the practice makes perfect mentality in mind, I also chose to make use of two additional review opportunities. The first came in the way of a kinesthetic pop quiz. I simply put several different questions on the overhead and asked students to "stand up if you know the answer". I found that 75-80% of my students were able to stand up each time, and when called upon were able to give a correct explanation of the concept or question being asked. For many, however, this game quickly got old and they resorted to raising their hands after the first three or four questions rather than standing up. One student noted on her feedback form that although this unofficial pop quiz of sorts was helpful in reviewing material that was a few days old, it was "embarrassing if you didn't know the answer." Rather than quizzes of this type, the students noted that they would like to play more trivia type games to test their knowledge. One final strategy that I employed was allowing the students to use a single notecard on their chapter 10 test in which they could record equations, examples, and notes. I provided the students with a list of items that they might find useful to include, and allowed them freedom to fill in whatever else they liked. This idea really came about as a result of a discussion that was had during the summer semester during learning theory. I believe it came about when we were talking about classic vs. official theories of learning and it was stated that as teachers our goal was to help students actually learn material rather than just memorize and regurgitate information. Ginny suggested that we try implementing various means of assessment rather than relying simply on tests. She also noted that it was acceptable to allow students to use their resources when testing including another student, the textbook, or class notes. Not surprisingly, the average test score increased by three points. I suppose the rise in the test scores from the previous test could be attributed solely to the use of a notecard, however, I also believe that other factors may have contributed including, but not limited to: student interest in the material, nature of the material, number of review opportunities offered, learning that resulted from re-writing class notes onto the notecard, etc. Regardless, I plan to ask students about the usefulness of this review notecard in an upcoming data set.

Overall, I am truly curious to know whether or not incorporating study skills and review activities into my daily lessons is really making a difference in improving students' study habits and increasing student learning. Although I do not believe that test and quiz scores alone can provide an answer, I have witnessed a general increase in students' scores. One student in particular was consistently receiving scores of 2/10 on quizzes had scored 9/50 on the first chapter test. I have seen her scores dramatically improve to 9/10 on the last three quizzes and 37/50 on the most recent test. I continue to listen for students ability to talk with other students using the language of science, to assist each other and work cooperatively, to make use of the problem solving skills they are most certainly acquiring, and to demonstrate that their knowledge base is continually growing larger as we progress through the trimester.

→ FIGURE I.3: Example Three: Analytic Memo (with critical colleague comments)

To: Chris

Date: February 1

RE: Data Set Two

        Rosaburg Elementary School

        3rd/4th Grade

From: Liam

During the months of September through December, I taught my students about the various elements of design: line, shape, form, color, and texture. We have learned the different vocabulary that is connected to each of these elements and viewed and discussed examples of artists' works that exhibit each of these elements. I've collected numerous artifacts for each student that demonstrates their ability to convey each of these elements in their art. By learning about each of the elements of design, my students would all possess a basic knowledge of art that provides a solid foundation to build upon in the coming year. The only question I asked myself was in which direction do I want to go?

At the beginning of the New Year, I reevaluated my whole art unit that I had previously mapped out. I decided to turn my focus from the tools that artists use to create art and instead focused on what makes someone an artist, and more importantly, a confident artist. I have been studying my students developing art identity but realized that I had become more interested in how they were becoming confident in the art that they were creating.

Ah, this is a challenge. I face the same dilemma with my writers. I tell them they are writer, or actors, or directors, and I mean it. They do a whole lot more creative writing, and even acting than more than 90% of our population, but they think I am full of it. The sad thing is that THEY don't think they are writers, or actors, or in your case, artists, because they are neither making tons or money, or gaining a popular star status from the creative endeavors that they do in school. In fact, they more than likely don't think their stuff is half as good as the person next to them. That seems to be one perspective that surrounds these students. Somehow, I feel that I need to work with my students to redefine what a "writer" is, or an "artist" is. It seems that if we can help students redefine their assumptions of artists and writers, we might start to crack away at the hyper sensitivity that faces developing creative pursuits, and allow them to be free to have fun, and have room to grow, to play, and look at the world as a writer or artist. I am curious—what data convinced you to change the focus of the project?

I figured the very best way to study my students as artists and whether they thought of themselves as confident artists was to just come out and ask them. My students participated in an informal art survey; answering questions ranging from "Are you an artist? Why or why not?" "What is confidence", and "Are you a confident artist?" Out of the 26 students surveyed, 17 students thought they were artists, and 14 of the 17 artists thought of themselves as confident artists.

Most students viewed confidence as believing in yourself, though it was also described as "bravery to do something", "having faith in yourself and [when you] really aren't afraid of doing what you want to do". Also mentioned were courage, pride, and trusting yourself. The students that responded no to the questioned asking them whether or not they were a confident artist explained that "I don't believe I can do it", "I think I'm not that good", "I do not draw with pride", or simply that they "hate art". I found it telling that those who thought of themselves as confident artists were the same students that said they loved art and on the other side, those that said they didn't like art, were the same students that thought they were not "good" at art.

Wow, it is nice to see many of your students as confident artists! For them, it is time to keep them challenged, interested, and confident enough to continue on through their school (which will not be easy, but there is always life outside of school, and if a seed is planted, perhaps time away from school will be used in artistic pursuits). But, I am guessing that you are going to be more focused on those students who do not like or feel they are not good at art. This will be the challenge. I have found that there are many students I have who say openly that they do not enjoy writing, and others say they do not like writing for school, but like to write what they like, without the pressure of grade or scrutiny. And yet when I bring in a tennis racket, or ask them to write about paradise, they get excited, or they at least write, for several minutes, and there seems to be a flow. The same can happen with art. Give someone a ball of clay, some wood and paint and glue, or even colored pieces of smooth glass and concrete, and you will find almost all students excited about 3 dimensional art. Our huge challenge is time to find the activities that appeal to these tough artists, as well as the money or supplies to make it happen. When they have fun, then they care less about perfection, and start to think differently, even with baby steps, about how they think of themselves as artists.

After reviewing my students' surveys, I was energized to provide an atmosphere that would be open and inviting to all my students' "inner" artist. Though we have continually talked about how there are no mistakes in art and viewed different representations of art that are far from "perfect", some of my students still do not realize that they are indeed an artist! I found a children's book that put into words some of what I had been trying to explain to my students. The book, *The Dot*, by Peter H. Reynolds, is about a little girl named Vashti that doesn't believe that she is good at art. Her art teacher urges her to "just make a mark and see where it takes you" and this allows Vashti to see her art in a whole new way.

I read this story to my students and asked them to think about what it means to be an artist. I then asked them to respond to a few questions that related to the story and their own artistic self. In the story, Vashti says, "I just can't draw!" I asked the students "Do you ever feel like Vashti?", "Who in your life encourages you to pursue art? What do they say to encourage you?", "What makes Vashti good at art?", and "Is Vashti an artist? Why?" Seventy-five percent of my students felt that at some point in their life, they felt discouraged and unable to be good at drawing. Though my question may have led them to consider their drawing ability, I wonder if their responses would have been any different if Vashti would have said "I just can't do art!"

This story seems like a great fit with what you are seeing in your classroom. It is nice to see that so many of your students connected with this story, and the struggle with their own feelings about being an artist. Do you think this story gave any of those struggling artists hope? Did any struggling artists approach their own art differently after this story?

My class and I have discussed that drawing is only one component of art. As long as you are creative, you can be successful in art, but still my students' focus on drawing as what defines art. One girl said she was an artist because "I can draw things, that's an artist." One boy wrote, "I'm not quite an artist because I don't draw much". One girl even mentioned how she's not because she just doodles. That last comment sounded all too familiar to me. That is exactly what I say! Throughout this whole process, I don't know if I've ever really stopped to consider myself as an artist. I love art and I especially love to draw. I have been told that I'm good, but I look at my drawings and say the exact same things, "I just doodle". I'm making excuses for my art! Do I sound like confident artist?

This is an excellent discovery. We as educators fall into the same trap as our students. We live in a culture where we do not think we are artists because we are not a master, or a professional artist. Same with writing. We look at great things and hardly measure up, and they break us down. We need masters to inspire, not to make us feel like we have no chance at art. We all understand and view art, our lives, and our world differently. We all have massive potential. We should stop trying to be great, like Van Goah, especially where there is only one Van Goah. We should all start trying to be great as only we can be great, using our own style and uniqueness. Does that make sense? We are the translators of artists to our students. If we translate to them that we do art, we enjoy it, and we are pretty proud of it, then they see that it is possible to do the same. If we model to students that we love art, but could never be great, the students will think that it is possible to appreciate art, but not become a great artist.

Enlighten by my own personal revelation, I would like to continue to examine what makes someone a confident artist. If I don't consider myself one, how do I expect the students, especially those that suffer from self-doubt, to be able to look in the mirror and see an artist staring back? I intend to create an open discussion of all the characteristics of an artist. Do they have to draw well? Have they sold a painting? Taken art classes? Know how to sculpt? I hope by talking more about this, the students will become even more aware of all the opportunities that the world provides to be creative and create art.

Great, do that, and keep letting them explore art, and experience the creation of art. They can even start to look at the world through the eyes of an artist. And make sure you realize that you are an artist, and that by teaching art you will grow and understand yourself as an artist more and more each day. Anyway, that's what I am learning from people in the writing field like, Routman (2003) and Atwell (1998)—I need to be a writer in front of my students—I need to model this. Is there any literature in art that support this as well?

APPENDIX J
STRATEGIES FOR THINKING ABOUT DATA

A downloadable version of these activities is available on the companion website.

The Loop Writing Process

Adapted from: Elbow, P. (1998). *Writing with Power: Techniques for Mastering the Writing Process* (2nd ed.). New York: Oxford University Press.

Elbow describes loop writing as a voyage—you leave on the journey, make discoveries along the way, and then return. Only when you return, the place where you started is changed. Consider a teaching incident, a management struggle, a project that did or didn't go well, how well students did or didn't learn, etc. Reflect on data that doesn't seem to connect with other data or what you believe is really happening in the classroom. Or, after studying a complete data set, mull the details around by loop writing.

The Voyage Out

Use any one of the following strategies to "leave the port" and travel with your data:

- Dialogues. This is a good way to promote multiple viewpoints of the incident or data set. Write a dialogue between two or three students discussing the lesson or the classroom incident. Write another dialogue between a student telling her mom or dad about the lesson. Write another dialogue between an author who has published on your action research topic and yourself concerning your data set. You can write dialogues between any number of participants, both those present in the classroom and those who may not be present but could have an interest, and thus consider multiple ways of looking at your topic.

- Narrative Thinking. If you are confused about the subject, write the story of your thinking. "When I first planned to teach this lesson, I thought . . . and then . . . this happened . . . and I thought that . . ."

- Story. Use a story format. Drop the formality of "memo writing" and begin with a story line, "It was a regular day in room 234 when the student teacher decided it was time for a change . . ." Sometimes, it is useful to write in third person, putting yourself outside of the situation to see it a little more clearly.

- Scenes. Write in "scenes." Focus on individual moments and write them as vignettes by stopping the action and focusing in on the moment. Don't necessarily write these in chronological order—write as they come to mind when you recall the lesson, incident, or data set.

The Voyage Home—or Looping Back to Where You Began

- Read what you have written.

- Take notes in the margins; use a highlighter.

- Write back to yourself in the attempt to create coherence out of your draft.

- Return to the guiding questions in the introduction to data analysis and attempt to answer them based upon your draft writing.

Open-Ended Writing

Adapted from: Elbow, P. (1998). *Writing with Power: Techniques for Mastering the Writing Process* (2nd ed.). New York: Oxford University Press.

- Write for 15–20 minutes without stopping. Put down as fast as you can all the thoughts, feelings, and facts you happen to have about the topic. Write fast. Don't think, "Oh, now I need to analyze, synthesize, deconstruct and consider context." Rather, just pour words onto a page about the incident, data, or question you have.

- Release your writing—let it go where it goes.

- Pause. Find the center or focus or main point in what you wrote. Write it down in a single synthesizing sentence.

- From this single synthesized sentence, let loose with a new round of writing. Use that focusing sentence for a new burst of nonstop writing. Don't try to consciously connect the sections of writing and, again, resist thinking, "Okay, it is time to analyze the data."

- Keep alternating this cycle until you feel you've gotten to that "something" that you knew was there in the data, knew you wanted to see in the incident, or possible ways to re-frame a dilemma.

- Now, draft a memo addressing your action research data.

Drawing, Mapping, and Graphing Your Thoughts

The end of one turn of the spiral becomes the beginning of another . . . We are designed for possibility.
—Gabriele Rico

Gabriele Rico, author of *Writing the Natural Way: Using Right-Brain Techniques to Release Your Expressive Powers* (2000), reminds us that we don't have to begin with words. Rico wrote her dissertation about the technique of clustering when teaching students about writing, and although she wanted to write a book on what she discovered, the words wouldn't come. Rico reportedly sat down on the floor with a big sheet of butcher paper and began her very own cluster. With "natural writing" in the center of the cluster, she covered the paper with associations. Seeing this kind of "big picture" gave her the words she needed. She color-coded the words into the 12 chapters of what would become *Writing the Natural Way*. She went on to create a cluster for each of the chapters followed by one-paragraph descriptions and a one-page book proposal. She did this in one day, sent the book proposal off, and three days later, she had a book contract. That's a testimonial!

We have used clustering throughout this textbook and we encourage its use in doing ongoing data analysis. The theory behind clustering is deceptively simple: Your right, creative brain knows something your left, logical brain doesn't know. Clustering allows the right brain to "talk" and in the process of doing so, you can make creative and important discoveries. If you are not familiar with clustering, here are some simple steps to follow in using it for ongoing data analysis:

- Use a blank piece of paper (the authors of this text like butcher paper and markers but blank 8 ½ × 11 and a pen or pencil will do).

- Write your question, critical incident, a summary word of your data set, or some other word phrase that represents your data in the center of the page.

- Let your brain wander! Don't try to be deliberate about getting to an "answer." Do word associations with the center phrase, branching out to other clusters, and branching, yet again. Let your brain spiral in and around and over itself. Continue doing this for as long as you can.

- Stop and take time to look at the entire cluster. What patterns do you see? What is repeated? Is there a single name, thought, concept, idea, or question that seems to persist? If so, you may want to cluster again.

- Respond to your own cluster by answering these questions:

    - I am surprised . . . .

    - I have discovered . . .

    - I wonder . . .

- Return to the task of writing the ongoing analytical memo now that you have "the words."

If you would like to know more about Gabriele Rico's work, with additional instruction on clustering, you can find this information at this website: http://www.gabrielerico.com/Main/AboutGabrieleRico.htm.

Structured Template for Ongoing Analysis

1. Divide your data by type (observation, interview, artifact, researcher's journal, other). Read through your data; make notes in the margins. *Analyze* your data by responding to

the following questions. Use the data in your responses. Do this for the data from each type.

- What seems to be happening in this data?

- What is *not* happening in this data?

- What is repeated in this data (words, behaviors, attitudes, occurrences)?

- What is surprising, perplexing, disturbing in the data?

- What information seems to be missing from the data?

2. When you complete this for each data type, *synthesize* your data by considering the following questions. Again, jot down responses. Use the data in your responses.

- What patterns emerge across the landscape of the data?

- What is the classroom context for these patterns?

- Where are the contradictions, paradoxes, and dilemmas in the data? (What does not seem to fit in the landscape?)

- What are the emotional and intellectual reactions to this data?

- What confirms and disaffirms what is thought about the research question?

3. Next, *deconstruct* this data set by responding to the following questions. Again, use data in your response. Also, include your hunches.

- Where have categories of either/or interpretations been made? How can these either/or conclusions be reconstructed using a different lens?

- What are the limitations of the analysis and synthesis? (What do you not know and what can you not know?)

- What assumptions are being made in the analysis and synthesis? What values and beliefs do these assumptions rely upon?

- What would students, parents, a cooperating teacher, an advisor, or authors in the literature say about the analysis and synthesis?

4. Now, *consider context*. Respond to the following questions about your data set. Use data in your response.

- How does the role of student teacher influence the data and the interpretation of data?

- In what ways did the action research project conclude in the way you as the teacher-researcher wanted? How does this reflect your own beliefs/values?

- How do the interpretations reflect your beliefs/values of what "good" teaching is, "good students" are, and "good" curriculum should be?

- How do the interpretations mirror values and beliefs you hold as a teacher-researcher given your ethnic, gender, and social standings? How are the interpretations limited by these same labels?

- How do the interpretations align with the stated school and community values and beliefs where the project was conducted?

5. Finally, look back over all of your notes. Take special note of areas that seem repetitive in your responses across the above categories.

- Do you need to change your data collection methods to better answer your critical question? What changes need to be made?

- Does the critical question still seem pertinent or relevant? Does this data change your perception and thus the focus of your research?

- What practices in your teaching do you need to change based upon this data?

6. Talk over these last three items with your critical colleague, mentor-teacher and/or instructor. Strategize and implement the next stages of your research.

Action Research. Action research for pre-service teachers is a process of learning to think and act critically, recognize and negotiate political systems, and to focus passion to grow one's identity as a teacher. Such a process evolves out of desire to become a caring, intelligent, transformative educator and includes honing the art and science of planning, assessment, and a critical reflective practice that includes the interrogation of one's own paradigm while in active exploration of ways of thinking and acting beyond those said boundaries. *The result of action research for preservice teachers is the beginning of a journey in becoming a teacher living the teaching/research life to simultaneously improve teaching practice, student outcomes, and systems of schooling to be more just and equitable for all children and adolescents.*

Analysis. The act of taking apart, breaking down or dissecting data.

Analytic Memo. A part of ongoing analysis of data in which the researcher organizes data, seeks patterns and themes, and writes a summative narrative. Analytic memos are often shared with critical colleagues

Anchor Text. An article, textbook, book chapter, or other literature resource that the teacher-researcher uses as foundation for the research.

Annotated Bibliography. A kind of bibliography that includes a short description of the work cited.

ANOVA. Analysis of variance; a procedure for determining if differences between two or more groups of scores are statistically significant.

Artifact. Any documentation gather as "evidence" during a qualitative research project; may include written work, video, art projects, photos and/or other forms of performance.

Assessment. In education the term is broadly applied to strategies, techniques, and/or methods for evaluating, comparing, contrasting, and/or reflecting on progress, performance, and/or development towards a set of criteria and/or goals.

Context. In this text, we use the word context to refer to the cultural, social and political values and beliefs of school and classroom settings.

Critical Colleague. A colleague in the research project committed to question, assist, support, and engage in dialogue with the researcher during a research project.

Critical Question. The primary question in an action research project.

Cultural Proficiency. "Esteeming culture, knowing how to learn about individual and organizational culture, and interacting effectively in a variety of cultural environments" (Lindsey, Robins, & Terrell, 2003, p. 85).

Curriculum Analysis. Action research methodology focused on analyzing curriculum with the goal of evaluating the curriculum for its weaknesses and strengths.

Data Collection Period. Action research projects are often divided into two or more data collection periods, in which one or more data sets are collected. Data collection periods are often separated by a "reflective pause" for ongoing analysis.

Data Set. A complete data set includes data from multiple sources such as: observation, interview, and artifact.

Deconstruction. The term is associated with Jacques Derrida. It is a way of thinking, of breaking down oppositional concepts to create alternative meanings.

Design Research. Action research methodology focused on trying out a specific intervention for some kind of student improvement.

Distant Colleagues. Colleagues found in the literature (research and other professional sources) who provide expertise for the research study.

Empirical Research. A term applied to research experiments using control and experimental groups, statistical analysis, and the control of variables to determine results.

Enlightenment. An intellectual movement associated with the 18th century—the belief that human reason can create a better world.

Epistemology. "Epistemology refers to how people know what they know, including assumptions about the nature of knowledge and "reality," and the process of coming to know" (Sleeter, 2001, p. 213).

Ethnography. A research methodology first associated with the social sciences; a study of culture.

Experimental Research. A subset of empirical research: it attempts to establish cause-and-effect relationships between variables. It does this by carefully designing an experimental test the results of which permits the researcher to reasonably claim the existence of a cause-and-effect relationship. Additionally, it limits its data to strictly quantifiable measurements to permit a rigorous, unambiguous and mathematical analysis of results.

Field Experience. The time a student teacher spends in a mentor's classroom teaching; can be referred to as student-teaching or an internship.

Informed Consent. The process of requesting and gaining permission from participants in a research study; informing participants fully of the research design and methods for data collection and evaluation.

Interview. A data collection method associated with qualitative research; a way of engaging with participants to learn about their experiences, feelings, attitudes, histories, knowledges, and/or opinions.

Literature Review. The expertise of distant colleagues found from research and other professional sources organized to create a framework for a research study.

Methodology. The approach one takes to research—the research design.

Methods. The techniques one uses to collect data during a research project.

Mentor-Teacher. Also referred to as a "cooperating teacher," this is the licensed teacher whose classroom a preservice teacher is assigned during field placements. This teacher provides mentorship in learning to teach.

Mixed Methods Research. A type of research that combines both quantitative and qualitative data and data analysis methods to answer a research question.

Modernism. A time period and a paradigm or way of thinking generally associated with the mid-1800s to the mid-1900s; in research, this includes the strong belief in "objectivity." World War I and II were significant events of this time.

Observation. A data collection technique associated with qualitative research; the act of see or watching behaviors and actions in order to gain a greater understanding of a phenomenon.

Paradigm. The set unconscious philosophical assumptions that form the foundation of any body of practice (Kuhn, 1970).

Postmodernism. A time period and a paradigm or way of thinking associated with the later part of the 20th century; a rejection of modernism.

Problematize. The act of questioning assumptions and seeking additional perspectives, about one's teaching practice.

Pragmatism. A philosophical approach to seeking knowledge that often combines or integrates differing or even opposite approaches in order to optimize solutions.

Preservice Teacher. Also known as "student teacher," this term refers to a student in a teacher education program who is a "teacher in training" or is conducting "practice teaching" in a mentor's classroom; may also be called an intern.

Qualitative Research. A broad category of research with a vast array of methodologies that generally rely upon some form of interview, observation, and/or artifact collection from which conclusions, additional questions, and/or results is formed.

Quantitative Research. Research that uses numerical data collection techniques, and is generally statistically-based, meaning various computations of numbers are used to prove or disapprove a hypothesis.

Quasi-Experimental Research Design. Quantitative research experiment in which research participants are not randomly assigned to the experimental and control groups.

Research Design. A document outlining the *who, what, how, when* and *why* of a research study; the roadmap to the action research project.

Reflective Pause. A time inserted between data collection periods in order to perform on-going analysis activities and write an analytic memo.

Reflexivity. When researchers inform their audiences about their historical, cultural, and geographical location, their personal involvement with the research, their biases (as they are aware of them), and of influences affecting the research design and analysis; a form of heightened critical awareness the researcher makes public.

Self-study. A research methodology based upon study one's self as a teacher in relationship to others; it is primarily focused on improving practice, and relies upon collaboration, multiple qualitative methodologies, and making the work public (LaBoskey, 2004).

Statistically Significant. A confidence rating based upon the use of ANOVA procedures to determine the amount of difference between two or more groups of scores.

Student Teacher-Researcher. A student in a teacher education program who is teaching as a guest in a mentor's classroom and is also conducting research.

Synthesis. The act of putting the data back together again after analysis; of creating wholeness, or integrating pieces to form a sense of unity.

Synthesis Statements. Statements based upon data and the literature that reflect what has been learned and questioned during an action research study.

Theory. Belief and/or hypothesis based upon philosophy and/or research.

Triangulation. A strategy associated with qualitative research used to increase the credibility of the results; generally, triangulation refers to gathering data from at least three different sources in order to better respond to the research question.

Trustworthiness. A term applied to qualitative research when the research has met criteria based upon acceptable description in the literature of credibility.

REFERENCES

Abraham, M., & Karsh, S. (Producers), Tolkin, N. (Screenplay Writer), & Hoffman, M. D. (Director). (2002). *The Emperor's Club* [Motion picture]. United States: Universal Pictures.

Anguiano, P. (2001). A first year teacher's plan to reduce misbehavior in the classroom. *Teaching Exceptional Children, 33*(3), 52–55.

Arhar, J. M., Holly, M. L., & Kasten, W. C. (2001). *Action research for teachers: Traveling the yellow brick road.* Upper Saddle River, NY: Merrill Prentice Hall.

Arminio, J. L., & Hultgren, F. H. (2002). Breaking out from the shadow: The question of criteria in qualitative research. *Journal of College Student Development, 43*(4), 446–460.

Aronowitz, S., & Giroux, H. (1985). *Education under siege.* Westport, CT: Greenwood, Bergin-Garvey.

Atkinson, P., & Hammersley, M. (1994). Ethnography and participant observation. In N. K. Denzin & Y. S. Lincoln (Eds.), *Handbook of qualitative research* (pp. 248–261). Thousand Oaks, CA: Sage.

Atwell, N. (1998). *In the middle: New understandings about writing, reading, and learning* (2nd ed.). Portsmouth, NH: Boynton/Cook Publishers, Inc.

Avildsen, J. G. (Producer/Director), & Schiffer, M. (Writer). (1989). *Lean on Me* [Motion picture]. United States: Warner Brothers.

Babkie, A. M., & Provost, M. C. (2004). Teachers as researchers. *Intervention in School and Clinic, 39*(5), 260–268.

Banks, J. A. (1997). *Educating citizens in a multicultural society.* New York: Teachers College Press.

Barad, K. (2007). *Meeting the universe halfway: Quantum physics and the entanglement of matter and meaning.* Durham, NC: Duke University Press.

Bass, L., Anderson-Patton, V., & Allender, J. (2002). Self-study as a way of teaching and learning: A research collaborative re-analysis of self-study teaching portfolios. In J. Loughran & T. Russell (Eds.), *Improving teacher education practices through self study* (pp. 56–69). London: Routledge.

Beck, I. L., McKeown, M. G., & Kucan, L. (2013). *Bringing words to life: Robust vocabulary instruction* (2nd ed.). New York: The Guilford Press.

Beijaard, D., Meijer, P. C., & Verloop, N. (2004). Reconsidering research on teachers' professional identity. *Teaching and Teacher Education, 20,* 107–128.

Bloom, L. R. (2002). Stories of one's own: Nonunitary subjectivity in narrative representation. In S. Merriam and associates (Eds.), *Qualitative research in practice: Examples for discussion and analysis* (pp. 289–309). San Francisco: Jossey-Bass.

Bradbury, R. (1994). *Zen in the art of writing.* Santa Barbara, CA: Joshua Odell Editions.

Brandt, D. S. (2004). Why we need to evaluate what we find on the Internet. Retrieved July 25, 2013, from http://oldsite.lib.purdue.edu/research/techman/eval.html

Britzman, D. P. (2003). *Practice makes practice: A critical study of learning to teach* (2nd ed.). Albany: State University of New York Press.

Bullough, R. V. J. (1992). *Emerging as a teacher.* London: Routledge.

Bullough, R. V. J., & Gitlin, A. D. (2001). *Becoming a student of teaching: Methodologies for exploring self and school context* (2nd ed.). New York: RoutledgeFalmer.

Butler, J. (1997). *Excitable speech: A politics of the performative.* New York: Routledge.

Calkins, L. (2006), *A guide to the writing workshop: Grades 3–6*. Portsmouth, NH: Heinemann.

Cambourne, B. (1995). *Toward an educationally relevant theory of literacy learning: Twenty years of inquiry. The Reading Teacher, 49*(3), 182–190.

Campbell, L., Campbell, B., & Dickinson, D. (2004). *Teaching and learning through multiple intelligences* (3rd ed.). Boston, MA: Pearson/Allyn & Bacon.

Carr, W., & Kemmis, S. (1986). *Becoming critical: Education, knowledge, and action research.* London: Falmer Press.

Chaudhry, L. N. (2000). Researching "my people," research myself: Fragments of a reflexive tale. In E. St. Pierre, A., Pillow, Wanda, S. (Eds.), *Working the ruins: Feminist poststructural theory and methods in education* (pp. 96–113). New York: Routledge.

Clandinin, D. J., & Connelly, F. M. (1994). Personal experience methods. In N. K. Denzin & Y. S. Lincoln (Eds.), *Handbook of qualitative research* (pp. 413–427). Thousand Oaks, CA: Sage.

Clandinin, D. J., & Connelly, F. M. (1995). *Teachers' professional knowledge landscapes.* New York: Sage.

Clandinin, D. J., & Connelly, F. M. (1996). Teachers' professional knowledge landscapes: Teacher stories—stories of teachers—school stories—stories of schools. *Educational Researcher, 25*(3), 24–30.

Clandinin, D. J., & Connelly, F. M. (2000). *Narrative inquiry: Experience and story in qualitative research.* San Francisco: Jossey-Bass Publishers.

Cochran-Smith, M., & Lytle, S. L. (1999). Relationships of knowledge and practice: Teacher learning in communities. In A. Iran-Nejad & P. D. Pearson (Eds.), *Review of research in education* (Vol. 24, pp. 249–305). Washington, D C: American Educational Research Association.

Cochran-Smith, M., & Lytle, S. L. (Eds.). (1993). *Inside/outside: Teacher research and knowledge.* New York: Teachers College Press.

Coladarci, T., Cobb, C. D., Minium, E. W., & Clarke, R. C. (2004). *Fundamentals of statistical reasoning in education.* Hoboken, NJ: John Wiley & Sons.

Coldron, J., & Smith, R. (1999). Active location in teachers' construction of their professional identities. *Journal of Curriculum Studies, 31*(6), 711–726.

Corey, S. M. (1953). *Action research to improve school practices.* New York: Bureau of Publications, Teachers College, Columbia University.

Cort, R. W., Field, T., & Nolan, M. (Producers), Duncan, P. S. (Writer), & Herek, S. D. (Director). (1995). *Mr. Holland's Opus* [Motion Picture]. United States: Hollywood Pictures.

Coyne, M. D., Kame'enui, E. J., Simmons, D. C., & Harn, B. A. (2004). Beginning reading intervention as inoculation or insulin: First-grade reading performance of strong responders to kindergarten intervention. *Journal of Learning Disabilities, 37*(2), 90–104.

Crotty, M. (1998). *The foundations of social research.* Thousand Oaks, CA: Sage.

Darwin, C. (1859). *On the origin of the species.* London: John Murray.

Deleuze, G., & Guattari, F. (1987). *A thousand plateaus: Capitalism and schizophrenia* (B. Massumi, Trans.). Minneapolis, MN: University of Minnesota Press (original work published 1980).

Denzin, H. K., & Lincoln, Y. S. (2003a). Introduction: The discipline and practice of qualitative research. In H. K. Denzin & Y. S. Lincoln (Eds.), *The landscape of qualitative research* (2nd ed., pp. 1–45). Thousand Oaks, CA: Sage Publications.

Denzin, N. K., & Lincoln, Y. S. (Eds.). (2003b). *The landscape of qualitative research: Theories and issues* (2nd ed.). Thousand Oaks, CA: Sage.

Derrida, J. (1983). The time of a thesis: Punctuations. In A. Montefiore (Ed.), *Philosophy in France today* (pp. 34–51). New York: Cambridge University.

Dewey, J. (1954). *The public and its problems.* Athens, Ohio: Swallow Press.

Dudley-Marling, C. (1997). *Living with uncertainty.* Portsmouth, NH: Heinemann.

Eisner, E. W. (1998). *The enlightened eye: Qualitative inquiry and the enhancement of educational practice.* Upper Saddle River, NJ: Prentice-Hall.

Eisner, E. W. (2002). What can education learn from the arts about the practice of education? *Journal of Curriculum and Supervision, 18*(1), 4–16.

Elbow, P. (1998). *Writing with power: Techniques for mastering the writing process* (2nd ed.). New York: Oxford University Press.

Elliot, J. (1991). *Action research for educational change.* Milton Keynes: Open University Press.

Elliot, J. (1994). Research on teachers' knowledge and action research. *Educational Action Research, 2*(1), 133–137.

Ellis, C., & Bochner, A. P. (2003). Autoethnography, personal narrative, reflexivity: Researcher as subject. In H. K. Denzin & Y. S. Lincoln (Eds.), *Collecting and interpreting qualitative materials* (pp. 199–258). Thousand Oaks, CA: Sage.

Ellsworth, E. (1997). *Teaching positions: Difference, pedagogy, and the power of address.* New York: Teacher College Press.

Feldman, A., Paugh, P., & Mills, G. (2004). Self-study through action research. In J. Loughram, M. L. Hamilton, V. K. LaBoskey & T. Russell (Eds.), *International handbook of self-study of teaching and teaching education practices* (Vol. 2, pp. 943–977). Dordrecht: Kluwer Academic Publishers.

Fletcher, R. (1993). *What a writer needs.* Portsmouth, New Hampshire: Heinemann.

Fletcher, R. & Portalupi, J. (2001). *Writing workshop: The essential guide.* Portsmouth, NH: Heinemann.

Foucault, M. (1972). *The archaeology of knowledge.* New York: Harper Colophon Books.

Foucault, M., Martin, L., Gutman, H., & Hutton, P. H. (1988). *Technologies of the self: A seminar with Michel Foucault.* Amherst: The University of Massachusetts Press.

Frank, C. (1999). *Ethnographic eyes: A teacher's guide to classroom observation.* Portsmouth, NH: Heinemann.

Freeman, Y., & Freeman D. (2009). *Academic language for English language learners and struggling readers: How to help students succeed across content areas.* Portsmouth, NH: Heinemann.

Fisher, D., & Frey. (2008). *Word wise and content rich: Five essential steps to teaching academic vocabulary.* Portsmouth, NH: Heinemann.

Gall, M. E., Borg, W. R., & Gall, J. P. (2003). *Educational research: An introduction* (7th ed.). Boston, MA: Allyn and Bacon.

Gardner, H. (1993). *Creating minds: An anatomy of creativity seen through the lives of Freud, Einstein, Picasso, Stravinsky, Eliot, Graham, and Gandhi.* New York: Basic Books.

Gardner, H. (2004a). *Frames of mind: The theory of multiple intelligences* (20th anniversary ed.). New York: Basic Books.

Gardner, H. (2004b). *The unschooled mind: How children think and how schools should teach.* New York: Basic Books.

Gay, G. (2010). *Culturally responsive teaching: Theory, research, and practice* (2nd ed.). New York: Teachers College Press.

Gee, J. P. (2001). Identity as an analytic lens for research in education. In W. G. Secada (Ed.), *Review of research in education* (vol. 25, pp. 99–125). Washington, DC: American Educational Research Association.

Geertz, C. (1973). *The interpretation of cultures.* New York: Basic Books.

Gergen, M. M., & Gergen, K., J. (2003). Qualitative inquiry: Tensions and transformations. In

N. K. Denzin & Y. Lincoln, S. (Eds.), *The landscape of qualitative research: Theories and issues* (2nd ed., pp. 575–610). Thousand Oaks, CA: Sage Publications.

Giroux, H. A. (2003). *The abandoned generation: Democracy beyond the culture of fear.* New York: Palgrave.

Gitlin, A. (2005). Inquiry, imagination, and the search for a deep politic. *Educational Researcher, 34*(3), 15–24.

Gningue, S. M. (2003). The effectiveness of long-term vs. short term training in selected computing technologies on middle and high school mathematics teachers' attitudes and beliefs. *Journal of Computers in Mathematics and Science Teaching, 22*(3), 207–224.

Goldberg, N. (1990). *Wild mind: Living the writer's life.* New York: Bantam Books.

Goodlad, J. I. (2004). *A place called school* (20th anniversary ed.). New York: McGraw-Hill.

Gorard, S. (2001). *Quantitative methods in educational research: The role of numbers made easy.* London: Continuum.

Gore, J. (1993). *The struggle for pedagogies: Critical and feminist discourses as regimes of truth.* New York: Routledge.

Graves, D. (1994). *A fresh look at writing.* Portsmouth, NH: Heinemann.

Graves, M. F. (2006). *The vocabulary book: Learning & instruction.* New York: Teacher's College Press.

Greene, M. (2001). Reflections on teaching. In V. Richardson (Ed.), *Handbook of research on teaching* (4th ed., pp. 82–89). Washington, DC: American Educational Research Association.

Haberman, M. (1991). The pedagogy of poverty versus good teaching. *Phi Delta Kappan, 73*(4), 290–294.

Haft, S., Wilt, P. J., & Thorman, T. (Producers), Schulman, T. (Writer), & Weir, P. (Director). (1989).

Dead Poets Society [Motion picture]. United States: Touchstone Pictures.

Hamilton, M. L. (2005). Researcher as teacher: Lessons modeled by a well-remembered scholar. *Studying Teacher Education, 1*(1), 85–102.

Hansen, J. J., & Wentworth, N. (2002). Rediscovering ourselves and why we teach. *The High School Journal, 85*(4), 16–22.

Haraway, D. (1996). Situated knowledges: The science question in feminism and the privilege of partial perspective. In E. F. Keller & Longino, H. E. (Eds.), *Feminism and science* (pp. 249–263). New York: Oxford University Press.

Harding, S. (1996). Rethinking standpoint epistemology: What is "strong objectivity?" In E. F. Keller & H. Longino (Eds.), *Feminism and science* (pp. 235–247). New York: Oxford University Press.

Hargreaves, A. (1994). *Changing teachers, changing times.* New York: Teachers College Press.

Hargreaves, A. (1999). The psychic rewards (and annoyances) of teaching. In M. Hammersley (Ed.), *Researching school experiences: Ethnographic studies of teaching and learning.* London: Falmer Press.

Hargreaves, A., & Jacka, N. (1995). Induction or seduction? Postmodern patterns of preparing to teach. *Peabody Journal of Education, 70*(3), 41–63.

Heidegger, M. (1972). *What is called thinking.* New York: Harper & Row.

Howard, G. R. (1999). *We can't teach what we don't know: White teachers, multiracial schools.* New York: Teachers College Press.

Hubbard, R. S., & Power, B. M. (2003). *The art of class-room inquiry: A handbook for teacher-researchers* (rev. ed.). Portsmouth, NH: Heinemann.

Johnson, R. B. (1997). Examining the validity structure of qualitative research. *Education, 118*(2), 282–291.

Johnston, P. H. (2004). *Choice words: How our language affects children's learning.* Portland, ME: Stenhouse.

Johnston, P. H. & Powers, B. M. (2012) *Opening minds: Using language to change lives.* Portland, ME: Stenhouse Publishers.

Joyce, B., Mueller, L., Hrycauk, M., & Hrycauk, W. (2005). Cadres help to create competence. *Journal of Staff Development, 26*(3), 44–49.

Katz, M. S., Noddings, N., & Strike, K. A. (1999). *Justice and caring: The search for common ground in education.* New York: Teachers College Press.

Kemmis, S., & McTaggart, R. (1988). *The action research planner* (3rd ed.). Geelong, Australia: Deakin University.

Kemmis, S., & McTaggart, R. (2003). Participatory action research. In H. K. Denzin & Y. S. Lincoln (Eds.), *Strategies of qualitative inquiry* (pp. 336–396). Thousand Oaks, CA: Sage.

Kessler, R. (2000). *The soul of education: Helping students find connection, compassion, and character at school.* Alexandria, VA: Association for Supervision and Curriculum Development.

Kincheloe, J. L. (2003). *Teachers as researchers: Qualitative inquiry as a path to empowerment* (2nd ed.). London: RoutledgeFalmer.

Kohn, A. (1994). *The risks of rewards.* ERIC/EECE Clearinghouse on Early Childhood Education. Retrieved from ERK database. (E)376990)

Kohn, A. (1999). *The schools our children deserve: Moving beyond traditional classrooms and "tougher standards".* Boston, MA: Houghton Mifflin.

Kozol, J. (1985). *Death at an early age: The destruction of the hearts and minds of negro children in the Boston Public Schools.* New York: New American Library.

Kozol, J. (1992). *Savage inequalities: Children in America's schools* (1st Harper Perennial ed.). New York: HarperPerennial.

Kozol, J. (1995). *Amazing grace: The lives of children and the conscience of a nation.* New York: Crown.

Kozol, J. (2001). *Ordinary resurrections: Children in the years of hope* (1st Perennial ed.). New York: Perennial.

Kozol, J. (2005). *The shame of the nation: The restoration of apartheid schooling in America.* New York: Crown Publishers.

Kuhn, T. (1970). *The structure of scientific revolutions* (2nd ed.). Chicago: University of Chicago Press.

LaBoskey, V. K. (2004). The methodology of self-study and its theoretical underpinnings. In J. J. Loughran, M. L. Hamilton, V. K. LaBoskey & T. Russell (Eds.), *International handbook of self-study of teaching and teacher education practices* (Vol. 2, pp. 817–869). Dordrecht: Kluwer Academic Publishers.

Lacey, C. (1977). *The socialization of teachers.* London: Methuen.

Lammott, A. (1994). *Bird by bird: Some instructions on writing and life.* New York: Anchor Books.

Lampert, M. (2000). Knowing teaching: The intersection of research on teaching and qualitative research. In B. M. Brizuela, J. P. Stewart, R. G. Carrillo & J. G. Berger (Eds.), *Acts of inquiry in qualitative research* (pp. 61–72). Cambridge, MA: Harvard Educational Review.

Lane, S., Lacefield-Parachini, N., & Isken, J. (2003). Developing novice teachers as change agents: Student teacher placements "against the grain". *Teacher Education Quarterly, 30*(2), 56–68.

Lather, P. (1991). *Getting smart.* New York: Routledge.

Lather, P. (1992). Post-critical pedagogies: A feminist reading. In C. Luke & J. Gore (Eds.), *Feminisms and critical pedagogy* (pp. 120–137). New York: Routledge.

Lather, P. (1993). Fertile obsession: Validity after poststructuralism. *Sociological Quarterly, 34*(4), 673–693.

Lather, P. (2004). This IS your father's paradigm: Government intrusion and the case of qualitative research in education. *Qualitative Inquiry, 10*(1), 15–34.

Le Guin, U. K. (1969). *The left hand of darkness.* New York: The Berkley Publishing Group.

Lenz Taguchi, H. 2010. *Going beyond the theory/practice divide in early childhood education: Introducing an intra-active pedagogy.* New York: Routledge.

Lewin, K. (1948). *Resolving social conflict: Selected papers on group dynamics (1935–1946).* New York: Harper.

Lincoln, Y. S. (2002). *On the nature of qualitative evidence.* Paper presented at the Annual meeting of the association for the study of higher education, Sacramento, CA.

Lincoln, Y. S., & Denzin, H. K. (2003). The seventh moment: Out of the past. In H. K. Denzin & Y. S. Lincoln (Eds.), *The landscape of qualitative research* (2nd ed., pp. 611–640). Thousand Oaks: Sage Publications.

Lincoln, Y. S., & Guba, E. G. (1985). *Naturalistic inquiry.* Beverly Hills, CA: Sage Publications.

Lincoln, Y. S., & Guba, E. G. (2003). Paradigmatic controversies, contradictions, and emerging confluences. In *The landscape of qualitative research: Theories and issues* (2nd ed., pp. 253–291). Thousand Oaks, CA: Sage Publications.

Lindsey, R. B., Robins, K. N., & Terrell, R. D. (2003). *Cultural proficiency: A manual for school leaders* (2nd ed.). Thousand Oaks, CA: Corwin Press, Inc.

Linn, R. (1996). *A teacher's introduction to postmodernism.* Urbana, IL: National Council of Teachers of English.

Loughran, J. J. (2004). A history and context of self-study of teaching and teacher education practices. In J. J. Loughran, M. L. Hamilton, V. K. LaBoskey, & T. Russell (Eds.), *International handbook of self-study of teaching and teacher education practices*

(vol. 1, pp. 7–39). Dordrecht: Kluwer Academic Publishers.

Luna, C., Botelho, M. J., Fontaine, D., French, K., Iverson, K., & Matos, N. (2004). Making the road by walking and talking: Critical literacy and/as professional development in a teacher inquiry group. *Teacher Education Quarterly, 31*(1).

Marsh, M. M. (2002). The shaping of Ms. Nicholi: The discursive fashioning of teacher identities. *Qualitative Studies in Education, 15*(3), 333–347.

McCotter, S. S. (2001). The journey of a beginning researcher. *The Qualitative Report, 6*(2), 1–22.

McLaughlin, M. W. (1993). What matters most in teachers' workplace context? In J. W. M. Little & W. Milbrety (Eds.), *Teachers' work: Individuals, colleagues, and contexts* (pp. 79–101). New York: Teachers College Press.

McNiff, J. (1988). *Action research: Principles and practice.* Basingstoke: Macmillian.

McNiff, J., Lomax, P., & Whitehead, J. (2003). *You and your action research project* (2nd ed.). London: Routledge/Falmer.

Merriam-Webster Online Dictionary. (2005). Retrieved May 25, 2005, from www.Merriam-Webster.com

Meyers, E., & Rust, F. (Eds.). (2003). *Taking action with teacher research.* Portsmouth, NH: Heinemann.

Mills, G. E. (2000). *Action research: A guide for the teacher researcher.* London: Prentice Hall International.

Mohr, M. M., Rogers, C., Sanford, B., Nocerino, M., MacLean, M. S., & Clawson, S. (2004). *Teacher research for better schools.* New York: Teachers College Press.

Moore, A. (1999). Beyond reflection: Contingency, idiosyncrasy and reflexivity in the initial teacher education. In M. Hammersley (Ed.), *Researching* school experience: Ethnographic studies of teaching and learning. London: Falmer Press.

Noffke, S. E. (1995). Action research and democratic schooling: Problematics and potentials. In S. E. Noffke & R. B. Stevenson (Eds.), *Educational action research: Becoming practically critical* (pp. 1–10). New York: Teachers College Press.

Noffke, S. E., & Stevenson, R. B. (Eds.). (1995). *Educational action research: Becoming practically critical.* New York: Teachers College Press.

O'Reilley, M. R. (1998). *Radical presence: Teaching as contemplative practice.* Portsmouth: Boynton/Cook.

Palmer, J. A. (2001). *Fifty modern thinkers on education: From Piaget to the present.* London: Routledge.

Palmer, P. J. (2003). Teaching with heart and soul: Reflections on spirituality in teacher education. *Journal of Teacher Education, 45*(5), 376–385.

Patton, M. (2002). *Qualitative research and evaluation methods* (3rd ed.). Thousand Oaks, CA: Sage.

Paulsen, G. (1989). *The winter room.* New York: Bantam Doubleday Dell Books for Young Readers.

Phillips, D. K. (2001). Learning to speak the sacred and learning to construct the secret: Two stories of finding space as preservice teachers in professional education. *Teaching Education, 12*(3), 261–278.

Phillips, D. K. (2002). Female preservice teachers' talk: Illustrations of subjectivity, visions of 'nomadic' space. *Teachers and Teaching: Theory and Practice, 8*(1), 9–27.

Phillips, D. K., & Larson, M, L. (2012). The teacher-student writing conference entangled. *Cultural Studies & Critical Methodologies, 12*(3), 225–234.

Phillips, D. K. & Carr, K. (2009). Dilemmas of trustworthiness in preservice teacher action research. *Action Research, 7*(2), 239–258.

Phillips, D. K. & Carr, K. (2007). Illustrations of the analytic memo as reflexivity for preservice teachers. *Educational Action Research, 15*(4), 561–575.

Purpel, D., E. (1999). *Moral outrage in education.* New York: Peter Lang.

Rankin, E. (2001). *The work of writing: Insights and strategies for academics and professionals.* San Francisco: Jossey-Bass.

Raisch, M. (2005). Action research aids Albuquerque. *Journal of Staff Development, 26*(3), 50–52.

Reason, P., & Bradbury, H. (2001). Introduction: Inquiry and participation in search of a world worthy of human aspiration. In P. Reason & H. Bradbury (Eds.), *Handbook of Action Research: Participative inquiry and practice* (pp. 1–14). Thousand Oaks, CA: Sage.

Reinharz, S. (1992). *Feminist methods in social research.* New York: Oxford University Press.

Richardson, L. (2003). Writing: A method of inquiry. In H. K. Denzin & Y. S. Lincoln (Eds.), *Collecting and interpreting qualitative materials* (pp. 499–541). Thousand Oaks, CA: Sage.

Rico, G. (2000). *Writing the natural way: Using right-brain techniques to release your expressive powers.* New York: Jeremy P. Tarcher/Putnam.

Roth, W-M., & Tobin, K. (2002). *At the elbow of another: Learning to teach by coteaching.* New York: Peter Lang.

Rilke, R. M. (1934). *Letters to a young poet* (M. D. H. Norton, Trans.). New York: W. W. Norton & Company.

Routman, R. (2003). *Reading essentials: The specifics you need to teach reading well.* Portsmouth, MH: Heinemann.

Rowling, J. K. (1999). *Harry Potter and the chamber of secrets.* New York: Scholastic.

Rudduck, J., & Hopkins, D. (Eds.). (1985). *Research as a basis for teaching: Readings from the work of*

Lawrence Stenhouse. London: Heinemann Educational Books.

Sax, C., & Fisher, D. (2001). Using qualitative action research to effect change: Implications for professional education. *Teacher Education Quarterly, 28*(2), 71–80.

Schon, D. A. (1990). *Educating the reflective practitioner* (2nd ed.). San Francisco: Jossey-Bass.

Schulte, A. K. (2002). *"Do as I say"*. Paper presented at the Fourth International Conference of the Self-Study of Teacher Education Practices, Herstmonceux Castle, East Sussex, England.

Senese, J. C. (2002). Energize with action research. *Journal of Staff Development, 23*(3), 39–41.

Senese, J. C. (2005). Teach to learn. *Studying Teacher Education, 1*(1), 43–54.

Shank, G. D. (2002). *Qualitative research: A personal skills approach*. Upper Saddle River, NJ: Merrill Prentice Hall.

Sharpes, D. K. (2002). *Advanced educational foundations for teachers: The history, philosophy, and culture of schooling*. New York: RoutledgeFalmer.

Shor, I. (1992). *Empowering education: Critical teaching for social change*. Chicago: The University of Chicago Press.

Simpson, D., Bruckheimer, J., Rabins, S. & Foster, L. (Producers), Bass, R. (Writer/Screenplay), & Smith, J. N. (Director). (1995). *Dangerous Minds* [Motion picture]. United States: Hollywood Pictures.

Sleeter, C. E. (2001). Epistemological diversity in research on preservice teacher preparation for historically underserved children. In W. G. Secada (Ed.), *Review of research in education* (vol. 25, pp. 209–250). Washington D.C.: American Educational Research Association.

Smith, A. G. (1997). Testing the surf: Criteria for evaluating internet information resources. *The Public-Access Computer Systems Review, 8*(3).

Smith, F. (1998). *The book of learning and forgetting*. New York: Teachers College Press.

Smith, J. (1993). *After the demise of empiricism: The problem of judging social and educational inquiry*. Norwoods, NJ: Ablex.

Smith, L. (1954). *The journey*. Cleveland, OH: World Publishing, Company.

Sobel, D. (1996). *Beyond ecophobia: Reclaiming the heart in nature education*. Barrington, MA: The Orion Society & The Mayrin Institute.

Spivak, G. C. (1993). *Outside in the teaching machine*. New York: Routledge.

St. Pierre, E. A. (1997). Nomadic inquiry in the smooth spaces of the field: A preface. *Qualitative Studies in Education, 10*(3), 365–383.

St. Pierre, E. A., & Pillow, W. S. (Eds.). (2000). *Working the ruins: Feminist poststructural theory and methods in education*. New York: Routledge.

Stafford, W. (1993). Are you there Mr. William Stafford? Retrieved June 4, 2005, from http://www.newsfromnowhere.com/stafford/wspoem04.html

Stenhouse, L. (1975). *An introduction to curriculum research and development*. London: Heinemann.

Stenhouse, L. (Ed.). (1980). *Curriculum research and development in action*. London: Heinemann.

Teddlie, C., & Tashakkori, A. (2009). *Foundations of mixed methods research: Integrating quantitative and qualitative approaches in the social and behavioral sciences*. Los Angeles: Sage.

Tilden, F. (1957). *Interpreting our heritage* (3rd ed.). Chapel Hill, NC: The University of North Carolina Press.

Torrence, M. (Summer 2002). Teaching as advocacy. *Montessori Life, 14*(3), 13.

U.S. Department of Education. (2004). No child left behind. Retrieved January 21, 2005, from http://www.ed.gov/nclb/landing.jhtml?src=pb

Valenzuela, A. (2005). Subtractive schooling, caring relations, and social capital in the schooling of U.S. Mexican youth. In L. Weis & M. Fine (Eds.), *Beyond silenced voices: Class, race and gender in United States schools* (rev. ed., pp. 83–94). Albany: State University of New York Press.

Vonnegut, K. J. (1970). Address to graduating class at Bennington College. Retrieved July 27, 2005, from http://www.geocities.com/quotequeen81/speeches/vonnegut.html

Weber, S., & Mitchell, C. (1995). *'That's funny, you don't look like a teacher': Interrogating images and identity in popular culture*. London: Falmer Press.

Weedon, C. (1987). *Feminist practice and poststructural theory*. New York: Blackwell.

Weiler, K. (1988). *Women teaching for change: Gender, class and power*. South Hadley, MA: Bergin and Garvey.

White, T. H. (1958). *The once and future king*. New York: Penguin Putman Inc.

Whitehead, J. (1989). Creating a living educational theory from questions of the kind, "how do I improve my practice?" *Cambridge Journal of Education, 19*(1), 1–11.

Whitehead, J. (1993). *The growth of educational knowledge: Creating your own living educational theories*. Bournemouth: Hyde.

Whitt, E. J. (1991). Artful science: A primer in qualitative research methods. *Journal of College Student Development, 32*, 406–415.

Wink, J. (1997). *Critical pedagogy: Notes from the real world*. New York: Longman.

Xpt Software & Consulting B.V. (2013). SimpleMind+ (Version 1.7.0) [Mobile application software]. Retrieved from http://itunes.apple.com

Zeichner, K. (2001). Educational action research. In P. Reason & H. Bradbury (Eds.), *Handbook of action research: Participative inquiry and practice* (pp. 273–283). London: Sage.

Zeichner, K. M., & Gore, J. (1995). Using action research as a vehicle for student teacher reflection: A social reconstructionist approach. In S. E. Noffke & R. B. Stevenson (Eds.), *Educational action research: Becoming practically critical* (pp. 13–30). New York: Teachers College Press.

Zeichner, K. M., & Liston, D. P. (1996). *Reflective teaching: An introduction*. Mahwah, NJ: Erlbaum Associates.

Zembylas, M. (2003). Emotions and teacher identity: A poststructural perspective. *Teachers and Teaching: theory and practice, 9*(3), 213–238.

Zukav, G. (1980). *The dancing Wu Li Masters*. New York: Bantam Books.

INDEX